Starting a
Home-Based Business

The *Entrepreneur* Magazine Small Business Series

<u>Published:</u>

The Entrepreneur Magazine Small Business Advisor
Starting an Import/Export Business
Making Money with Your Personal Computer
Starting a Home-Based Business
Small Business Legal Guide

<u>Forthcoming:</u>

New Entrepreneur's Answer Book
Complete Guide to Integrated Marketing
Organizing and Promoting Seminars
Successful Advertising for Small Businesses

ENTREPRENEUR MAGAZINE

Starting a
Home-Based Business

John Wiley & Sons, Inc.

New York • Chichester • Brisbane • Toronto • Singapore

This text is printed on acid-free paper.

Copyright © 1996 by Entrepreneur Media, Inc.
Published by John Wiley & Sons, Inc.

Library of Congress Cataloging-in-Publication Data:

Entrepreneur magazine : starting a home-based business.
   p. cm. — (The Entrepreneur magazine small business series)
  Includes bibliographical references
  ISBN 0-471-10980-0 (cloth : alk. paper). — ISBN 0-471-10979-7
 (pbk.)
  1. Home-based businesses—Management. 2. New business
enterprises. I. Entrepreneur (Santa Monica, Calif.) II. Series.
HD62.38.E573 1995
  658.1' 141—dc20   95-38736
Printed in the United States of America

10 9 8 7 6 5 4 3

ACKNOWLEDGMENTS

ENTREPRENEUR MAGAZINE GROUP

Editor	Charles Fuller
Assistant Editor	Ken Ohlson
Copy Editors	Imran Husain
	David Pomije
Contributing Editors	Gina Farrell Gladwell
	Frances Huffman
	John Song
	Anne Callot
	Maura Hudson Pomije
	Meredith Kaplan

CONTENTS

INTRODUCTION

A revolution is in progress. Throughout America, a growing number of people are saying good-bye to their corporate jobs and heading home—not to look for other jobs, but to create their own businesses right in their own homes.

A lack of security in the corporate world has pushed thousands—even millions—of Americans to opt for business ownership. Why is starting a business at home becoming an increasingly popular option? Because it costs a lot less than traditional start-ups, it offers flexibility, and it gives entrepreneurs more time to spend with their families.

With advances in computer and telecommunications technology, almost any kind of business can be run from the home. By simply hooking up a computer, a modem, and a fax machine, you can turn your home into a money-making business site.

THE GROWTH OF HOME-BASED BUSINESSES

Home-based businesses are responsible for generating $382.5 billion in annual revenues, and for creating more than 8,200 new jobs and entrepreneurial positions each day. It is estimated that a new home-based business is started in the United States every 11 seconds.

No one knows exactly how many home-based businesses there are in the United States. The reason is twofold: (1) no one has come up with a generally accepted definition for home-based business and (2) no one has undertaken the task of counting them all. There are estimates, though. Link Resources, a prominent New York City-based market research firm, has estimated that at least 24.9 million home-based business owners in the United States were operating either full- or part-time in 1993. Of that total, Link estimated that 12.7 million were self-employed individuals whose home-based business was their primary occupation, an increase of 600,000 over 1992 figures; the remaining 12.2 million were part-time home-based business owners, half a million more than in 1992. Although industry growth estimates vary, experts agree that the number of home-based businesses will increase dramatically in the coming years.

Operating a full- or part-time business is an attractive alternative for entrepreneurs. Once viewed as a convenient but somewhat humbling alternative to traditional corporate or industrial employment, home-based businesses are now enjoying newfound prestige. Millions of people who for years held positions in established business firms, government agencies, or factories are now running their own businesses out of their homes. Because of their sheer numbers, home-based businesses command respect from all sectors of the economy. But just what is a home-based business?

Collectively, home-based business enterprises have been called "cottage industries," a term associated with the pre-electronic age. Home-based businesses now cover a wide range of business concepts, from service units and mail order to light manufacturing. They generally don't require an extensive amount of space or capital (equipment) investments. They can be started and operated on a shoestring budget, and usually that's just the way they are run. Meanwhile, their potential for growth is unlimited.

ADVANTAGES OF HOME-BASED BUSINESSES

The appeal of home-based businesses is irresistible. Consider these advantages:

- *Lower operating costs.* Starting a business is an expensive undertaking, and most entrepreneurs are anxious to place as little strain on their budget as possible. Running a business from home not only eliminates the cost of renting office space, but also allows homeowners to deduct a portion of their mortgage payments as an expense of doing business (see Chapter 10, "Record Keeping and Taxes," for updates on home-based business deductions). Additional charges for utilities and phone at an away-from-home office, transportation costs such as gas, tolls, or communication, and insurance premiums are considerably reduced or even eliminated because they're already a part of your household expenses.

- *Flexible work schedules.* Owning and operating a home-based business often allows more flexibility. You may be able to set your own hours (depending on clients' expectations), which will give you time to do things you couldn't do if you were confined to someone else's rigid work schedule. You can care for your family, do errands, and complete other tasks while still running your business.
- *Location.* Working from your home, you can avoid the catch-22 of being employed at or having a business located in the city: you either have to live in the city and face high rents, congestion, and noise, or move to the suburbs and face long and expensive daily commutes. Being at home also frees you from the problems of a location-sensitive business. With most home-based businesses, you can live almost anywhere.
- *The electronic office.* The advent of the personal computer was a watershed for home-based businesses. Computers, along with facsimile machines, modems, on-line services, and feature-rich telephones have turned the ordinary home office into a fully functional "electronic cottage."

GETTING DOWN TO BUSINESS

These advantages explain why so many people are turning to the home-based option. But take note: it isn't an easy option. When contemplating the start-up of a home-based business, keep in mind the key word: *business.* Unless you view your home-based venture as a business at all times, it will be hard to realize any long-run success.

For many people, a home-based venture is a hobby, not a business. They don't actively market their products or services, they don't know how they will sell them, and they don't know how to take advantage of the vast distribution channels available to home-based ventures. These individuals are perfectly content with the little successes and satisfaction they derive from their home-based *hobby;* they are not operating to make money. They may wish they were making a lot of money, but until they take the next step and transform their hobby into a business, they will continue to spin their wheels and go nowhere.

If you decide to start your business from your home, don't look on it as a hobby. You are the moving force behind your business, and you should approach your start-up at home with planning and commitment worthy of a CEO of a major corporation. Here's what you'll need to do:

- *Write a business plan.* Construct a detailed, complete business plan that includes your short-term and long-term business goals.

- *Know your zoning laws.* Check the zoning laws in your neighborhood, to see whether you can operate legally from your home or whether you can shuttle clients in and out of your house all day.
- *Obtain proper licenses.* Obtain all the appropriate licenses and other legal documents required of any business. Just because you operate your business out of your home doesn't mean that you can cut corners with the government.
- *Create a separate office space.* Differentiate between the space in your home that is your office (work environment) and the space in your home that is your domicile (living environment). You can't expect to use the same space for both functions. The boundary line between your office and your home must be clearly established so that when you are "at work," you are occupying the appropriate space, and when you "leave the office for the day," you do just that.
- *Learn time-management tricks.* Pay special attention to how you manage your time and your money. To run a business from home, you must be extremely well organized.
- *Create a professional image.* Maintain the appearance and manner of a professional at all times. Answering the door in dirty blue jeans won't help you win the confidence of potential clients or customers who come to visit you.
- *Take advantage of technology.* Master the technological tools that can make your business day easier and more productive. Computers, faxes, modems, voice mail, on-line services—they can all help you perform your work more efficiently in your home office. Now that you're on your own, you probably won't have a secretary or staff to help you with administrative or clerical tasks. If you have to learn to use a computer, computerized databases, a remote-controlled answering machine, or whatever, then *do it.*
- *Take charge.* Never forget that you're the boss now; you control the speed and direction of your entrepreneurial future. Take responsibility for your business's successes and failures. Recognize good decisions and learn from inevitable mistakes.

ARE YOU READY?

What's your perception of a home-based entrepreneur's life? Do you imagine yourself setting your own schedule and sleeping late? Do you envision yourself working minimal hours and enjoying the solitude of being on your own? Do you foresee getting together with friends and spending time with your kids during the day? If you do, your vision of home-based entrepreneurship isn't very realistic.

Thousands of people who are fed up with 9-to-5 drudgery look to a home-based business as the ultimate alternative. Some of those who become home-based-business owners find satisfaction in their work, but many others are completely bowled over by the responsibilities that come with working from home. Why? There's a lot more to home-based business ownership than many people imagine. Being in control means finding and doing enough work to be a success. There's no one else to assign it to.

Starting a home-based business is a challenge. There are times of loneliness, there are constant distractions, and there are problems with time management. Can you face that challenge and make the home-based alternative work for you? Preparation is the key. Too many small-business owners start a home-based operation without any understanding of whether a home-based business is right for them or whether there's a market for their products or services. Evaluate yourself honestly before getting serious about a home-based business.

Are You Cut Out for a Home-Based Business?

To be a successful home-based business owner, you need to possess some key traits. Chapter 1 discusses them in greater detail, but here's a quick list:

- *Be a self-starter.* Nobody will be there to tell you what to do or when to do it. Getting the job done is entirely up to you.
- *Be disciplined.* Learn to avoid the distractions of working at home and to concentrate on the job at hand.
- *Be an excellent time manager.* Know how to manage your time so you can complete all the necessary tasks without interfering with your family life.
- *Be organized.* Keeping track of customers, orders, and projects is essential to home-based success.
- *Enjoy working alone.* In a home-based start-up business, other colleagues won't be around to help with projects, brainstorm ideas, or shoot the breeze.

Keeping these traits in mind, think about what type of business is going to be right for you. The key word in that sentence is *you*. There's nothing wrong with looking through a business opportunity magazine and picking out the business that will be most profitable and least costly to start, but will it fulfill your own personal interests and needs? Income and success are important to anybody starting a business, but unless the business is enjoyable and fulfilling, chances are it won't be any different from going to a job that you hate each day.

There's another underlying factor to consider when choosing a business. If you enjoy the business you are in, you will receive more satisfaction from your work and will have a sense of having "a good job." Your enthusiasm for your work will be apparent to the people you'll be dealing with. Many times, that attitude can be infectious. Customers like dealing with people who are enthusiastic about their work.

Choosing the right business for your home-based venture begins with you. What are your goals? What do you want to accomplish by going into business from your home? Generally, your goals and objectives will center on the following categories:

Income

What type of income do you want to generate from the business? Many people go into business to obtain financial security. When setting financial goals, consider what you would like to earn during the first year of operation and each year thereafter. Build yourself a five-year projection that denotes your desired financial position by the end of that period of time.

Type of Work

It's no secret that the more you like your work, the greater satisfaction you will derive from your efforts and the more successful you're likely to be. What do you enjoy doing the most? What work experience do you have? Do you like working outdoors? in an office environment? with computers? on the phone? with a great number of people? Start by listing the jobs, hobbies, and social activities that give you the greatest satisfaction, then write down the skills you need to master in order to do those jobs. Now give your imagination free rein and list the activities that come to mind. Arrange them in an order of priority. You will then have a good foundation on which to determine the right business for you.

Lifestyle

Lifestyle is a rather ambiguous term. Think of it as encompassing several areas of your life that relate to how you want to live. When setting lifestyle goals, you need to consider whether you want to do a lot of traveling, whether physical labor is a priority (or is even something you can do), what type of hours you want to work, what personal assets (such as your house or car) are available for investment into the business. What personal goals do you want to accomplish through your business? Status within the community, time to be with your children, the freedom to set your own hours? If a business that interests you won't provide you with the type of status you desire, then the time to discover that is *before* you go into business, not after.

Ego Gratification

Let's face it, people go into business to satisfy their egos as well as their bank accounts. Owning a business can be very ego-gratifying because of the perception other people have of you. How important is ego gratification to you, and what industries will fill that need?

PRODUCT-ORIENTED VS. SERVICE-BASED BUSINESSES

Now that you know what you are bringing to the business and what you want from the business, you can begin to examine some opportunities that are consistent with your evaluations. This is the research phase. You've already listed some activities, but can those activities be turned into a business? Now is the time to find out.

There are basically two types of businesses you can operate from your home: a service business or a product-oriented business. Product-oriented businesses usually fall within two categories: producers of self-manufactured goods, and producers of goods manufactured by others and sold through a distribution network. Services also generally fall into two categories: those that can be performed from the home, and those that are performed on-site or "in the field." Chapter 2 discusses these opportunities in greater detail.

Services and products cover a broad spectrum of opportunities. Many home-based entrepreneurs have applied their own unique vision to existing ideas to create totally new businesses. You may be able to do the same. Look through newspapers, magazines, books, association directories, and other resources, and create a list of opportunities that will be suitable for you.

THE PROS AND CONS OF STARTING A HOME-BASED BUSINESS

There are many reasons why people begin businesses from the home. Some start their venture as a hobby, realize its potential, and commit themselves full-time to turning it into a business. Others want to run their own business and be their own boss, but don't have any aspirations beyond what their home-based venture will provide them. Others don't necessarily want to start from their home, but they have failed to raise the start-up capital needed to lease a commercial location. Whatever your reasons for starting from home, take a look at the pros and cons first.

Advantages of a Home-Based Business

There are many advantages to starting a business from home. A very small initial investment is required, ongoing expenses are minimal, you don't have to worry about commuting, bad weather won't affect you, and there are good tax write-offs.

For most people, the biggest factor in favor of owning home-based businesses is the reduced start-up and operating costs. Because no front-end cost is involved in the rent or purchase of property, leasehold improvements, phone or utility deposits, property taxes, etc., you save a considerable amount of money. Depending on the type of business you create, the savings may reach tens of thousands of dollars.

Besides the savings on rent, operating expenses are lower because of reduced overhead. In fact, you may be able to deduct the expenses connected with your home office. (See Chapter 10, "Record Keeping and Taxes" for more information.)

Disadvantages of a Home-Based Business

There are some problems associated with running a business from home. You'll have to deal with all kinds of interruptions during the day—charity seekers, door-to-door salespeople, phone solicitations, and unexpected callers, often in person, who know you're home and assume you can "spare a little time" for them. Every interruption breaks the concentration of the home-based entrepreneur and makes it that much harder to continue with the task at hand or to complete it in the budgeted time.

There are also a lot of in-house distractions. You may never have thought of washing the car, cleaning the basement, or mowing the lawn until you've been bogged down in a project and needed an excuse to get away from work for a while. These chores may suddenly seem more enticing than the difficult business of making your venture a success.

You may also have a problem attracting employees—whether you need full-time, part-time, or temporary workers—to your home-based business. Most full-time workers are interested in job security, and, let's face it, a home-based office doesn't present itself as a very secure enterprise. Legitimacy is a big issue among individuals who are seeking employment and agencies that provide temporary workers. No matter how elaborate your work area is or how separate it is from the living quarters, most people you deal with will have that question of legitimacy in the back of their minds.

This image problem can make it difficult to deal with suppliers, subcontractors, and distribution sources. They're often reluctant to deal with home-based entrepreneurs. They will want your business, but they will also want to be sure that they're going to be paid. After all, they're in business to make money as well, and they can't afford to deal with businesses that don't meet their obligations.

Despite the popular notion that *real* businesses exist only in lavish corporate environs, home-based ventures can be prosperous, especially when the business you're in doesn't require customers to visit your office. Service businesses, such as interior design or event planning, are perfect for home-based operation because owners visit clients on *their* premises. A mail order business is another option. Distribution channels are through the mail, so all you need is a central location with adequate storage space for your inventory of goods.

To improve the image of your home-based business, you can create the illusion that you are located in a business complex by renting a box from a private mail box center and advertising that address as your business's central location. For instance, you can rent a mail box in Newport Beach, California, and advertise your mail box number as a suite number. By hiring an answering service and providing instructions on how incoming phone calls are to be answered, you can make callers think they are dealing with a large, established company.

The point is, there are ways to overcome the obstacles and maximize the benefits of operating a business from your home. By preparing a rock-solid business plan, taking advantage of current technology, using effective marketing strategies and promotional tactics, and enlisting the help of individuals and information sources that can increase your knowledge of their market or industry, you can create a successful home-based business.

1

HOMEWARD BOUND: OVERCOMING SPECIAL CHALLENGES

An ever-growing number of employed persons are realizing the limits of working in corporate America. After years of battling their way through daily commutes in gridlock traffic, tolerating office politics, and sacrificing their personal lives to meet deadlines and satisfy others' expectations, they have decided that enough is enough.

Home-based business is providing a way for these people to realize their potential. Perhaps the oldest method of entrepreneurship, it is growing in popularity every day.

If you have been compelled to forfeit your personal or family life in order to make a living, you can now look forward to having the best of both worlds.

As people head home in droves to start businesses, another perceptible change is in progress. People used to think that if someone worked at home, it was because he or she couldn't get a job or had been laid off or fired. Now, working at home and starting a home-based businesses has become not only acceptable but a sign of individual capability.

THERE'S NO PLACE LIKE HOME

Home-based business have experienced dramatic growth in recent years. These are some of the many advantages it offers:

- Freedom, flexibility, and administrative control.
- Increased productivity.
- Decreased operating costs.
- Greater individual earning potential.
- Reduction of stress.
- More time with family.

Thanks to technology, people can work as productively from a spare bedroom, den, or garage area as from any commercial facility.

With the apparent focusing of the American consciousness on efficiency and value, home-based entrepreneurs can be proud of their ability to avoid the high costs associated with industrial/commercial start-ups. Their new found flexibility allows them to devote more time to their families.

THE HOME-BASED ENTREPRENEUR

The word *entrepreneur* conjures images of bold risk-takers, creative pioneers, and determined spirits—individuals who look at things a little differently from everyone else. Through entrepreneurs, a collective spirit has worked its way inexorably into the rich fabric of American history. The word is French in origin, but the entrepreneur has definitely become an American phenomenon and represents one of our greatest natural resources.

Just what kind of person is a home-based entrepreneur? There is no stereotype. All kinds of people are starting businesses from home—twentysomethings, octogenarians, city dwellers, suburbanites, country folk, college grads, and high school dropouts. All types of people can find success from home.

Entrepreneurs share at least one thing in common: *the willingness to take a risk and start a business.* Cut from a different cloth, home-based entrepreneurs are not professional managers who want to work for someone else. They are self-starters who want to take control of their own destiny. Now, more of them are finding that the home offers an environment better suited to that goal.

HOME-BASED HURDLES

Home-based entrepreneurship comes at a price. Although there is a great deal to gain by making your home the shared focus of your personal and professional life, you must be prepared to work hard, make sacrifices, and press the limits of your self-control in order to make your venture successful. It goes without saying that every entrepreneur encounters obstacles during start-up. By taking the home-based route, you can avoid many of the hurdles traditional businesses face, such as facility and location requirements and costs. At the same time, you take on a whole different set of responsibilities:

- Developing a professional image.
- Managing your business and your household.
- Separating your personal and professional commitments for the sake of your business.
- Coming to terms with isolation.
- Fitting a company into a home environment.

Each of these items will be discussed at greater length in other chapters of this book. All of these responsibilities will require your attention. Neglect any one of them and your enterprise may never get off the ground.

This chapter will help you understand some of the intangible aspects of working from home. It offers you some proven strategies for tackling some of the less obvious problems you may confront.

As home-based entrepreneurs with families will attest, running a business from home naturally creates a spirit of pride within the household. This "all for one, and one for all" way of seeing the business as a family extension makes the family willing to endure financial and personal sacrifices to benefit from the long-term goals of the business.

Entrepreneurs who achieve success are able to strike a careful balance between family and business life: the two enhance each other, bringing out the best in both. The family goes into the venture enthusiastically, and that enthusiasm grows stronger as the business grows stronger. Successful home-based entrepreneurs have learned to place the concerns of the family at the forefront of their lives while not letting these concerns interfere with business decisions that must be made.

IS THE HOME-BASED OPTION FOR YOU?

How many times have you thought to yourself, "I'm going to do it. Today, I'm going to get started with my plans for my own business," only to shuffle that ambition into the recesses of your mind for future consideration? The thought of starting a business is frightening for most people—even those who eventually do it successfully.

Starting a business forces you to come to grips with the feasibility of your ideas and the proportions of your own strengths and weaknesses. Self-doubt and second-guessing of your potential for success and financial security are often the results. That's why the question "Are you ready?" becomes much more poignant. Only by confronting your fears and hesitations can you begin to evaluate your strengths and weaknesses, your likes and dislikes, and the type of business that might be most suitable for you.

Facing your insecurities also forces you to ask yourself why you want to be in business for yourself. Although the answer may appear obvious to you, upon closer examination you may discover other, more pertinent reasons. Did you know that the primary motivating factor for many people isn't money, but opportunity—opportunity not offered to them by the corporate world? A home-based start-up is one of the best ways for entrepreneurs to maximize their opportunity while minimizing their costs.

The corporations' loss is definitely an economic benefit to the small business community as growing ranks of entrepreneurs contribute their unique visions and talents. According to the Small Business Administration (SBA), home-based business is the fastest growing segment of small business.

Starting a home-based business is the American Dream for a growing number of entrepreneurs. To take advantage of that dream, however, you first have to place your feet on the road and start walking. Here are the factors you must consider before embarking on your own business venture:

- Your primary reason for being in business for yourself.
- The amount of risk capital available.
- The amount of credit available.
- Your skills.
- Your likes and dislikes.
- The amount of effort you are willing to expend.
- Your financial goals.
- Whether you can begin full- or part-time.

Numerous money-making concepts are presently on the market. You may have an original idea that you would like to develop. Ultimately, the decision of what type of business you're going to start rests with your own ambitions.

What type of business will give you the most satisfaction? Which concept will allow you to achieve your goals, and is that idea marketable? You should aim to start a business that you will *enjoy* running, one that is in a growth industry that has accessible markets in your area, and one that will allow you to develop financial freedom.

Self-Assessment

An old proverb states, "Businesses don't fail, people do." A business is merely a reflection of the people running it. If the people running the business are strong in one area and weak in another, the business will show that. This correlation is even more apparent in small businesses.

As the owner of a small business, you will have to handle many different responsibilities within the operations of your company and cope with a variety of situations. For some of these situations, you will have only limited experience, if any at all. As an entrepreneur, you have to know your strengths and weaknesses so you can compensate in some way for the areas in which you are not proficient.

To determine your entrepreneurial strengths and weaknesses, take the time to evaluate the major accomplishments in your personal and professional life and the skills that enabled you to complete those tasks. This evaluation involves three steps:

1. *Create a personal resume.* Start by listing your professional experience. For each job you've held, write a short description of the various duties you were assigned and the degree of success you experienced. Next, list your educational background and any extracurricular activities you participated in during your scholastic career. Finally, write down your hobbies.
2. *List your personal attributes.* Are you personable? Do you feel comfortable around other people? Are you self-motivated? Are you a hard worker? Do you possess good common sense? Are you good with numbers? Do you have effective verbal and written communications skills? Are you well-organized?
3. *Detail your professional attributes.* List the various management roles and tasks you expect to face: sales, marketing, financial planning, accounting, advertising, administrative, personnel management, and research. Alongside each function, write down your competency level—excellent, good, or poor.

Key Attributes

Use the following sample checklist to audit your personal and professional attributes. By putting together a resume and a list of your attributes, you will have a fairly good idea of your likes and dislikes and your strengths and weaknesses. Once you know these things, you will be able to identify what qualities you will bring to the business and what areas may require training or additional help.

Some of the key attributes you need to possess are:

1. *Initiative.* You need to be able to work well independently. Much of the support available when you work for someone else won't be found at home. You can't turn to a supervisor or coworker and ask for help. Therefore, it is very important for you to be a self-starter and to be able to critique your own work.

2. *Risk taking.* Without the ability to take risks, you won't go very far with your home-based venture. There are no guarantees that your business will succeed. If you want the security of a guaranteed income, remain an employee of another company.

3. *Creative thinking.* Most people associate the entrepreneurial spirit with an ability to innovate. Entrepreneurs are willing to try something new, to look at things differently, to find a niche and fill the void.

4. *Motivation.* Just because you work for yourself doesn't mean you can work less. Instead, it may mean working longer hours and wearing many more hats than when you worked for someone else.

5. *Experience.* You're going to need experience in both the field of business you choose to start and in general business principles. A great many entrepreneurs have great ideas and a lot of talent, but don't know the first thing about running a business. Remember, most home-based businesses are run by one or two people. There won't be anyone in your business to turn to for answers, and there won't be anyone looking over your shoulder to make sure that you do the right things—on time. If you don't know the basics of running a business, you'd better do some quick self-education.

6. *Organization.* Plan your time and organize your activities efficiently. Develop a schedule and adhere to it.

7. *Ambition.* You don't have to be ambitious to the point of greediness, but you should have enough ambition to keep going in the face of adversity. Remember, some people won't take you seriously because you operate from your home, but you can't let that get you down. You have to be persistent enough to get around their prejudice regarding home-based businesses.

Some of these attributes are inherent; others can be learned. Successful home-based entrepreneurs strongly suggest joining associations, subscribing to magazines, and reading small-business books (especially in your area of concern). See the appendixes at the end of this book for lists of these resources. Ask other people in the same type of business about situations they've encountered and how they handled them. Learn from their mistakes so you won't make them yourself.

Setting Objectives

Many entrepreneurs go into business to meet a set of personal goals they've established for themselves. For some, it's as simple as having the freedom to do what they want *when* they want, without anyone telling them otherwise. For others, achieving financial security is a major personal goal. Whatever they may be, your personal objectives play an integral part in selecting a business that will be right for you.

After all, if you start a business that doesn't meet your personal objectives, chances are you won't enjoy it, and sooner or later, it will become just a job. You'll lose interest or you won't put enough work into it to make the business work.

When forming goals, whether personal or business-related, consider their most important characteristics:

1. *Specific and detailed.* Whether your goal is to start a business, raise capital, or lose weight, you must be very specific: size, shape, color, location, and time.
2. *Positive and present tense.* A financial goal is not just to pay bills or get by, but to be financially secure. Set a specific minimum of at least X amount of dollars in a given period.
3. *Realistic and attainable.* If you set a goal to earn $100,000 a month and you've never even earned that in a year, your goal is not very realistic. Begin with a "first step"; a figure that's realistic. Once your first goal is met, you can project larger ones.
4. *Short-term and Long-term.* Short-term goals should have the above characteristics and be attainable in a period of weeks or months, up to one year. The long term can extend much longer, though it should still be realistic. You are the only one who can set these parameters. You must decide what is a realistic time frame and what is not.

Once you've set your personal goals, decide which ones are most important to you. This will help you examine your entrepreneurial desire and how it relates to other important aspects of your life.

Risk Assessment

Every business venture, regardless of timing, products, services, personnel, and capitalization, has inherent risks attached. The first two tasks you should complete are (1) assessing those risks and (2) taking steps to diminish them.

Once you have a clear picture of the risks involved, you can make an educated decision on whether to proceed.

The following paragraphs describe some techniques for assessing risks.

Research Similar Types of Businesses

Look at their locations, advertising, staff requirements, and equipment. They are also your competition; get an idea of what you will be up against.

Research the Current Market Trends

What seemed like a hot idea over the past few months may only be a fad. Find last year's phone book and call several of these types of businesses. Are they still around? If you live in a small community or want to expand your research, your local telephone company may have a library of phone books from other cities.

Know Your Strengths and Likes

Does this type of business suit you? Is it too physical? Not physical enough? Do you know experienced persons who can handle the areas that you personally have little or no expertise in?

Create a Family Budget

How long can you live without a paycheck, in case you need to put all your income back into the business? What other income can you reasonably expect while you're in start-up? Make sure your family understands what you are doing. Ask for their support. They are sharing in the risk, and they will be more willing to assist you if they understand exactly what you are doing.

Know How Changes in the Economy Will Affect Your Business

Is this the type of business that could be damaged if inflation rises by two points? What's the history of this type of business during various economic waves?

Write a Business Plan

Once you are serious about starting, your business plan will be your blueprint. It can be simple or complex, depending on the type of business, number of investors, and so on, you may be dealing with. But it is *necessary*, if you really want to increase your odds of success as an entrepreneur. See Chapter 3, "Planning for Success," for a detailed description of how to write a business plan.

START-UP COSTS AND EQUIPMENT

When starting a business, proper planning and research are absolutely necessary. There is no other way to success. Many people get into business, put up the needed money, and then fail without ever knowing why. If you don't take the time to research your prospective business, you may fall victim to one of these common start-up blunders:

- Insufficient capital requirements.
- Optimistic market opportunities resulting in an overestimation of projected sales.
- Saturation of the market by the competition.
- Poor access to markets because of a bad location.
- Inadequate equipment projections.

Don't let any of these blunders occur. Do the required market research, as detailed in Chapter 3, "Planning for Success," and do the necessary business planning.

On a personal scale, your first research and planning steps are to assess your start-up requirements and calculate how much income you are going to need to get your business off the ground.

How Much Money Will You Need to Start?

There are a great many philosophies regarding the actual start-up costs associated with a business. Some entrepreneurs have begun successful operations with next to nothing, often using the start-up financing techniques discussed in Chapters 3 and 4. There is nothing wrong with that approach if you're willing to sacrifice yourself and spend a great amount of time and energy making your home-based business work. But *undercapitalization* is one of the primary reasons for business failure, and statistics show that businesses that are started for less than $10,000 have a greater chance of failure.

This doesn't necessarily mean that $25,000 or $50,000 is a good start-up figure either. If you need $500,000 to cover all your start-up costs and get your business off the ground and you only spend $100,000, chances are you are going to fail. The key question is not "How much?" but "Is it enough?"

You must make sure that *all* your start-up costs are accounted for—not just your opening expenses, but your initial operating expenses as well. Generally, these numbers can be gathered from similar businesses operating in an area that is comparable to the one where you wish to open, or from trade associations, trade periodicals, suppliers, and other industry sources described in Chapter 3, "Planning For Success."

Although every business has unique costs associated with it, some start-up costs are general to most home-based businesses; these are described in the following paragraphs.

Phone and Utilities

Some telephone and utility companies require deposits; others do not. A deposit should not be required if you have established a payment record with the company as a homeowner or tenant. Telephone deposits are determined by the number of phones and the type of service required. Unless you need a large number of phones and lines, the deposit is likely to range from $50 to $350. Deposits for gas and electricity (when required) will vary according to your projected usage. It is possible to lower them by not overestimating your initial consumption of these utilities.

Equipment

Equipment costs will vary from operation to operation, depending on how equipment-intensive each one is. Common equipment needs are office machines and supplies. To determine what your equipment costs will be, list all of your requirements for efficient business operations. Next, price those items by obtaining quotes or bids from several vendors. Government purchasing agents usually require three closed bids, which is a good minimum number of quotes to start with. Use the quotes you receive to estimate your start-up equipment costs.

Fixtures

The broad category of "fixtures" can include such items as partitions, paneling, signs, storage shelves, cabinets, lighting, shelves, tables, stands, wall systems, showcases, and related hardware for product storage or display. The cost of fixtures depends on a number of variables: location within the home, size and present condition, the type of merchandise to be sold, what kind of image you want to project, and whether new or used fixtures are purchased.

Inventory

Like equipment, inventory requirements change from business to business. Even if you have a service business, you'll still need to store your inventory of office supplies, such as stationery, invoices, and purchase orders.

Leasehold Improvements

Leasehold improvements are immovable installations within your residence that result from remodeling. They include carpeting and other flooring, insulation, electrical wiring, plumbing, bathroom installations, lighting, wall partitions, windows, ceiling tiles, painting, security systems, and some elements of interior design. Because the cost of improvements can vary tremendously (from $5 per square foot to over $20 per square foot), you must investigate your needs carefully.

Licenses and Tax Deposits

Most cities and counties require business operators to obtain various licenses or permits to comply with local regulations. The costs for licensing will vary from business to business in conjunction with the particular start-up requirements. In addition to licensing fees, you'll also need start-up capital for tax deposits. Many states require an advance deposit against future taxes to be collected. In California, for example, if you project $10,000 in taxable sales for the first three months of operation, you must deposit 6.5% ($650) with the state tax bureau when applying for your sales tax permit number.

Marketing Budgets

Most businesses require a strong "grand opening" push to get off the ground and build a customer foundation. Most companies determine their first year's advertising budget as a percentage of projected gross sales. They peg their ad budgets at 2% to 5% of their projected gross sales.

Professional Services

During start-up, you'll probably need the help of a lawyer and an accountant to make sure you meet your legal and tax filing requirements. Fees for these professionals will range according to their expertise and your geographic location.

Pre-Opening Payroll

If your involvement in the business will be full-time, you'll have to set aside at least one month of pre-opening salary for yourself, in addition to a three-month reserve. This payroll reserve will also apply to any employees you might hire during the business start-up phase.

Insurance

Plan on allocating the first quarter's cost of insurance to get your business rolling. A word of caution: If there is ever a time for realism, exercise it when estimating these costs. It is better to have a cushion of excess money to support the start-up of your business than to have insufficient capital.

How Much Income Will You Need?

To determine how much money you have available to invest in a business, evaluate your credits (assets) and debits (liabilities) by using the Personal Balance Sheet on page 22. List all your assets and their value in the top portion of the form: house, car, jewelry, and so on. Then list all your debts in the bottom portion: credit cards, mortgage, bank notes, personal debts, auto loans, and so on. Compute the ratio between total assets and total liabilities to determine your net worth or degree of indebtedness. This ratio is assets:liabilities, or line A:line B. The ratio should approach 2:1, or, if you are like most people nowadays, 1:2. This is generally referred to as the acid-test ratio or quick ratio. If your assets exceed your liabilities, you should be able to keep the creditors from knocking on your door.

TIME MANAGEMENT

The responsibilities of a home-based business owner are vastly different from those of a corporate employee. When you work for someone else, you are responsible only for carrying out your particular duties. A home-based entrepreneur, however, must also pay the bills, seek out new clients, and market the company.

To perform all these tasks and still maintain a professional image, a home-based business owner may need to make some sacrifices. A key factor is how you manage your time. This takes discipline and knowing when and what to delegate. Time management is important not only to the psyche of the owner, but also to the bottom line. Without it, your business can suffer. Follow the guidelines below to stay on schedule.

Logging Your Personal Time Use

Realizing the importance of time allocation and its influence on your business is definitely the first step in establishing a time-management system for yourself. You'll want to begin by exploring your personal

PERSONAL BALANCE SHEET

STATEMENT OF FINANCIAL CONDITION AS OF_____ , 19___

ASSETS   TOTALS

Cash, checking and savings		
Marketable securities		
Non-marketable securities		
Real estate owned		
Partial interest in real-estate equities		
Automobiles		
Personal property		
Personal loans		
Life Insurance—Cash value		
Other Assets—Itemize		
TOTAL ASSETS **A**		

LIABILITIES   TOTALS

Secured loans		
Unsecured loans		
Charge-account bills		
Personal debts		
Monthly bills		
Real-estate mortgages		
Unpaid income tax		
Other unpaid taxes and interest		
Other debts—Itemize		
TOTAL LIABILITIES **B**		
NET WORTH (A - B=C) **C**		
TOTAL LIABILITIES & NET WORTH **D**		

DEGREE OF INDEBTEDNESS

Note:
If total liabilities exceed total assets,
subtract assets from liabilities to determine
degree of indebtedness (B - A=E)

TOTAL LIABILITIES	**B**	
TOTAL ASSETS	**A**	
DEGREE OF INDEBTEDNESS	**E**	

uses of time. Once you become more acutely aware of the ways in which you spend your time, you can remedy your less efficient approaches to various tasks.

The only way to track your use of time is to keep a log. Record your work segments in this log for as long as it takes to get a good reading of your typical usage of the workday. (One or two weeks should be sufficient.) Aside from its obvious concrete benefits, keeping a log is an extremely important practice because it creates awareness of the way in which you run your business.

Here are some questions you can ask yourself at the end of each logged workday, to make the most of the process:

- What time did I start my most important project today? (There's a saying in business: "The way the first hour of the day goes, so goes the day.")
- Could I have started it sooner?
- Did anything distract me from completing it? What? Why?
- Could I have avoided the distraction?
- Did I recover immediately? (Often, a 10-minute distraction will require another 30 minutes to resolve.)
- What might I have done differently today?
- What, right now, is my single biggest time-management problem?

That last question is very important. Time wasters must be identified and eliminated by looking within yourself and assessing your time profile candidly.

CONQUERING TIME WASTERS

Let's deal with interruptions. There are two types: necessary and unnecessary. That distinction is more important than it might appear. To test this, just ask yourself, "If I did not have a single interruption for a month, where would my business be?"

Many interruptions are necessary; the way in which we choose to handle them allows them to bog us down. If we go into a situation knowing full well that there are going to be interruptions because they're part of the business we're in, then we can create ways in which to deal with them effectively. For instance, instead of allowing your incoming calls to be the variable that ultimately determines your daily schedule, you can let your answering machine or answering service take all calls and then choose which ones you will return at a specified time during the day. In that way, your time is yours rather than some-one else's.

After you have completed your daily log of activities and identified your own personal time wasters, divide them into categories so you can classify and conquer them. Most time wasters can be categorized as self-imposed or system-imposed.

1. *Self-imposed time wasters.* "Self-imposed" distractions are those you create yourself. These include:
   - Insufficient planning.
   - Failure to anticipate.
   - Poorly defined goals.
   - Unrealistic time estimates.
   - Procrastination.
   - Attempting too much.
   - Mistakes (your own).
   - Involvement in details.
   - Ineffective delegation.
   - Overcontrol.
   - Reverse delegation.
   - Going directly to people (when intermediates could handle).
   - Calling people unexpectedly.
   - Excessive socializing.
   - Inability to terminate visits.
   - Preoccupation.
   - Emotional upset.
   - Lack of discipline.
   - Fear of offending.
   - Inability to say no.
   - Arguing.
   - Failing to listen.
   - Slow reading.
   - Distracting objects in work environment.
2. *System-imposed time wasters.* "System-imposed" stands for any-thing that the business system or other external forces (like other people) bring upon you. These include:
   - Insufficient planning by others.
   - Lack of company policy.

- Inconsistent values within company.
- Lack of authority.
- Meetings.
- Delays.
- Waiting for others' decisions.
- Poor communications.
- Lack of feedback.
- Unclear problem.
- Mistakes (other people's).
- Mechanical failure.
- Overlong visits.
- Low-priority memos.
- Overstaffing.
- Understaffing.
- Lack of clerical staff.
- Lack of competent staff.
- Ineffective secretary.
- Negative attitude.
- Distractions.

You may discover, upon further inspection, that many things that are believed to be system-imposed are really self-imposed—or a combination of the two. For instance, if a neighbor drops in to chitchat, you have a time waster caused by others. But if you invite that kind of behavior by being open to it or failing to discourage it, then you are also bringing it upon yourself, at least to the degree to which it occurs. Observe your own behavior in these instances. Did you in any way initiate these visits or prolong them?

Keep Visits Brief

A drop-in visit is common in the home office setting, and it can be a real time-waster. Here are some tricks you can utilize to ensure that its toll on you is minimal. First, arrange your furniture in a way that does not make people feel overly welcome and comfortable. (If you deal regularly with clients, however, this advice does not apply.) If someone remains a chronic, unwelcome drop-in, diplomatically let him or her know that you have work to do and will socialize only after office hours. It might help to have a script arranged if you are afraid of floundering. Don't feel bad. Remember that this is one aspect of running a business. The other party should feel apologetic for not demonstrating more sensitivity where you are concerned. Another method you can implement when people stay just a bit too long is to have a few closings at hand that will help them get the picture. You might say, "Before you go . . ." or, "Before we wrap up, is there anything else you wanted to cover?" Be as businesslike as possible at all times.

Keep Phone Calls Brief

The telephone should be handled in much the same way. A lot of people keep stopwatches or clocks handy and when a certain number of minutes have elapsed (7 to 10 minutes seems common), they begin winding up the conversation with closings like those mentioned above. Let people know you're ready to conclude. Take charge. State your goals at the beginning and summarize them at the end.

If you think you receive an excessive number of phone interruptions, solving the problem may require you to do the following:

- *Prioritize calls.* It may not be clear where the phone interruptions are coming from or how many there are. In a telephone log book, write down each phone interruption as it occurs. After a few days, review when the calls came in, their sources and relevance, and the time spent on the phone. Look for trends. Is there one particular caller or group of callers? Once you have this log of callers, you will be able to take action to resolve the problem, either by timing the calls, winding up the conversation by introducing one of the closings above, or making a list of pertinent callers to get back to at a time when you aren't so busy.
- *Screen calls.* If you have employees or an answering service, they may have been informing clients that you are the only person to talk to regarding their questions, when in actuality they may be able to help the callers just as effectively. Be sure your employees (or answering service) know how to handle specific items or problems so you won't be interrupted. This will save time for you and the callers.
- *Avoid telephone tag.* Avoid wasting your time in returning phone calls to people who are continually not available.

When the person you are calling is not in:

- Ask when is the best time to contact the person. Get specific information.

- Ask to speak to the person's secretary or administrative assistant, or a coworker. These individuals may be able to address the purpose of your call, or at least they will work more closely with the person you are trying to reach and can suggest ways of reaching him or her.
- Ask whether the person you are calling can be paged. The person you are calling may simply be down the hall talking with a coworker or away from his or her desk for just a few moments.
- Tell the person you are talking to as much as you can about the purpose of your call. When your call is returned by the person you're trying to reach, he or she can have answers ready for you.
- Give a specific time when you will be available for the return phone call; for example, "I will be in from 9:00 to 11:45 A.M. and in the afternoon from 3 to 5 P.M."
- Make a telephone appointment for a specific time, such as 3 P.M., to return the call or have it returned to you. Many people treat telephone appointments with the same attention given to in-person appointments. The only difference is that the meeting takes place on the phone.

In these situations, ask yourself, "Does this encounter help me complete my objectives?" If not, it must be dealt with swiftly and efficiently. (The aforementioned diplomacy will go a long way in making sure that people continue to work with you rather than deciding to go elsewhere. If they fail to understand the importance of getting work done rather than socializing, then perhaps they are not the right people for you to work with.)

Keep Meetings on Schedule

The above principles also apply for meetings. Even though you probably won't have employees in the beginning, you will have meetings with clients, vendors, and suppliers. You will want to set a businesslike tone without being officious. Many people mistake "businesslike" for unfriendly. In the ideal working environment, people work together on goals in a businesslike fashion. This cooperation shows up in the bottom line time and time again. Set time limits on your meetings, and make everyone present aware of them. Make sure the purpose of the meeting is clear. Develop and distribute an agenda, and establish firm time limits for each subject to be discussed. Encourage people to get their points across in as little time as possible. Another way to cut down on meeting time is to make sure that only the people who really need to be there are present. Make sure your meetings start on time. Much time is wasted when people who show up on time must stand around waiting for a scheduled meeting to begin. And don't schedule meetings unless they are really necessary. Most people spend too much time in meetings simply because too many unnecessary meetings are held.

Do your homework before any meeting. Jot down notes on the agenda, and organize your thoughts so that you don't waste time once the meeting begins. Request that others do the same. Postpone the meeting if everyone is not prepared. Take personal responsibility for the productivity of a meeting. Participate in ways that fulfill both the purpose of the meeting and your own needs.

When you need to keep notes of a meeting, try to record them as the meeting progresses. You won't have to invest time doing it afterwards, and you'll be less likely to leave out pertinent points. Write legibly. If necessary, have the notes typed immediately afterward so that they can be of value right away to you and to the people to whom they are distributed.

Organize Your Paperwork

Most desks are a mountainous mess and that disorganization contributes to the time crunch in an obvious way: valuable time is spent just finding things. In the long run, many people begin to believe that they are as inefficient as their messy desks. In other words, organization and time are quite closely linked.

Solutions to the problem of office organization have filled volumes. Here are a few tips:

- Handle each piece of paper once.
- After you have looked at it, don't add it to the growing piles; do something with it.
- If you think you will need it for information, file it with other background information (and make sure you go through this file and weed out what you don't need every month or so.)
- If it requires immediate action, place it in one of the stackable letter trays on your desk. They should be labeled "To Read," "To Do," "To Pay," and "To File," or given similar tags.

You'll find that these are the four main filing categories of papers. All of the other papers should sail right into the most efficient receptacles ever created for paper: the wastebasket.

You may feel comfortable using form letters for some of your correspondence. They may not be personal or impressive, but form letters provide fast and concise information that may be more valuable than a personalized letter. They also save the time it takes to personally compose a new letter for a repetitive situation.

Keep your correspondence as brief as possible, cutting out superfluous words and phrases. Whoever said, "If I had more time, I would have written a shorter letter," understood that clear writing is a skill that requires a lot of practice and attention. Say what you mean; don't make your reader interpret vague references and suggestions. Use your dictionary. Be clear about what you want and you're more likely to get it.

You can do other things you can do to discourage clutter. Establish a message center on a bulletin board or some other central place, so that messages don't get misplaced. Make sure your phone lists are current, and keep pads and working pens by the phone. (How often have you spent time searching for those?) And spend 10 minutes at the end of each day tidying up. This will ensure that you will not only start each day in a fresher state of mind, but you will prevent mounds of clutter from accumulating.

Identify Your Objectives and Priorities

Earlier, the issue discussed was priorities. In keeping your time log, for instance, you will be forced to determine which of your activities are more important for meeting your greater objectives, and which are less important. That kind of prioritizing must be done because it is the only way you can determine which of your waiting tasks should be done ahead of the others.

But, by definition, you must determine your objectives before you can prioritize them. If you've already written your business plan (discussed in Chapter 3), you will have a clear vision of your ultimate goal.

Your business plan should highlight your short- and long-term goals for your home-based venture. One short-term goal might be "Turn over the initial inventory by June." A long-term goal might be "Expand the business to overseas markets within the next 10 years."

By creating a list of both of these types of goals, you can determine which ones take precedence over others. The more comprehensive your list is, the more thorough your planning becomes. Your list should serve as a guideline, but it isn't engraved in stone. You can revise it as is necessary to maintain your focus.

Your list will come in handy during your daily operations. Time waits for no one, as the saying goes, and it puts double pressure on a person torn between two projects that seem equally important. Should you take care of the filing or make an appointment to finalize a client's contract? One may seem more immediate because assorted paperwork is piled on your desk, but the other could put money into your bank account. Weigh the two tasks according to your needs, and according to how significantly they will contribute to your long-term goals.

Once you have outlined your long-term and short-term goals, explore what you must do to accomplish them. You might make a daily "To Do" list, with each specific duty highlighted. You should incorporate both your personal tasks and your professional responsibilities in the list, and indicate when you need to carry out each activity. For example, making your bed in the morning is not as important as making a call to a client in another time zone. Some activities can be delayed; others cannot.

Next to your list of activities, put numbers indicating their order of importance. If you need to carry out an activity by a specific time, list a deadline. These notations will help you keep your schedule in order. On some days, you may find that two or three things need to be done at the same time. When that happens, try to delegate some tasks, or, if possible, adjust your schedule.

Delegate Skillfully

We've mentioned delegation as a method of time management. In this section, you will learn why it's important to use this often-overlooked tool.

Delegation is vital to a one-person operation. Without it, important first clients could be lost forever, and your reputation could be damaged. Delegation is a learned skill, not a trait business owners are born with. It's important for you to seek out as many clients as possible and perform work for them, but you can have too much of a good thing. With delegation, you can take a step back and evaluate your operation more objectively, fine-tuning your business as you go along.

There are three types of projects you may encounter:

1. Projects only you can complete.
2. Projects you or someone else can complete.
3. Projects only others can complete.

No matter how hard you try, you will never be able to handle all the projects you want to finish yourself. For many home-based business owners, however, this outcome is not for a lack of trying. Some people are afraid to let go of work because they feel that (1) it won't get done, (2) it won't get done properly, or (3) both. This is where home-based operators should take a second look at the part-time employees they hire or the service bureaus they contract with. Are they really not worthy of additional work because they can't do it? Or can they do it, but the owners are just afraid to delegate? Can you hire someone to deliver important paperwork instead of doing it yourself? Will you allow a service bureau to mail out your products instead of trudging to the post office each day yourself?

Delegation is not a dirty word. It can help home-based business owners manage their own time and help others learn about the company they work for. Here are a few simple steps you can take to put delegation into practice on a day-to-day basis:

1. Choose part-time employees or service bureaus that will perform the task adequately.
2. Identify the task that is being delegated.
3. Specify when you will check on their work, be available for questions or problems, and so on. Encourage and reward employees or service bureaus for their work by giving them more.

CONQUERING PROCRASTINATION

Just about everybody procrastinates, so there's no room for guilt or bad feelings where this issue is concerned. There are steps you can take to conquer this element of modern life. Without understanding and dealing with procrastination, writing down goals for the rest of your life will help only minimally. You've got to get over the hump that may be preventing you from carrying them out.

What is procrastination? Simply put, it's the act of doing low-priority things (or nothing) when you know you should be doing high-priority things. One of the many reasons for procrastinating is that you simply don't have your priorities straight. After you have completed your detailed priority list, assigning a sequence to the tasks should no longer be a problem. The most common reason that people procrastinate is that they are putting off the prospect of dealing with a potentially unpleasant task. (Often, they actually enjoy the work once they take the first step and dive in.)

What are the best ways to face unpleasant tasks head-on? If you own your own business, try calculating the amount of money that your delay is costing you. Delays are very expensive. If you delay handling an inquiry, for example, you could lose a customer and the potential for hundreds of dollars. If you delay servicing a machine when it needs it, you could end up with a very costly breakdown. Sit down and calculate the costs. Seeing the actual dollar amount will be surprisingly effective. If you lose a machine for a day, for instance, you're looking at lost productivity hours as well as emergency repair bills. And the frustration of knowing that the work loss could have been prevented probably won't help much.

Promise yourself a reward for finishing an unpleasant task. Even a small one might help you get there sooner. Just as you wrote down your goals, let other people know about your tasks, particularly the ones you are having difficulty accomplishing. That method could help your resolve as well. Give yourself a deadline—an early one, if possible—and stick to it.

One of the best ways to tackle difficult projects is to break them up into smaller, more manageable pieces. Anything is bearable for a few minutes of time. Arrange to do an unpleasant task for just 5 or 10 minutes. Chances are that once you get started, it won't be so difficult. You may even find yourself enjoying it. The hardest part is always getting started. The dread that accompanies a future project always seems to build on itself, making the project much worse than it was to start with. The trick is to *get started,* any way you can. Divide the task into time segments or individual units.

If you are avoiding a certain task because you fear you may not be good at it, that is an entirely different issue. If you can assign the task to someone else, then do so, rather than wasting time debating whether you can do it. As a home-based business owner, you can assign certain tasks to independent contractors who are experts in their fields: advertising, sales, public relations, computer graphics, and so on. You'll be using the delegating principles outlined earlier to maximize your efficiency.

These techniques provide excellent ways of dealing with the procrastination that haunts everyone. They can be put into practice time and time again. The underlying element that must be changed, though, is your overall attitude about the things you have to do. You must realize that they've simply got to be done. Your "Do it Later" attitude has to become a "Do it Now" attitude. Most entrepreneurs count themselves among the "Do it Now" people. If they aren't born that way, they make sure they become that way. Things don't just happen for entrepreneurs. *Entrepreneurs make things happen.*

The first step is taking initiative—turning an idea or thought into reality through action; making something happen that might not otherwise occur.

The initiative process is characterized by the following:

- Action rather than waiting passively for something to happen.
- Willingness to move from the known (the status quo) to the unknown.
- Independence rather than dependence.
- More emphasis on risk than on security.
- Expansion rather than restriction.
- Concern with opportunities to assist and support, and de-emphasis of personal rights (your rights at times need to be secondary to getting the job done).
- Greater willingness to take an extra step. If everyone does only his or her share, there will always be a percentage left undone. People need to do more than their share, contributing whatever is needed to complete each task.

Entrepreneurs are masters of their own time. They have separated their priorities from their commitments, they have learned how to set long-term and short-term goals, and they have learned to schedule their valuable time in a way that allows them to act on those goals and still retain the flexibility necessary to be open to change and growth. In short, they have learned to manage time.

Time Management Tools

Here are some of the many products available to keep you focused and working efficiently:

Filing System
You may need a filing cabinet, file folders, an in/out basket, and dividers for alphabetizing invoices or other documents. A host of other filing tools are available to help you put paperwork in its place—and find it when needed again.

Calendar
Among the many options are a wall calendar, a date book, or a dry-erase chart. Some of these items are more useful when you're at your home office; others help you keep track of your deadlines while you're on the road. Look for date books that divide the day into hours, to gain the greatest control and most detailed record of your time.

Contact Management System

You can use a variety of up-to-date tools to manage relationships with your clients, such as contact management software, e-mail and voice mail systems, and answering machines.

BALANCING HOME AND BUSINESS

Though the advantages are attractive, maintaining a successful home-based business is no cakewalk. In the beginning, especially, demands on your time and assets will be considerable, and dedication to the success of the business is critical. These demands may increase the stress already present in operating any business, and can take their toll on family relationships, creating tension both during and after work hours.

The privacy and freedom gained from home-based business ownership often lead to problems. The absence of outside scrutiny also means insulation from outside input and suggestions, and can result in stagnation and a failure to keep up with the newest market trends. All of these factors can prevent growth and future market success.

Separating family and business life is an important step toward the successful management of both. By setting boundaries for proper roles and behavior in each setting, it is possible to head off role carry-over problems before they occur. When lines are drawn, family members know what to expect from you when the arena changes from home to work.

Family/Business Boundaries

You can establish fair and reasonable family/business boundaries in a variety of ways. Work out guidelines together, creating a family/business "creed" or "mission statement." Central to the theme of the document should be the fact that business decisions must be based on what is best for the company, and that family politics and problems should not interfere with your business operations. By the same token, business should not dominate your home life.

All family members should be present when the creed/statement is done. Family goals should be set first, and can be placed in the document as a preamble to the guidelines. Once goals are set, specific guidelines for achieving this success should be outlined.

Once goals and guidelines have been set, it's a good idea to create *physical* boundaries as well. Separate areas of the house should be designated as work-only areas, separate telecommunications should be installed for business use, and traffic and noise levels must indicate respect for business hours in the home. Chapter 6, "Setting Up Your Home Office," gives some valuable suggestions.

You don't have to be a miracle worker to keep family and business separate. Here are some simple tips to keep the two from crossing over:

- Close the door to your office while you are working. This is a sign to family members not to bother you.
- Close the door to your office when you have finished working for the day. This will keep you from rushing into your office at all hours of the night.
- Don't let your children answer your business phone. You may think it's cute; customers won't.
- Make sure children know you are not to be bothered while you are "at the office."
- Don't answer your business phone after hours. Your recorded answering message should state your business hours.
- Don't do household chores during business hours.
- Schedule short breaks in your workday.

Turning Your Home into a Business Site

Some home-based entrepreneurs feel that starting up a business is as easy as making a declaration that they are in business. Every part of the house is used to accommodate the business. Every drawer is used to stash receipts, invoices, and other items that deal strictly with the business. Friends, family, and just about any other persons stopping by the house are free to interrupt the businessperson at the drop of a paper clip. These home-based businesses suffer from a poor image. Their legal and tax obligations are neglected until the last minute. Is it any wonder that many of them don't stay in business?

Not all home-based entrepreneurs conduct business in this manner. In fact, with the influx of corporate refugees into the home-based arena, a new wave of professionalism has hit the home office. Specific rooms are now set aside as offices only. Within those home offices, business is conducted away from the disturbances of family, friends, and day-to-day distractions. Accountants and lawyers are consulted. Separate phone lines are installed, and cutting-edge office equipment is put in place. What eventually transpires is a metamorphosis of a room in a house into an office where business is conducted in a professional manner.

An Office Is an Office

The first thing you have to do when setting up a home-based business is to establish—for yourself, your family, and your friends—rules that separate your home life from your work life. The first rule involves the office space. It marks the boundary where home life stops and work life begins. When you are in your office, you are conducting business.

Your home and business should not mix: They should coexist. Isolating your office from your family life allows you to conduct business without distractions. You can start creating boundaries by approaching your home business as a *business*. That means developing a sense of professionalism. Even if your clients will never see your home office— or you—remember that *being* polished is the best way to conduct your home-based venture as a business.

As briefly alluded to earlier, one of the most significant but least tangible problems home-based entrepreneurs face involves creating and maintaining a professional image. Here are some things you can do to build professionalism:

- Keep regular business hours so that work seems like work.
- Build a separate entrance or arrange for direct access to your office so that visiting clients or business associates won't have to traipse through your house to get to your office.
- Establish family time and work time. Don't let personal matters intrude on your work time if you can, and don't let business matters interfere with the time you've set aside for your family.
- Make provisions for child care if business demands are such that you cannot adequately care for your children and the business at the same time.
- Rent a mailbox at the post office or at a private mailbox service, to establish a commercial address rather than a residential one.
- Install a separate phone/fax line for your business.
- Maintain all business records inside your office.
- Have letterhead, stationery, business cards, envelopes, note pads, and other office supplies printed with your business name, logo, and P.O. Box address on them.
- Develop some sort of messaging system—an answering machine, an answering service, or a voice mail service—so that clients can leave messages in your absence.

The home-based business basics listed above may seem very conventional and somewhat restrictive, until you realize what you expect from the businesses you deal with. What would your reaction be if a toddler answered the phone when you called a corporate client? How would you feel if a supplier sent you an invoice written on a piece of scratch paper? As a businessperson, you take certain things for granted. You assume that the businesses you deal with will fulfill certain professional conventions.

As a home-based businessperson, you may feel tempted to skirt those conventions. In fact, being unconventional may be what prompted you to work at home in the first place. Even so, disregarding the basic rules of business won't work to your benefit in the long run. "Making do" without printed stationery and a well-planned phone system may not cut into your productivity, but it won't boost your image much. For most home-based businesses, taking advantage of every opportunity to foster a professional image is critical.

A retail operation develops its image in a variety of ways. Its merchandise, its location, its signs, its window dressing, its salespeople— all of these factors add up to the public's perception of the operation. But if you conduct business from your spare bedroom or den, you have access to none of these attention-getting devices. Your business image depends on whatever limited interaction you may have with clients (and potential clients)—and that means *every detail counts*.

How will your business come into contact with the outside world? One way is in print, so pay close attention to your logo, stationery, and business cards. Although a company logo may seem like a trivial decoration, a cleverly designed, attractive logo can go a long way toward helping your company stand out in your customers' minds. If you aren't artistically inclined, hire a professional to design your typography.

BALANCING FAMILY AND BUSINESS

If you find it's almost impossible to pry yourself away from your desk when the clock chimes closing time, you're not alone. Home-based business owners know quite well the temptation to keep working through the night.

In fact, several factors inherent in running a home-based business fuel workaholism. At an outside office, there are clear divisions in the day—you see people leaving at 5 P.M., and the cleaning crew comes in around 7 P.M. At home, you don't have the obvious cut-off points, so the next thing you know, it's 8 P.M.

Home-based business owners may be overworked simply because so many of them are start-up or one-person operations. Still, workaholism left unchecked leads to some real dangers. Excessive business hours can be a tremendous intrusion on family life.

The key word is *balance.* Having your work at your fingertips 24 hours a day can be an advantage if handled correctly. Being able to work at night after putting children to bed is a definite plus.

To keep some balance between your business and your family life, follow these guidelines.

Define Your Work Hours and Stick to Them

Whether you work "normal" office hours or work in the evenings, stick to your routine. Let your business associates know that you don't answer phones after hours. Sometimes you will have to violate the boundaries, but if you make long hours the exception rather than the rule, you'll be fine.

Create a Specific Work Plan for Each Day

If you don't set goals and limits, work expands to fill available time.

Set Up Good Support Mechanisms

Purchase equipment, phone lines, a fax machine—whatever you need to make your home office more efficient. Arrange an account with a delivery service such as Federal Express, or invest in a postage meter if you're far from the local post office. In that way, you won't waste time running errands.

Take Breaks during Your Workday

It is important to get away from your office from time to time during your workday. Take a walk around the block, have a cup of tea, or play a quick game with your children.

Close the Door to Your Business

If your office door is open and you can see the work piled up on your desk, you are far more likely to head back into your office to make more calls or do paperwork.

Don't Talk about Business during Family Time

If all you talk about is your business, your family may grow to resent your entrepreneurial efforts. When you leave your office at the end of your workday, leave your business behind you.

Expect the Unexpected and Work to Avoid It

In any new business venture, conventional or home-based, situations happen that are out of your control. Your house may need cleaning, or the garage door may need fixing. You can spread out the most serious events by dividing responsibility for day-to-day activities with your spouse and/or children.

Schedule Quality Time with Your Family

It may seem strange to make appointments to spend time with your children or your spouse, but it's a good practice. Making sure you and your family spend time together while you're not working is key to holding your family together and keeping them supportive of your business. If you spend all your time working and neglect your family, you may cause irreparable damage to your relationships with your spouse and children.

Talk to Your Family

If your family is distracting you from your business, you may need to discuss your problems with them. Let them know that you enjoy their company, but that your work is vital to their happiness. Ask for their advice and assistance. In this way, your family will consider themselves part of the solution instead of part of the problem.

Keep Yourself Focused on Your Work

Home-based business owners know well the feeling of being left out as their family members catch a movie, go out to dinner, or play in the park. Resist the temptation to join them at times when business is more important, and you'll be better able to enjoy yourself when you're not working.

Strengthen Your Life Away from Home

The most successful home-business owners are able to restrict contact with their families while they are working. Think about meeting clients at their offices, taking them to lunch, or working at the library occasionally.

DEALING WITH CHILDREN

Many parents choose to start a home-based business in an effort to spend more time with their children. And although some people are able to successfully meet that goal, others find it difficult to master the roles of parent and at-home entrepreneur.

Combining business ownership and parenthood under the same roof can lead to trouble. Children can create interruptions that take your attention away from your business, and they can undermine the image of professionalism you try to convey. On the other hand, your business can become all-consuming, keeping you from giving your children the attention they need.

Making Your Office Child-Proof

To better balance the responsibilities of raising children and running a successful home-based business, keep the following general rules in mind.

Don't Rule Out Child Care

If you want your business to grow rapidly, it may be necessary to make some kind of child-care arrangements, at least occasionally. Besides traditional preschools or day-care centers, consider "trading off" some babysitting time with another home-based business owner/parent who will watch your child while you work, and vice versa.

Teach Your Children to Respect Your Business

If your children are very young, the responsibility lies with you; a 2-year-old can't understand how important it is not to run screaming down the hall while you're on the phone. Schedule calls during your children's nap time or when they're settled in front of "Sesame Street." With older children, though, you should make it clear that you are in charge of a business and you can't be interrupted every 10 minutes with problems they can take care of themselves.

Address the Phone Issue

One of the greatest challenges facing home-based business owners with small children is preventing them from picking up a phone extension in the middle of a business call and giggling. To avoid this problem, your best bet is to get an answering machine and, if at all possible, a separate business line.

Consider Starting a Child-Related Business

If you sell toys or baby products, your clients will most likely be parents, who will be more sympathetic to your situation. An added bonus: your kids will be delighted if they get to play with samples of your inventory.

Get Your Children Involved

Let children apply stamps or labels to envelopes or let older children sort mail by name or ZIP code. Children can be very enthusiastic about the most routine tasks. Remember to keep tasks age-appropriate. If you give a 3-year-old a task he or she can't perform well, the child will get upset, you'll be frustrated, and you'll probably have to redo the task yourself, thereby wasting a lot of time and energy. Giving children tasks they can perform well allows them to feel important. They will have a sense of contributing to your business and you will be able to get some tedious chores off your plate.

Situate Your Office Away from Your Children's Play Area

Trying to force your children to tiptoe quietly around your home office usually won't work. Just because you are running a business from your home, don't expect your kids to act like grown-ups. Kids will be kids. They'll be noisy, they'll run around the house, they'll interrupt you, and they'll demand your attention while you are trying to work. To remedy the situation, put your office in a room or space that isn't in the center of your children's play area. With your operation located in a den down the hall or in a basement, you can keep your office free of the common laughs and shrieks.

Deal with Problems Immediately

Children and parents may experience some friction when an office is run from the home. Children may resent having to be quiet when Mom or Dad is on a business call, having to pick up their things when a client stops by, having strangers stopping by the house, or having a parent who is working all the time. The business owner may resent constant interruptions and noise. Don't let these problems fester: address them early. If children complain that you are spending too much time "at work" and not enough time with them, it may be time to reevaluate your schedule. Sit down with your children to discuss the problems and come up with solutions that are satisfactory to both of you.

WORKING WITH YOUR SPOUSE

When married couples start home-based businesses together, office romance takes on a whole new meaning.

More and more couples are considering home-based businesses as their route to living happily ever after. Unfortunately, a large number of these couples overlook the fact that they have much more at risk than just business failure. If things go awry, they could end up in divorce court.

Most husband-and-wife business owners agree that the personal relationship has to be a superstrong if the business is to survive. Young marriages often make for unsuccessful businesses. In general, an established marriage has a better chance of making a business succeed at home.

When entrepreneurial success is at stake, love alone can't keep your business together. To make your partnership work, Dennis Jaffe, owner of Heartwork, a family business consulting firm in San Francisco, and author of *Working with the Ones You Love* (Berkeley, CA: Conari Press) says, "You must do a fierce audit to determine whether each of you has what's needed to run a business. Desire isn't enough."

Though it may seem an obvious step, many couples don't objectively examine whether they have the complementary skills to make the business partnership viable. Just because you love each other doesn't mean you have the skills to run a business together.

Before starting a home-based business with your spouse, ask yourselves the following questions:

- Do you enjoy working together?
- Do you communicate effectively?
- Do you have skills that are complementary?
- Can you discuss problems without getting personal?
- Do you agree on the goals for your proposed business?

If you answered no to any of these questions, you should reevaluate your plans to go into business together.

One of the major issues facing married home-based business owners is defining clear boundaries—both physical and psychological. To preserve your sanity, you must be able to separate the pressures of your work life from your personal life and vice versa. The first step toward attaining this goal is to agree to solve problems together instead of blaming each other for them. You must learn to communicate effectively under pressure. And when problems can't be nipped in the bud, couples have to agree not to deal with business situations at home on weekends.

You must also strive to keep your independence from each other intact. It's difficult to complain about your business partner after a stressful day if your partner is the person you're talking to. Spouses need separate friends, individual hobbies, and sometimes just plain old space. After being together all week long, some time apart on the weekends is a good idea. There has to be some separation, otherwise there's a danger the marriage will become nothing but the business.

There is one area that demands solidarity: housework. You have to be as explicit about home responsibilities as you are about business responsibilities.

Even if you believe you have all the ingredients for a fruitful partnership, don't take any chances. Draw up an agreement that outlines what will happen to the business in case of divorce.

Once you get past all the messy details, a business-and-marriage partnership can be extremely rewarding.

COPING WITH ISOLATION

An often-overlooked negative aspect of working from home is the sense of isolation you can feel during the workday. You might take for granted the buzz that permeates a traditional office. The sounds of phones ringing, the drone of employees talking, and the barking of an irate manager may all serve to drive potential business owners into work for themselves. However, these noises may not seem too bad compared to the silence of an empty house. Without human interaction, people tend to feel lonely and isolated. Without someone with whom to discuss your ideas or from whom you occasionally receive a pat on the back, a home-based business owner can become discouraged.

There can never be a replacement for the human interaction found in the traditional office. If you can accept this fact, you can work to find your own motivational stimuli and you will function just as effectively as you did as an employee.

Only you can take steps to find others who can motivate you in your work. There are certain activities you can engage in to find prospective clients and build professional alliances. A few of these are highlighted below.

Meetings

Meetings are an important aspect of any business, but they serve a dual purpose for the home-based business owner. First, and most obviously, they allow you to communicate directly with your present and future clients. Second, they help you establish rapport with people who can help you in both your professional and personal life. By taking the time to schedule and attend a meeting outside of your office, you demonstrate your willingness to go out of your way to present your products or services to your clients. A home-based business owner who takes the time and effort to put together a presentation and deliver it in person shows a confidence not necessarily conveyed over a phone line or on paper.

Meetings should be structured; don't schedule them just for the sake of getting out of the house. However, if you find yourself frequently speaking to certain clients on the phone, ask yourself whether it would be better to meet them in person.

Working Lunches

Some meetings are impossible to schedule during normal work hours. Your clients may be too busy to host a sales call, or inundated with proposals from many of your industry colleagues. This is where a little extra effort on your part is advisable and will serve to break up the daily routine you may find monotonous.

Business meals are generally more relaxed than more formal meetings, and an invitation to lunch could put your client in a more receptive mood toward what your company has to offer. You can also establish friendships and professional networks this way.

Even if your business isn't conducive to meetings, you can still schedule some luncheons with business partners and focus groups—or with a friend—to break up a hectic day.

Professional Organizations

Some business-related organizations have been created specifically to get people out of their work environments and into more comfortable settings for personal interaction. The National Association of Home-based Business, for example, offers regional meetings and annual events specifically for home-based business owners. Members can meet for dinner and discuss their companies, receiving suggestions for solving problems from other members. Other trade-related groups can offer you information on your specific industry and help you find your business voice through their lobbying efforts. Chambers of Commerce and networking associations can also fulfill your need for social interaction. See Appendix A for details on these associations.

There are trade associations for nearly every industry you can think of, from craft-making to mail order to desktop publishing. A publication by Gale Research, *The Encyclopedia of Associations*, is especially valuable. Many libraries have this publication in their reference sections. See Appendix B for other useful books.

Consider subscribing to any trade publications serving your industry. Not only will they keep you abreast of news concerning your industry; they can also provide information on other organizations you should join. Appendix C lists many helpful publications.

Community newspapers, local business journals, and other publications can keep you informed on local events affecting your business, and let you know about any local associations you might want to join.

Organize Your Own Group

Even the most reserved of entrepreneurs can start up their own focus group, networking club, or trade organization in their area. You would fill a need not currently being addressed by the industry, and that in itself could cause others to join. With a little promotion through a local business journal (perhaps a calendar listing of the date, time, and location of your meeting) or even a flyer at the local library or business resource center, you may find some interested parties.

A meeting can be a structured event or simply an informal "meet and greet" at your home. Once your group becomes a little more established, you may want to alternate locales or request permission to use a room in the local library or a meeting hall. Low attendance doesn't signify failure; indeed, some groups are better small. The point is that you would be networking with your peers on a personal and professional level.

The Art of Networking

Home-based operation in and of itself is not conducive to networking; as mentioned above, isolation is one possible negative side effect of working from home. This does not mean, however, that networking is impossible. Indeed, you should realize that you have an opportunity to network every time you interact with another human being.

Let's take one entrepreneur's typical workday as an example. A desktop publisher starts her morning by taking her son to school, stopping briefly at the gate to talk to his teacher about a science project. Her next stop is the office supply store, where she picks up her order of toner cartridges, a ream of paper, and a stack of file folders. After a brief stop at a client's business to drop off a contract with the secretary, she is off to meet with a printer about a newsletter job. She then goes home to work on a brochure for a landscaping service. She encounters a question related to the job, so she calls the client and gets his assistant, who promptly answers the question. She finishes the assignment in enough time to pick up her son from school, after which she runs into an old friend picking up his daughter. They talk for a moment, and she leaves to drop her child off with her husband, after which she attends a meeting for her marketing focus group.

How many times during this workday was the desktop publisher faced with a networking opportunity? Answer: At least six, if you don't count immediate family members.

Every person you encounter could be a potential client. You never know whether people you've talked to on a regular basis could use your services unless you tell them what you do. Whenever appropriate, make sure everyone knows your business specialty. Even if they don't need your services, they may know someone else who does. At the same time, do not make yourself or your work the center of the conversation.

On a practical note, take samples of your work (if possible) and plenty of business cards wherever you go. You never know when you might find an excellent potential client.

2

HOME-BASED BUSINESS OPPORTUNITIES

The kind of home-based business you decide to pursue and the way in which you pursue it are strictly personal decisions. However, other considerations may be entirely *im*personal.

Existing and expected competition, market growth, start-up capital, personal income, and hundreds of other factors are *quantifiable* (measurable) and, therefore, unrelated to personal sentiment. The trends that took hold last year or the growth of a certain industry over the past decade are undeniable facts. But, what you or anyone else thinks is poised to be the next high-growth business is purely speculative. Then again, you may not be looking for the next Great Opportunity: a lot of aspiring entrepreneurs simply don't want to work for anybody else. The point is that the choice is entirely your own. If home-based businesses offer anything, it is the freedom to choose what you want to do and how you want to do it. Most home-based ventures can be part-time (many of them start that way) or full-time; typically, they are labor-intensive and require minimal cash investment. Many are solo operations requiring no additional employees, and all of them offer the dual reward associated with owning a business: emotional satisfaction and the potential for financial prosperity.

Ideally, the business you choose should be based on both personal (intuition or insight) and impersonal (market research) factors. You may believe that a particular market is going to take off, based on evidence you have gathered, but you decide not to enter into that market because it doesn't seem right for you. Conversely, you may have a hunch about an entirely new service business that you feel will be in high demand a year from now, and decide to take the risk although there is no proof that it's viable. Either situation may hold success or failure for you; the key is to balance your personal beliefs with a strong dose of forethought and research. A new product or service will not sell if you cannot find or create a market for it, and a proven business won't be successful if you don't believe in it.

This chapter serves as a bridge between the two focal points of this book: you, and the business you plan to start. It starts by exploring more of the personal issues you will face as a business owner working from home. It continues with a thorough analysis of the different ways to find the business that will be right for you. Will you do best with an original idea, an invention, a licensed business opportunity, or a franchise?

THE PART-TIME PATH

Once you understand the dynamics of home-based business—the demands it will place on your personal life and professional life—you have to decide how much time you are going to devote to making your dream a reality. (As you will see, the other critical decision is how much money you can afford to feed it.) Some entrepreneurs are content with keeping their full-time jobs and running a part-time home-based business simultaneously, or they may have so many obligations already that four hours a day is all they can give to their venture (at least for the time being). Others, start a home-based business with the intention of making it a multimillion-dollar corporation, and they pour every waking hour into making it grow.

Advantages of a Part-Time Business

Starting a business from home on a part-time basis has certain advantages. A part-time home-based venture:

- Supplements your current income.
- Reduces the risk of starting a business by decreasing the amount of effort (and money) you have to expend.
- Allows your business to grow gradually, in proportion to the demand for your product(s) or service(s).
- Offers an easier transition out of your current employment and into full-time home-based operation.

Part-time is by far the safest way to proceed, especially with a first-time entrepreneurial venture. Not only do you have complete control over the mechanics of the business (structure, personnel, advertising, production, and so on), but you also regulate the amount of time you spend operating it. If your full-time job or your personal life suddenly requires more of your attention, you have the flexibility to tend to those matters without sacrificing your business operations or your income. However, if you try to run a full-time business in addition to holding a full-time job, it can be all-consuming.

Besides exacting less of your time, a part-time home-based business allows you to get started for less money. You are not burdened with the pressures that full-time operators experience: they need to achieve high production and sales levels immediately, in order to offset the substantial costs incurred while putting the business together. For instance, a gift-basket service operating part-time can sustain itself on just a few orders a month because the owner is still earning income from his or her full-time occupation and is not relying on the income generated by gift-basket sales.

If gradual growth and a casual atmosphere are what you seek, then a part-time home-based business is what you want. You may be content with your current employment, and simply want to develop a business idea at home in your spare time as a means of supplementing your income. In that case, there is no reason to give up your other work just yet. By giving your idea just a couple of hours a day, you can get your business rolling.

The transformation from full-time employee to full-time entrepreneur is substantially less difficult when you are already well beyond start-up. It's no secret that becoming an entrepreneur by quitting your job one day and starting the next day from scratch is a high-risk proposition. The common misconception is that entrepreneurs leverage their livelihood by starting their own businesses. Home-based business is helping to change all that. By working slowly from home, you can create new opportunities for yourself without having to sacrifice anything in the process. *But you will have to work at it.*

Disadvantages of a Part-Time Business

Along with the attractive features of running a home-based business on a part-time basis, there are certain obstacles that threaten your success:

- Owners of part-time businesses often are not taken seriously by suppliers, potential investors, and prospective customers.
- Many part-time businesses suffer from slow growth.
- Some people find it difficult to maintain part-time status.

- A lot of home-based part-timers experience burnout and begin to neglect their businesses.

These problems do not diminish by ignoring them. As mentioned in Chapter 1, there are hurdles to clear, puzzles to solve, and questions to be answered. You have to take a realistic view of your current living conditions—your employment, your family, and the amount of spare time you can afford to dedicate to the new enterprise, before determining which path you should follow.

Even when they start part-time, many home-based entrepreneurs find it difficult to maintain that status. Most are goal-driven individuals who expect results and are prodded by a belief that there is always more to be done. Naturally, when you succeed to any degree, it is not easy to stop and be content with what you have; after you have reached a certain production level or gained enough clients, you have to become less aggressive in your quest for growth if you plan to keep your home-based business a part-time endeavor.

There are people who don't take their businesses seriously. Having fallen prey to the same hollow belief held by others—namely, that home-based operations (especially *part-time* operations) are not as competent as their commercial counterparts—they give only a few hours a week to the business. Some get a feeling that they cannot measure up to other businesses; others grow tired of the responsibility. Both responses develop from a lack of confidence in themselves or their business or both. You have to believe in your business if you expect anybody else to do the same.

FULL-TIME OPPORTUNITIES

It is difficult to say whether any business is ever really "part-time." Most part-time entrepreneurs (especially those who are home-based) spend a lot of time thinking about their businesses—planning marketing strategies, practicing sales pitches, coming up with ways to streamline operations—even when they're not actually working in the home office. For obvious reasons, many owners of thriving part-time businesses eventually make the shift over to full-time status.

Limiting the amount of time you spend at your home-based business gives you the flexibility and freedom to work when you want and slowly grow accustomed to being a business owner. Ultimately, though, it also reduces your opportunities for expansion. Some of America's most well-known companies started as an entrepreneur's part-time dream, but they didn't stay that way for long. You will have to work at your home-based business full-time if you want to take it as far as it can go.

Advantages of a Full-Time Business

Like part-time operations, full-time home-based businesses have their share of benefits and drawbacks. These are a few of the reasons why some entrepreneurs prefer starting home-based businesses full-time:

- Greater time commitment allows more time to develop business ideas.
- Motivating factors (personal freedom, recognition, money, and so on) are more considerable.
- Opportunity for more rapid growth.
- Greater sense of professionalism.
- No other job or career to distract from making the business a success.

The more you invest in a particular pursuit, the more important the outcome becomes to you. Entrepreneurs who bring their businesses up to the full-time level, whether immediately from start-up or three years after starting part-time, will invariably care more about their business's well-being because they have put more time, effort, and money into it. If a full-time schedule will help you keep pace with an increase in demand for your product(s) or service(s), the result will be a jump in revenues (provided your costs remain comparatively equal). The same thing can happen when you go to a full-time schedule in order to increase your market share.

As mentioned before, it is easier for businesses headquartered in commercial offices to convince potential customers and clients of their professionalism. For similar reasons, it is easier for a full-time home-based business owner to convey professionalism. Part-timers will always come in second.

Disadvantages of a Full-Time Business

Starting a venture on a full-time basis does have some disadvantages:

- Greater risk.
- Loss of second income.
- Higher start-up costs.

Although the risks of a full-time operation are greater compared to those of a part-time operation, they are countered by the offer of unlimited growth opportunity and financial gain. This is the age-old "risk versus return" dilemma: where the dangers are greater, there is more of a possibility for gain. The cost of starting up at full capacity, whether you are product- or service-based, is more substantial than if you start part-time. Likewise, the potential rewards are more substantial.

To decide whether you should start full-time or part-time, you'll need to examine your goals and assess your financial situation.

CHOOSING AN INDUSTRY

When you know what you want from a business and what you will bring to it in terms of experience and personal effort, it is time to begin the selection process. Before focusing on a particular business, choose an industry category: service, retail, or manufacturing.

Service Businesses

Most home-based businesses are service-oriented. Not only do service businesses require the least amount of start-up capital because there are no inventory requirements, but they also require less space, for the same reason. Often, you can start with as little as a phone and a desk.

Many people start a service business that provides the very service they used to provide for an employer. For example, someone who worked in personnel for a large corporation might start a search firm or temporary help agency. Someone who worked as an advertising account executive might launch a advertising agency. Or someone who worked in a particular industry may forgo full-time employment to become a consultant in that same field—often keeping the former employer as a new client.

In a service-oriented business, plan on a lot of contact with clients, in addition to conducting a lot of marketing. Taking care of your clients and smoothing over any potential problems are essential functions for the owner of a service business.

If you have a service business, clients don't need to know that you are working from home. If you must meet with clients, either visit them at their location or home, or schedule meetings for breakfast, lunch, or dinner in a local restaurant.

Retail Businesses

You may think it's impossible to run a retail operation from home, because most retail businesses require a store or shop where goods are displayed and sold. Zoning laws prohibit you from turning your home into a "store" where customers come to purchase your wares, so a retail operation in the traditional sense *is* out of the question. However, you can operate a product-based business in which you sell to the public or to other businesses. As an alternative to having customers visit your home to make purchases, you can sell your products through other avenues: mail order, telemarketing, or visits to customers' homes or places of business.

To run a successful product-based business, you have to do more than find a great product. You must learn to *sell* that product. Selling involves a lot of customer contact and requires a great deal of persistence on your part. If you have qualms about giving sales presentations to customers or calling potential customers to tell them about your product, you may not be cut out for this type of business.

Manufacturing Businesses

You don't need a large factory and hundreds of workers to enter the manufacturing industry. Manufacturing can be as simple as creating hand-painted T-shirts or ceramic vases from your living room or garage. To run a small manufacturing business from home, you'll need to become adept at your craft in addition to mastering how to sell your wares, store them efficiently, and manage your inventory (making sure you never run out of stock or get stuck with stacks of product you can't sell).

Many entrepreneurs enjoy creating a product and selling it from home. However, a manufacturing business may require additional start-up capital to pay for any equipment or materials you need to make your product. With this kind of business, you may also have other needs, such as hiring part-time or even full-time employees to help you fill orders.

One entrepreneur who is now a well-known fashion designer got her start selling T-shirts from her one-bedroom apartment. She expected to sell a few hundred shirts, but was caught by surprise when she received orders for thousands of them. She had to hire people to handle fulfillment while she did the design work. Keep this in mind if you plan to start a manufacturing business.

SELECTING A BUSINESS

To find a business that's right for you, start by developing a list of potential opportunities that appeal to you. Hundreds of money-making concepts are available.

Next, research those ideas to see whether they are viable. You can find ideas anywhere—on TV, in the newspaper, at the golf course. By becoming more observant in your daily activities, you may come across a great business idea.

Following is a collection of some of the best sources of new business ideas. Any one of them may reveal the home-based business that's right for you.

Start with Yourself

To choose a business that will be right for you, assess your experience, your interests, and your personality. Starting a business that builds on your experience, that interests you, and that fits your personality will give you a much better chance of succeeding. If you start a business that doesn't interest you, how can you expect to get customers interested in it? And if you try to launch a business that you have no experience in, you'll have the double hurdle of trying to learn about the industry and selling your business at the same time.

Take into account the following:

- All kinds of work you have done in the past.
- Your strengths and weaknesses.
- Any previous experience you have had in owning a business.
- Your personality traits.

If you're employed now or have been in the past, think about ways your job could be made easier or more efficient through the use of some new product or service. If you've already come up with a new product or service that will make a salesperson's day more productive or a clerical worker's day more efficient, you may have found your business. American business history is filled with people who identified a need and filled it with their own products and services. And that tradition continues today.

Look at Other Successful Businesses

There's a wealth of wisdom in the adage, "Don't reinvent the wheel." Far too many entrepreneurs exhaust hours of effort in a vain attempt to build a better mousetrap. It's been done! A far better strategy is to look for a successful concept that you can learn from and adapt to your market's needs. Although you have to be careful not to infringe on any patent, trademark, copyright, or other form of legal protection, there are countless examples of shrewd entrepreneurs who have made significant money by coming up with their own version of a currently successful product or service. Next time you're in the supermarket, stop by the freezer section and count the brands of designer or upscale ice cream. You can do the same thing with chocolate-chip cookies, beer, running shoes, teddy bears, computers, and other products. In the service sector, someone may have created a unique business concept on the east coast that you can introduce to the southwest.

Just because a product or service already exists, it doesn't mean you can't get a share of that market too. The key element in selecting a successful concept is market share. Has the original product or service already captured and capitalized on a significant share of the available market, or do you see a sizable portion of the market as yet untapped? If you can see that a market is far from saturated, then it contains future profits that you can tap into. If an original product or service has captured a significant share of the market, you'll have to enter into head-to-head competition and you may not survive. If you run across a new product or service that interests you and appears to have good profit-making potential, do some research to see whether there's room for another player in that market. If so, you've found your opportunity.

Scan the Media for New Ideas

Dailies that cover the major markets where new trends and ideas are regularly developed should be scanned frequently. These include the *New York Times*, the *Los Angeles Times*, the *London Times*, and any other daily that reports on the global market.

Newspapers are an important source to tap, but don't neglect trade magazines and journals. You can't subscribe to every trade magazine or journal in print, but it would be worthwhile to read some of the more important and relevant ones like the *Wall Street Journal* and *Kiplinger's Personal Finance Magazine*. In this area, *Entrepreneur* and *Business Start-Ups* are also excellent sources. If you already have a good idea of the type of industry in which you would like to concentrate your efforts, then subscribing to a good trade publication in that area would be very helpful.

Most dailies and trade journals run classified ads on the back pages of each issue. Look through them for a product or concept that would be worth pursuing.

Don't forget television. A quick glance at your local cable listings will reveal a wide range of business programming. Again, this programming is designed to inform and educate the public about new products and ideas. If you don't have the time to catch each of these shows, program your VCR to tape them. You can quickly review the tapes at a later time, scanning them just as you would skim through a textbook for pertinent information.

Appendix B lists magazines, newsletters, and TV and radio shows relevant to home-based businesses.

FINDING A PRODUCT

Inventor Shows and Trade Shows

Trade and inventor shows, as well as conventions and civic groups, are also important; they can yield a wealth of information in just one day. Many trade shows and conventions are sponsored by trade associations within particular industries. To find an appropriate association for the industry you are interested in, look through the *Encyclopedia of Associations*, published by Gale Research. You can order the three volumes from the publisher, or research them in your local library.

An inventor show is a classic source of new products and ideas. Traditionally, inventors are great at formulating ideas and creating products from those ideas, but they hit a snag when it comes to marketing. This is one reason why so many new inventions, innovations, and products that obtain patents never go any further. Many inventors—particularly those without good marketing skills—may be looking for someone like you to help them get their products on the market. These inventors would welcome your licensing inquiries; some of them might even consider selling the rights to a new product, especially if some obstacle prevents them from producing it themselves.

If you're searching for a business idea or new product, inventor shows are a smorgasbord. At any one show, you can preview a staggering number of new products—some of which may end up being the next Hula Hoop or Frisbee success story. Whatever sources you decide to investigate, this is one that you should not miss. The sheer numbers of new products displayed at any inventor show simply improve your odds of finding a winner. An inventor show is eye-opening and fun, and will provide you with a pretty fair education on what's available because it will showcase a large selection of new products. Even if you don't find a particular product you want to pursue, you may be able to discern upcoming market trends from the types of products displayed at such a show.

To find out when the next inventor and/or trade show will occur in your area, contact your local convention facility. The space for shows of such size must be reserved well in advance, and if there's one planned during the next year, the facility manager's office will be able to give you the dates.

Your local Chamber of Commerce is another information source. Most Chambers sponsor inventor shows and serve as forums for interaction between inventors and manufacturers.

Don't forget to check for any local inventors' organizations. Inventors in most areas meet regularly to socialize, talk shop, and receive mutual support for their efforts. Not only will such a group know exactly where and when the upcoming inventor shows will occur, but you may also be able to tap into a great find before the next show and get a head start on all your potential competitors.

Appendix A lists some associations that can provide information on inventors' shows.

Foreign Products

Every country produces fine products that are wonderful examples of innovation, practicality, and profitability. Foreign items that can't be bought easily in the United States often hold great appeal and command high prices. For some Americans, foreign products possess an exotic, almost irresistible appeal. Products such as Irish lace, Swiss watches, Colombian coffee, and Limoges china are perennial favorites among American consumers.

Another fact must be considered in obtaining new products from foreign sources: no matter how old or common a product might be in its country of origin, in a new market it's a new product. Many of the finest products in the world are limited to specific countries because international distribution systems for them do not exist.

The world market is a cornucopia of products; many are waiting to be discovered by clever entrepreneurs who can introduce them into new areas. To investigate how and where you can obtain such profitable finds, contact a foreign consulate in your area or the Department of Commerce in Washington, DC. Many foreign countries that have products available for export also publish trade magazines. Ask for them either at your library or at a specific consulate.

Manufacturers

You'd be remiss in your new product investigation if you failed to contact original equipment manufacturers (OEMs). Just as a very old foreign product can be brand-new in an untapped market, a product that a manufacturer has decided to take out of production can also be a great seller. Similarly, many manufacturers begin the production process on a product and then, for a variety of reasons, decide not to commit to full-scale manufacturing of it. This withdrawal doesn't always imply that the product is faulty or that a market for it doesn't exist.

By contacting manufacturers, you will significantly advance your knowledge of the marketplace. You'll learn which products are being introduced, which concepts are being capitalized heavily, and which projects the manufacturers have decided not to fund. You could easily discover a new product for which a manufacturer is seeking distributors. A large, multiproduct operation may opt to discontinue an item because it no longer generates national sales figures in the entire U.S. market. It may, however, still possess plenty of salability in a regional, state, or local market. When you contact a manufacturer and learn that the company has decided to discontinue Product X, chances are you'll also learn the basis for the decision. The large company's extensive and expensive market research may easily become available to you. Besides learning what products might fit your designs, you might also obtain very valuable information on what products won't sell.

The Government

The U.S. government publishes mountains of information that most of us ignore—information that can be very profitable to you. To get acquainted with this unending flow of data, locate a U.S. government directory of publications. The amount of material available—much of it at no cost whatsoever—will stagger your imagination. As more and more Americans employ computers in their businesses, the government has started to establish databases that can also be of immense help to you.

To give a quick example of how government data can be useful in business, let's take a look at the space program. Research developed for the space program has provided consumers with many material benefits. Teflon, for example, a direct result of our efforts to adapt to the environment of space, has found myriad applications in everyday life. Such by-products of NASA programs are routinely written up in NASA publications and technical briefs.

Another fertile source of information is the *Patent Abstracts Bibliography,* published twice a year by the National Technical Information Service, which details all new patents and applications for new patents. It's a perfect information source for entrepreneurs who are interested in new products to license.

For more immediate information, you may wish to obtain *The Official Gazette* of the U.S. Patent Office. This publication, generated weekly, lists patents that have been granted (as opposed to those merely applied for). You can subscribe to this information source as you would a newspaper or magazine, by contacting the Superintendent of Documents, P.O. Box 371954, Pittsburgh, PA 15250-7954; (202) 512-1800.

Other relevant publications you may want to have mailed to you are the *Atomic Energy Commission Tech Briefs, National Aeronautics and Space Administration Tech Briefs, Topical Announcements,* and *FAST Announcement Service on Selected Scientific and Technical Reports.* All of these publications can be ordered through the National Technical Information Service, U.S. Department of Commerce, 5285 Port Royal Road, Springfield, VA 22161; (703)487-4600.

Obtain a list of public domain patents from the U.S. Patent Office. After a 17-year period, patents are no longer valid and can be developed without any licensing requirements or royalties to the original patent holder. Remember, however, that just because a patent has expired doesn't mean that the product will cease to exist. A perfect example is the single-element typewriter patented by IBM. Once the period of protection ended and the patent expired, many manufacturers produced their own versions of this product—most of which sold quite well.

The Small Business Administration (SBA), specifically its Small Business Investment Companies (SBICs), is also a fine source of information. The SBA licenses SBICs for the sole purpose of funding new companies. It's only logical that a new company would welcome inquiries about its products from potential marketers, distributors, wholesalers, or retailers. Discovering such a source is a classic win–win situation. The fact that each party needs the other to be successful creates the foundation for a symbiotic business relationship. Contact with an SBIC can be a direct route to your success. A list of the currently operating SBICs is located in Appendix E of this book.

EVALUATING BUSINESS OPPORTUNITIES

At this point, you've gone through your first stage of research and you now have a list of opportunities a mile long. All of them look appealing, but which one is going to be the best one for you? You have to do some serious "auditing" before you begin your final screening procedure.

This auditing is actually a simple test to determine whether you feel comfortable with a particular business. The goal is to narrow down your list of opportunities to three or four that elicit the most potential based on your audit. You will then screen this small group of opportunities according to your personal objectives, experience, and lifestyle.

The worksheet on page 60 will help you determine which opportunity will be right for you. At the top of the form, list each opportunity in

BUSINESS EVALUATION WORKSHEET

This worksheet will help you determine which homebased opportunity is most compatible with your personal objectives, experience, and lifestyle. Before you can complete it, you will need to do some research on each opportunity you are considering. Along the top of the form, list each homebased business opportunity in its own column. Answer each question along the left-hand side of the form with a "Yes" or "No." Look over your answers for each business after you are done. At the bottom of the form, indicate how compatible each business is with your goals and background. If two (or more) businesses seem equally compatible with your goals, you should investigate all of them more thoroughly, then make your decision.

	A	B	C	D
Have your experience and background given you any skills you can bring to this business?				
Are you familiar with the operations of this type of business?				
Does the business meet your investment goals?				
Does the business meet your income goals?				
Does the business generate sufficient profit?				
Do you feel comfortable with the business?				
Does your family feel comfortable with the business?				
Does the business satisfy your sense of status?				
Is the business compatible with your people skills?				
Is high growth projected for this industry?				
Can you accept the financial risk of starting this particular business?				
Does the business require long hours?				
Is the business location-sensitive?				
Does this business require any equipment which you would be unable to use or store at home?				
Would zoning laws interfere with your ability to operate this business from your home legally?				
OVERALL COMPATIBILITY				

a separate column. Along the left-hand side of the form are questions. For each question, rate the potential of each opportunity on a scale of 1 to 3, with a rating of 3 being the best. Once you've answered all the questions, total each opportunity's rating. The one with the highest rating will most likely conform to your goals and lifestyle.

You may want to investigate mail order, franchise, and licensed business opportunities.

Mail Order Opportunities

Mail order is not a get-rich-quick type of business, in spite of all the hype that may lead you to believe you can "Make a Million in Mail Order Overnight!" Even so, the beauty of a home-based mail order business is that you can get into it easily.

One of mail order's pioneers in the 1880s was Aaron Montgomery Ward, who started his business by mailing a one-page flyer announcing bed ticking, ladies' watches, hoop skirts, and household linens. The venture sparked sales and marked the debut of one of the nation's oldest and most successful mail order operations.

Since then, mail order has grown into an industry that now surpasses $73.6 billion in annual sales, according to Marke/Sroge Communications, a catalog consulting firm in Chicago. If you add business purchases to that, the figure soars to $126.6 billion. The mail order industry has been the scene of tremendous growth and exciting change over the past few years. More than 12.5 billion catalogs were mailed to consumers in 1994, and the number of people who shopped by phone or mail reached nearly 100 million, according to the Direct Marketing Association.

Because mail order is not merely a business but a method of doing business, the market is as wide and varied as the aggregate customer base of American business. Virtually any product with a specialized market niche is a potential mail-order candidate. The market ranges from political and charitable fund-raising to sweepstakes "winners" and virtually everything in between.

Why are mail order sales growing so rapidly? Busy consumers want the time-saving convenience of being able to shop from a catalog at their leisure. People can shop from a mail order catalog from home, the office, even the beach.

Starting a mail order business from home is ideal because it can be done on a small scale with just one product. From there, it can grow substantially. It's very possible to start a small mail order business from home with a few hundred dollars and make a good living; you may not set the world on fire and become another Montgomery Ward, but you'll be your own boss, you'll be small enough not to attract big-time competition, and you could well be earning between $50,000 and $100,000 or more per year. Small mail order operations are an exciting way to achieve the American dream of going into business for yourself because they require a low start-up ($100 to $1,000 in some cases; $5,000 to $10,000 in others) compared to conventional retail businesses that require upward of $50,000 in front-end capital.

Businesses that started out as part-time ventures and eventually expanded into full-time moneymakers include House of Camelot, a costume jewelry sales operation started by a husband and wife from a kitchen table and a cash outlay of $1,500. Five years later, the business topped $3 million in gross sales.

Another example is Holiday Gifts, Inc., a part-time business for its first three years of operation. The business began with a single ad in *House & Garden;* the product sold was the Melody phone, a device that plays music while a party is on hold. The ad brought in business, but the mail order entrepreneur lost a few hundred dollars his first year. It wasn't until three years later that he began making a profit; however, by his tenth year, he was making seven figures annually and had a print advertising budget of $450,000.

The secret to starting part-time is to offer a product or information source that has a limited market; otherwise, the majors will easily steal your idea and your potential audience. A limited market need not be small in size, however. One example of a limited-market mail order operation is the business started by L.L. Bean, seller of hunting, fishing, and camping equipment for more than 65 years, with a mailing list of customers approaching 2 million. Another is the Orvis Company of Manchester, Vermont, an outdoor equipment and apparel manufacturer and retailer that owns the title of oldest mail order company in the United States (selling through the mail since 1856).

Making a Million in Mail Order

Once you've moved from a part-time venture into a full-time home-based business, the income potential is virtually unlimited. Sears and Montgomery Ward started out as mail order operations and are now large retailers. But they started years ago, when the competition wasn't so rough. What about now?

More recent examples include the National Liberty Insurance Company, started in 1959 by insurance agent Arthur De Moss. His idea was to sell health insurance by mail, offering low rates to those who didn't drink alcohol. He made a $55,000 profit for his first year in business; within 10 years, he was running a $20 million company. Other examples are: Lands' End, a distributor of clothes, shoes, and luggage, which is earning more than $100 million annually; Harry and David, which sells quality fruit and fine foods from its Medford, Oregon, headquarters (their average sale is $60, and annual gross sales exceed $45 million). One of the largest operations is Fingerhut Corporation, which sells a variety of merchandise from clothing to appliances and home furnishings. Their gimmick is an installment plan: some customers pay only a few dollars a month. Fingerhut's annual income? Well over $500 million. Recently, they've been acquired by a company that owns eight other mail order operations.

The money to be made in mail order accounts for the fact that there are over 450,000 active mailing list permits nationwide.

Home-Based Start-Up

Again, perhaps the best place to start a mail order business is from your home. Unlike retail operations, where location is everything if you want to establish strong sales, a mail order operation (like any good home-based idea) can function just as well from a home-based office as from a commercial location. It doesn't matter if your facility is located in the heart of Manhattan or in Elko, Nevada; your product or products will sell just as well through proven mail order techniques.

For your mail order location, you need only a comfortable home office from which to conduct your business and a postal box for receiving orders. Other than that, the only other things you need to be aware of are the locations of your fulfillment house, suppliers, and printer.

Equipment

The mail order industry is huge; many different companies nationwide are selling a vast array of products. The type and sophistication of the equipment used in their operations are directly influenced by their strategies and size and the extent of their mailings.

Very small companies that sell a product to a catalog house, which markets it for them, need only an effective record-keeping system to track the sales derived from that source. Other small companies reach their customers through advertising in traditional media such as magazines, newspapers, television, and radio. They fulfill their orders by writing to the advertised address of the fulfillment house or phoning the telemarketing service used in the marketing campaign. Because of the nature of these businesses, very little capital investment in equipment is required. Owners either utilize a manual record-keeping system and ticker files or place the order information on a computer.

Some small companies prefer to handle everything from production of the ads and catalogs to maintenance of their own mailing lists and processing of their own orders. Several years ago, it would take quite a few people to handle all of these functions, but advancements in both computer hardware and software allow a small company with just a few employees to handle adequately everything that needs to be done. Investment is minimal, often under $15,000.

Small home-based operations can get by with a minimum investment in equipment by using the outside services that provide their professional expertise to the mail order industry. For the more ambitious, the purchase of a computer and specialized off-the-shelf software will provide the type of capabilities required to produce ads and catalogs, and fulfill orders, for a modest cost. Any way you choose to set it up, a mail order business is certainly one of today's most lucrative home-based business options.

Home-Based Opportunities in Franchised Business

If you think franchising is only for the fast-food giants, think again. Thousands of entrepreneurs are operating successful franchises from their own homes. The fast-growing franchise industry now includes hundreds of service-oriented opportunities that can be run successfully from home: interior decorating, pool cleaning, restaurant delivery, auto detailing, tax preparation, and more. ProFusion Systems, a plastic- and leather-goods repair franchise, is just one of many franchises which you can operate from your home.

According to industry statistics, a new franchise opens somewhere in the United States *every 17 minutes,* and total franchise sales have reached trillions of dollars. About one-third of all retail sales in the United States are made in franchised outlets. John Naisbitt, co-author of *Megatrends 2000* (William Morrow & Company, Inc., New York), has predicted, in a study commissioned by the International Franchise Association (IFA), that 50% of all retail sales will be made through franchised outlets by the year 2000. Service-related and mail order franchising will enjoy similar increases.

Just what is a franchise that it can earn such a staggering prediction for potential growth? It is a written agreement that allows a business owner to expand his or her business by granting franchisees the right to offer, sell, or distribute goods or services under the franchisor's trademark and use a proven marketing plan or system.

For people who want to start a business from home but have little business experience, or who want a little more security and support than they would have going it alone, franchising may be the way to go.

Advantages of Franchising

Becoming a franchisee isn't for everyone. Some people like the extra support available and the fact that there's already a proven way to do business. Others want to create their own business from scratch and don't want anyone telling them how to run their business—that's why they're becoming an entrepreneur instead of working for someone else. Being a franchisee falls somewhere in the middle of working for someone and being your own boss. You get a taste of both worlds.

There are a number of advantages and disadvantages of buying a franchise you can run from home. The following paragraphs describe some of the advantages.

- *The Risk of Failure Is Reduced.* You're buying a business concept that has already had most of its problems and kinks resolved.
- *No Previous Experience Is Necessary.* At least for most franchises, novices are welcome. Complete training and an operational blueprint of the business are usually provided, thereby eliminating most of the costly trial-and-error blunders that accompany new start-ups.
- *Immediate Name Identification.* You're able to capitalize on the national recognition of a franchise.
- *Turnkey Operation.* Many franchises have a proven product or service and a proven system of operation.
- *Franchising = Risk Reduction.* Reducing the risk of going into business is one of the prime attractions of buying a franchise. The franchisor can help you get a running start by offering you:
  — Standardized products and systems.
  — Financial and accounting systems.
  — Collective buying power.
  — Supervision and consulting.
  — National and local advertising programs.
  — Uniform packaging.
  — Ongoing research and development.
  — Financial assistance.
  — Operations manual.
  — Sales and marketing assistance.
  — Planning and forecasting.
  — Inventory control.

Franchise Drawbacks

Weighing down all the advantages, however, are these drawbacks to buying a franchise:

- Loss of control.
- High cost.
- A binding contract.
- The franchisor's problems (they become your problems).

Because you won't have complete control of the franchise, you have to ask yourself whether you are good at taking direction. The franchisor may have spent years developing a system for the business that has stood the test of time. You won't be able to change anything unless you have prior approval from the franchisor, and then there may be resentment involved. If you resist changes or can't take orders, you won't like franchising.

Low-Investment Home-Based Franchises

The financial requirements for buying a franchise can be quite substantial. However, home-based franchise opportunities tend to require less cash—sometimes, only a few thousand dollars. However, some franchises require you to purchase your supplies from them and will expect you to pay advertising fees and royalty fees on your revenues.

Among the types of low-investment home-based franchises are the following:

- Home and commercial cleaning services.
- Porcelain resurfacing.
- Home inspection.
- Ceiling cleaning.
- Carpet cleaning.
- Window cleaning.
- In-home pet care services.
- Mobile bookkeeping, accounting and tax services.
- Interior decorating.
- VCR maintenance and repair.
- Mobile vinyl, leather, and plastic repair and dyeing.
- Tutoring and test-preparation services.
- Transportation consulting services.
- Halloween hayrides.
- Plant care.
- Lawn and tree care.
- Restaurant cleaning.
- On-site oil changes.

- Merchant advertising.
- Mobile car care/quick oil and lube.
- Tub, sink, and tile resurfacing.
- Mystery shopping.
- Personal shopping service.
- Videotaping weddings.
- Desktop publishing.
- Word processing.

More information on buying a franchise can be found in the *Franchise Opportunities* chapter of *Entrepreneur Magazine's Small Business Advisor*.

Licensed Business Opportunities

If you want to buy a business that you can run from home and that won't cost a bundle, you may want to look into what's called a business opportunity. Just what is a business opportunity? Here's a simple analogy: Think back to elementary school when your teacher was explaining the difference between a rectangle and a square. A square is also a rectangle, but a rectangle isn't necessarily a square. The same relationship exists among business opportunities, independent businesses for sale, and franchises. All franchises and independent businesses for sale are business opportunities, but not all business opportunities meet the requirements of being a franchise nor are they in the strictest sense of the word independent businesses for sale.

In business opportunity ventures, as in franchises, the seller makes a commitment of continuing involvement with the buyer. So what's the difference between a franchise and a business opportunity venture? As a general rule of thumb, a franchise receives more support from the parent company, gets to use a trademarked name, and is more stringently controlled by the franchisor. Business opportunities, on the other hand, don't receive as much support from the parent company, generally aren't offered the use of a trademarked name, and are independent of the parent company's operational guidelines. The Fuller Brush Company might be one of the best-known business opportunities.

There are numerous forms of business opportunity ventures. Some are turnkey operations similar to package format franchises. These business opportunities provide everything you could possibly need to start a business. They help select site location, provide training, offer support for the licensee's marketing efforts, and supply a complete start-up inventory.

Unlike a package format franchise, however, these types of business opportunity ventures aren't trademarked outlets for the parent company. The company's name, logo, and how it is legally operated are left solely to the licensee. Often, the only binding requirement between the seller and buyer is that inventory is purchased solely through the parent company.

The most common types of business opportunity ventures are discussed next.

Licensee

This broad term applies to a host of business arrangements. Under a license agreement, the licenser gives the licensee the right to use the name and trademarks of the business in order to sell goods associated with the licenser. A license can be either limited in its scope or a full franchise agreement.

Distributorship

In this arrangement, an independent agent enters into an agreement to offer and sell a particular product, but is not entitled to use the manufacturer's trade name as part of its own trade name. Depending on the agreement, the distributor may be limited to selling only that company's goods or may have the freedom to market several different product lines or services from various firms.

Rack Jobber

Various companies' products are sold through a distribution system that involves rack jobbers. In a typical rack-jobbing business opportunity, the agent or buyer enters an agreement with the parent company to market its goods to various stores by means of strategically located store racks. Under the agreement, the parent company obtains a number of locations in which the racks are placed on a consignment basis. It is up to the agent to maintain the inventory, move the merchandise around to attract customers, and do the bookkeeping. After an agreed-on interval, the agent presents the store manager with a copy of the inventory control sheet, which indicates how much merchandise was sold. The distributor is paid by the store or location that has the rack—less the store's commission. Rack jobbers might distribute small items like various automotive accessories (such as air freshener), keychains, breath mints, etc.

Wholesaler

A wholesaler is similar to a distributor but does not engage in sales on a retail level. Rather, the wholesaler sells the products of other businesses to retailers and other distributors who have direct interaction with the end user.

Vending Machine Routes

The investment for this type of business opportunity venture is usually greater because the businessperson must buy the machines as well as the merchandise being vended. Although similar to rack jobbing, the situation is reversed in terms of the payment procedure. The vending machine operator must pay the location owner a percentage based on sales. The big secret to any route deal is to get locations in high-foot-traffic areas that are as close to one another as possible. If your locations are spread far apart, you waste time and traveling expense servicing them—and this expense can be the difference between profit and loss.

Advantages of Licensed Business Opportunities

Many business opportunities can be run from the home, so you may want to investigate some business opportunity listings before you jump into business for yourself. When you buy a business opportunity, you should get a headstart in the business world. Some advantages of buying a business opportunity include:

- A proven system of operation or product.
- Intensive training programs.
- Better financing options.
- Professional advertising and promotion.
- Ongoing counseling.
- Purchasing power.

However, counterbalancing some of the advantages to buying a business opportunity, there are also disadvantages.

Disadvantages of Licensed Business Opportunities

Keep in mind that most companies sell business opportunities because it is a way to expand their distribution channels without using additional capital. There are hundreds of variations of business opportunity contracts; consequently, not all the negative points mentioned will apply to every situation.

Under ideal conditions, business opportunities are a good, low-investment way to get into business with minimum risk and a good chance for success. But nothing in this world is perfect, so here are some problems you might run into:

- Exclusivity clauses. A business opportunity might require that you not distribute products made by any other companies, which can reduce your potential income.
- Parent company bankruptcy. You might build up a good distribution business, only to have your supplier go out of business.

You should carefully check any business opportunity venture you are considering. Get a list of operators from the parent company and call them. Have a lawyer look over any agreement drafted by the parent company. Make sure you receive a disclosure statement. Then carefully evaluate the licenser. Don't let anyone hurry you. Make sure the business opportunity is backed by a responsible company.

LOW-INVESTMENT BUSINESS OPPORTUNITIES

Business opportunities often require a smaller investment than a franchise. And home-based business opportunities can get you into business for only a few hundred dollars. Here is a list of some kinds of home-based business opportunities that don't cost a bundle:

- Cosmetics distribution. Examples: Goubaud de Paris, Nectarine, and Heritage Products.
- Home delivery of baby products.
- Disc jockey music service.
- Advertising services. Examples include Billboard Bags, Inc., which sells shopping-bag advertising, and Fiesta Cartoon, Maps Inc.
- Direct mail services. Examples include Adpak USA and Coupon Connection of America, Inc.
- Jewelry distribution. Examples include Lasting Impressions Inc. and World Jewelry Importers.
- Building services. Perma Crete, for instance, sells resurfacing products.
- Children's identification systems. Examples include Child Shield, U.S.A. and Ident-A-Kid Services of America.

- Maintenance. American Roof-Brite, for instance, is a roof- and shingle-cleaning service.
- Food vending machines. Haymco Marketing Inc. and Vend It All are two examples.
- Security systems. These systems include door peepholes, sold by Du Seung Trading Co., and self-defense spray, sold by Personal Security Inc.
- Telecommunications systems. You can establish 900 numbers through Avalon Communications, or sell pagers through Corvest Marketing.
- Water systems. Electron Pure Ltd. and Waterwise Inc. are two business opportunities in this category.
- Screen-printing services. Examples include Nationwide Screen Printing and Print Profits Inc.
- Windshield repair. Two business opportunities are Glas-Weld Systems Inc. and Ultra B-O-N-D Inc.
- Auditing services. Auditel International Inc. and Public Utility Consultants are two auditing opportunities.
- Medical claims processing. Claim-It Systems Inc. and Medical Billing Associates Inc. are two examples.
- Personalized children's products. About You Books and Best Personalized Books Inc. offer personalized books for children.
- Toner cartridge recharging. Alpha Laser Cartridge Inc. and the Laser Group Inc. are two examples.
- Travel agencies. TPI Travel Services and Travel Service Network are two travel-agency business opportunities.
- Housesitting services. Home Sitting Seniors Inc. and Pet Sitters, Plus! offer housesitting business opportunities. (Pet Sitters, Plus!, as the name implies, also offers pet-sitting services.)
- Yard signs. Do-It-Yourself Party Yard Signs and Main Event Lawn Sign Inc. are two business opportunities in this category.

WHAT TO ASK BEFORE BUYING A FRANCHISE OR LICENSED BUSINESS OPPORTUNITY

Talking openly with franchisors/licensers and franchisees/licensees is crucial to making a smart investment decision. It's important that you ask a franchisor/licenser to see the disclosure document, which outlines all the details of the agreement. In addition, here are some basic questions you should ask the franchisors/licensers:

1. How will the company help me once I open my doors?
2. How exactly does the company arrange for the supply of product to the business? May I see the current price sheets?
3. How does the franchise/business opportunity handle disputes? Through arbitration or mediation? How has the approach worked for solving problems?
4. What are the names and addresses of all owners who have left the system in the past two years for any reason (including transfer, expiration of term, or mutual termination)? (Get a copy of the list.)
5. Does the company have the results of any marketing studies that have been conducted in my projected market?
6. What is the single largest challenge faced by franchisees/licensees in this system?

Ask franchisees/licensees these questions:

1. How much support do you get from the franchisor/licensor?
2. What kinds of problems do you encounter?
3. What is your day like?
4. How many hours a day do you work?
5. How much money are you making, in gross revenues and salary?
6. How effective is the advertising campaign?
7. How is the business perceived in the community?
8. How much freedom do you have to make decisions?
9. Are you happy with your investment?
10. Were you disappointed with any aspect of your entry into the business?
11. Were you well-trained for the challenges of the business?
12. Have you had any problems with product supply?
13. How did you finance the business?
14. What does your cash flow look like?
15. How much do you spend on advertising each month?
16. Are there any aspects of the business you don't like?
17. What do you like most about it?
18. If you had the opportunity, knowing what you know now, would you make this investment again?

Once you have the answers to these questions, you will be able to make a more informed decision on whether a franchise or business opportunity is for you, or whether you would prefer to go it alone with your own home-based business.

More information on buying a franchise can be found in the *Business Opportunities* chapter of *Entrepreneur Magazine's Small Business Advisor.*

THE 23 BEST HOME-BASED BUSINESSES

All of the following businesses are well-suited to home-based operation. Research by *Entrepreneur* also indicates that all of them have high growth potential, because they take advantage of various trends, as explained in each business profile below. For these reasons, we have chosen these businesses as the 23 best home-based businesses.

1. Multimedia Services

With personal computers becoming increasingly equipped with complete multimedia systems that combine print, sound, graphics, and video in a single package, demand for multimedia systems is mounting. According to Information Workstation Group, a multimedia consulting and market research group, the industry will be a $30 billion market by 1998. Several segments of the industry remain ripe for entrepreneurial picking, such as business services in which entrepreneurs provide businesses with custom presentations or interactive training. To get started, you'll need a sophisticated computer set-up and a good dose of computer savvy.

2. Online/Bulletin Board Services

Thousands of entrepreneurs are merging onto the information superhighway with online services that are data-based, chat-oriented, business-minded, or strictly for shopping. According to Simba Information Inc., an information publishing firm based in Wilton, Connecticut, worldwide sales for online services exceeded $11.3 billion in 1993, up 11.9% from 1992. Arlen Communications Inc., a research firm in Bethesda, Maryland, estimates 5.2 million U.S. households have used online services. Basically, online bulletin boards are accessible to anyone with a personal computer, modem, and phone line. Today, there is

BBS software that anyone can run from home. Creating an online bulletin board service is entrepreneur-friendly because of its small initial investment—usually, around $15,000.

3. Business Plan Consulting

As start-up and expansion capital has dwindled, a new opportunity has sprung up for entrepreneurs who help others win the battle for funding by helping them prepare business plans. All banks, venture capitalists, and private investment groups require business plans from the entrepreneurs who court them. Business plan consulting has emerged as one of the fastest-growing service industries. Experience in writing and packaging business plans is essential for success in this industry. Start-up requirements are modest—as low as $10,000. A computer, fax, modem, answering machine, and telephone are all you need. Consultants generally charge a flat fee based on how much information the client is able to provide at the outset and how much it will take to put the plan together.

4. Computer Maintenance and Repair

Keeping the more than 100 million computers across the United States and Canada in tip-top shape is a growing business. Most computer owners don't know how to complete routine maintenance and cleaning of their computers, and that's where you might come in. With a home-based business, you go to homes and offices to clean computers. A strong knowledge of how computers work is essential in this business. Count on an investment of about $6,000.

5. Resume Writing Service

Here's a business you can start for as little as $3,600. As corporations downsize, competition for jobs is becoming keener. That translates into a rising demand for professional resume writers. The most successful resume writers do more than simply type someone's work history on nice paper. Today's resume writers go the extra mile, gathering in-depth information about their clients' backgrounds, skills, strengths, and weaknesses. To make it in this industry, you need copywriting skills, a knack for interviewing people and drawing out key information, the ability to think like personnel directors, and a talent for layout and design.

6. Business Consulting

Job loss is a common reason why people start their own businesses. Inevitably, most of these home-based business converts start consulting services to put their general managerial know-how to good use. With companies seeking independent consultants as a cost-effective replacement for middle managers, you can earn hundreds of dollars a day sharing your expertise. Or, you may choose to specialize in another needy market: helping small businesses write business plans and fine-tune their marketing and sales strategies.

7. Utility/Phone Bill Auditing

Utility/telephone bill auditors provide an invaluable service for businesses, especially at a time when revenues are so unpredictable: They save companies money that may be slowly slipping away through inaccurate charges on gas, water, sewage, and telephone bills. For as little as $8,000, you can get your business off the ground. After stocking up with a computer, tariff copies, a fax machine, and a telephone, and developing a knack for bill auditing through seminars or business opportunity courses, you sift through your clients' monthly bills and retrieve money that is rightfully theirs. This relatively new industry has become so popular that it's now sprouting additional appendages. Keep your eye on mortgage and medical claims auditing as well.

8. Travel Agency

With Americans spending more than $200 billion on travel each year, travel agencies are flying high. Travel agents book more than 90% of all foreign travel and 60% of all domestic travel, an indication that this business is ready for takeoff. To be competitive, you must have an automated system and, if possible, one that is integrated with an automated accounting system. A good phone system and ticketing equipment are musts. If you love to travel (and who doesn't?), this is your dream business.

9. Restaurant Delivery

First came room service, then pizza delivery. Now, restaurant delivery allows consumers the convenience of savoring an entree from their favorite restaurant without ever leaving the sofa. Restaurant delivery services are finding that singles, two-income families, and seniors, who don't have either the time or the inclination to cook, mean healthy business. You will need a car, a telephone, a two-way radio, and hot boxes for storage en route. In exchange for expanding local restaurants' clientele, you can charge up to 30% of the food bill. This type of business is still fresh, so get it while it's hot!

10. Seminar Promotion

To function in our fast-paced society, people need a mass of information compressed into a short amount of time. Enter the seminar promotion business, in which promoters provide businesspeople and individuals seeking general self-improvement with quick and relevant data. You can do the bulk of your work—planning the events from start to finish, enlisting expert speakers, publicizing the programs, and advertising to attendees—at home. Then you simply rent a room at a conveniently located facility, and let the seminars begin.

11. Mobile Windshield Repair

Much windshield damage is repairable, making this a top business in the repair-don't-replace '90s. Potential clientele is practically endless; after all, you'd be hard pressed to find someone who wouldn't rather pay $35 to $55 to repair a windshield than $200 to $2,000 to replace it. Serving clients who have fleets of commercial vehicles, such as delivery services or car rental agencies, is a key to success in this field. You can either get equipped with resin, razor blades, glass cleaner, and a vacuum or pressure machine and master the art of windshield repair yourself, or hire others to do the work while you set up the jobs. By taking the service to the customer, you not only lure more clients with the added benefit of convenience, you also decrease your overhead and start-up costs by being able to run the business from home.

12. Home Health-Care Agency

Just as house calls are associated with the 1940s and 1950s, home health care agencies have become the answer to America's raging health care crisis in the 1990s. Home health care caters to a society that's fed up with costly hospitals. Seeking a more affordable and comforting option, these clients are turning to home health care providers. For home-based business owners, operating a referral service or providing low-level home care is usually best, and you must check zoning and insurance requirements before starting out. Considering that 1 out of 4 people will reach senior status by the year 2020, and people are living longer than ever, this industry is expected to reach revenues of almost $45 billion within the next 10 years.

13. Import/Export

As an importer/exporter, you have the power of conducting international business without ever leaving your neighborhood. Exports alone have grown 10% to 15% annually in the past 3 years, according to the American Association of Exporters and Importers. Meanwhile, small export businesses are enjoying a bigger piece of the pie, with average annual sales growth of 30%. By serving as a consultant for foreign countries seeking to export their goods, an intermediary between manufacturers and wholesalers from different countries, or an exporter or importer yourself, you can have the whole world in your hands. (For additional information on this business opportunity, see *Entrepreneur Magazine: Starting an Import/Export Business.*)

14. Home Computer

If, like most people, you have a personal computer at home, you have access to hundreds of opportunities right at your fingertips. A home computer allows you to develop software, contract computer-related jobs from large corporations, provide general computer consulting, publish newsletters, do word processing or mailing lists, or create numerous other businesses. Not only does a computer put the capabilities of home-based businesses on the same par as large corporations, it also puts you a step ahead of your competition. With lower overhead, you can charge less and lure more clients. (For additional information on this business idea, see *Entrepreneur Magazine: Making Money with Your Personal Computer.*)

15. Medical Claims Processing

With a start-up investment of only $5,000, you can get into this industry, which is barely a decade old. Like a tax preparer, a medical claims processor helps clients fill out insurance claims and makes sure they get the benefits they deserve. A new angle on this young business: Help physicians collect their receivables and you'll collect a whole new clientele. Because you take your service to the client or simply file claims electronically, you can run this business from home with only a computer, a telephone, an answering machine, and a copier.

16. Language Translation

With global markets merging more than ever, language translation services are discovering it *is* a small world after all. The $20-billion plus industry has much room for home-based business owners, who need only a telephone, a computer, and a fax to link their service to the world. Plan on an investment of at least $11,000. As a language translator, you can meet the high demand of multinational corporations, local governments, publications expanding to overseas markets, and thousands of other businesses operating in the global marketplace. In any language, this business promises great rewards.

17. Carpet Cleaning Service

Want a business with a widespread customer base? Try carpet cleaning. Every homeowner and every business owner with installed carpeting is a prospect for a carpet cleaning service. Although you may be tempted to begin this business by renting equipment from the supermarket, you need to invest in the proper equipment: a steam-cleaning machine and a variety of brushes. You'll also need a vehicle to transport your equipment. Once you establish your carpet cleaning business, you can expand by providing complementary services, including upholstery, wall, ceiling, or drapery cleaning.

18. Co-Op Mailing Service

Here's a low-investment business you can start from home on a part-time basis. By putting together coupon mailers for local retailers, service businesses, civic or political organizations, and mail order companies, you can help them sell their products and services to customers. American businesses—large and small—now spend a total of $25.5 billion on direct mail advertising each year, and you can be a part of it with a coupon mailing service.

19. Financial Aid Services

Because of rising tuition costs and state budget cuts, college students are being forced to find financial aid to help them pay for an education. Students apply for billions of dollars in grants and student loans every year, and, as a financial aid expert, you can help students and their parents locate available funds. Some professional experience with the financial aid system is certainly helpful in this field. You can conduct most of your business over the phone, marketing your services to a local clientele or seeking out a nationwide customer base. To maintain detailed databases, you will need computer equipment and database software.

20. Secretarial Services

As American corporations downsize by laying off employees, they are turning to independent contractors to provide many of the services they once hired full-time employees to perform. Secretarial services—including word processing, desktop publishing, mailing list management, bookkeeping, telephone answering, and tape transcription—are some of the duties companies now seek entrepreneurs to perform. Small businesses and other home-based ventures that can't afford to hire someone on a full-time basis are also potential clients for this type of business, which you can get off the ground for less than $10,000.

21. Specialty Travel and Tours

Travelers are increasingly seeking vacations that cater to their specific interests: bicycling, river rafting, wine tasting, Irish poets, and so on. As a specialty tour operator, you can either host tours in your own region (such as stays in plantation homes in Georgia, if you live in the Atlanta area) or set up shop anywhere and send vacationers on trips around the world. Before sending people on trips, you must be an expert on the types of tours you offer—don't send a group of tourists to Russia if you've never been there. You can start this type of business, on a very small scale, with an investment of about $30,000.

22. Coin-Operated Vending

For a business that requires little customer contact and can be started with as little as $7,300, take a look at coin-operated vending machines.

You can establish routes and place machines that sell candy, soda, videotapes, coffee, hygiene products, even baseball cards. The target market for vending machines is vast: corporate offices, mechanics' shops, billiard halls, auto malls, bowling alleys, high schools, colleges, dormitories, miniature golf courses, and so on. Prices for machines start at about $1,000, but you can find good deals by ordering several machines at a time or by purchasing reconditioned units.

23. Video Production Service

Video has become a staple in American society. People routinely hire professionals to tape their weddings, birthday parties, and other celebrations. Companies of all sizes pay videographers to produce "video brochures" and other marketing materials. Keep in mind that you need experience in the field to produce high-quality videos. Start-up costs, however, may be prohibitive for some entrepreneurs—a camera, lights, cables, tripods, editing equipment, and other items can add up to nearly $60,000.

3

PLANNING
FOR SUCCESS

Before you take the plunge into home-based business ownership, you need to do some planning. By thinking through the basic aspects of your business, you will have a better understanding of your business and of what will be required of you to make it successful. You will also be forced to think through some of the problems you are likely to confront. By doing this mental exercise, you will come up with some solutions to those problems so they won't threaten your business if they do arise.

PREPARING A BUSINESS PLAN

Writing a business plan—an outline of your business's characteristics and goals—is a necessary step in the development of any business. Usually, entrepreneurs write a business plan in order to obtain financing. However, even if you aren't seeking outside financing, it's a good idea to put your plan on paper. A business plan becomes an operating tool that will help you manage your business efficiently.

Your business plan doesn't have to follow a specific format, but it should include the following:

- *Business description.* This section should include a brief summary of the basics about your business: products and/or services your business will offer, structure (home-based, product- or service-oriented), number of employees, customers, owners or partners.
- *Business format.* Is your company going to be a sole proprietorship, a partnership, or a corporation? Who are the key players and what are their roles within the business?
- *Market research.* A description of your market, your customers, and your competition. Include the size of your industry, its growth prospects, trends, and sales potential.
- *Marketing strategy.* Ways you will reach your target market. Describe your pricing strategy, your sales presentations, and how you will generate new leads.
- *Financing.* How you plan to finance your venture and how much money you will need to get it off the ground. Indicate fixed and variable overhead expenses. Also include cash flow projections for the first year.
- *Sales projections.* Realistic sales goals for your first year, including prices for your products and/or services.
- *Production goals and strategies.* How the work will be accomplished, who will be in charge of what tasks, how much materials and labor will cost, and how much you should produce within a certain time period. Include short-term (one-year) and long-term (five-year) goals for your business. Goals can include revenues, market share, number of employees, number of customers, distribution channels, and similar projections.
- *Competition.* Who are your competitors? What are their strengths and weaknesses? How much of the market share do they have? How do you plan to get your share of that market away from them? What gives your company an advantage over the competition? Is your product or service superior in quality? Are your distribution channels better? Are your prices more attractive to consumers? Are your promotions more effective? Does your advertising draw in more customers?

A completed business plan takes your business idea out of the realm of dreams and helps guide you to making it a reality. The plan puts in writing exactly what you need to accomplish in order to make your business a success.

Remember, your business plan is only a guide, and it will change as your business grows. You may realize that your goals were unrealistic and need to be reevaluated, or that you are growing faster than anticipated and must alter your projections accordingly. Think of your business plan as your map to success.

To create an effective business plan, some market research is essential. This chapter will show you how to conduct market research that will help you define your business, your market, and your competition.

CONDUCTING MARKET RESEARCH

If you think market research is something only Fortune 500 companies do, you're wrong. Research is, in fact, far more important for small businesses. A Fortune 500 company can introduce a new product that flops and still survive because its other products are strong sellers. A small home-based business that's attempting to get off the ground with one product or service can't afford to advertise to the wrong target market or set a price that's too high or too low.

Market research will help you discover who wants your product or service (senior citizens, young people, men, women, fitness fanatics, golfers, other businesses), how much they are willing to pay for it, the best ways to let customers know your company exists, and how your company will be viewed in the marketplace (as a luxury service or product, as a great bargain, as a necessity, and so on).

Conducting market research isn't difficult, but it may be time-consuming. From the moment you consider starting a business, start researching. It can be as simple as asking friends and acquaintances what they think of your business concept. Do they see a need for it? How much would they pay for such a product or service? How often would they use/buy it? How would they expect to hear about it? Do they know of other companies offering the same products/services?

That's just the beginning. More in-depth research about your customer base and your competition will be vital to your success. To make sure you get the most from your market research, you have to follow nine simple steps.

1. State in general terms the problems you want to solve before starting your business: defining the target market, analyzing the competition, determining your prices, reaching your customers, and so on. Brainstorm your situation and make a list of all the problems you can foresee.

2. Determine which problems can be solved through existing research sources. For instance, you might be able to find information about your competitors at your local library, so why waste time gathering information yourself? On the other hand, research may be available, but at a price. If the prices of industry surveys or customer demographic surveys are out of your budget, you'll have to tackle those tasks yourself. Note the appropriate sources next to each problem on your list.

3. After you've consulted your available research sources (this book's appendixes give some leads), restate your list of problems in Step 1 as *specific* market research goals. A notation to "Find out about the competition" is too vague. Instead, your list might now read: "Determine what percentage of the market Company X is already reaching." "Identify how Company X is reaching its customers—advertising (where and how often?) and promotions (what kind and how many?)."

4. Identify the type of data you need to gather to meet those goals. Most business owners focus on information about customers, competition, and the industry. Within these broad topics, there are many subtopics, which we will cover later in this chapter.

5. Plan how you will acquire the desired information. Are you going to rely entirely on existing research from the library or conduct some of your own? Will you phone people, create a survey to send out in the mail, or search for information using computer databases? (You'll probably use more than one method.)

6. Decide whom you should contact to obtain the data required. Will you phone potential customers? If you come up with a written survey, will you hand them out to potential customers? Will you call trade associations to get information on your industry?

7. Conduct your research and gather the information. You'll have to take the time to read printed material, conduct personal interviews, do telephone surveys, mail out questionnaires, and/or test samples (if you have a product).

8. Analyze the data. Look at the information you have gathered and arrange it in categories: pricing, advertising, customer demographics, and so on.

9. Develop conclusions based on your information analysis, and determine a course of action. Nail down your pricing strategy; develop an advertising strategy that will reach your customers; and write a description of your target market, including age, geographic location, gender, buying habits, and average income.

WHAT TO RESEARCH

Market research should help you determine how you will do the following:

- Define your product or service.
- Define your market: who are your customers?

- Identify what motivates those customers to buy.
- Price your product or service.
- Reach your customers through advertising, publicity, and sales calls.
- Compete with other companies providing the same products or services.
- Position your product in the marketplace.
- Cope with outside forces, such as the economy.
- Understand your industry and how your company fits in.
- Evaluate your community.

Each of these benefits is discussed in the following sections.

Defining Your Product or Service

Going into business without a clear idea of what you'll be selling spells disaster. You need to know exactly what you are offering your customers. Let's say you've decided to sell gift baskets, but that's as far as you've gone. Your next decisions involve what the baskets will look like, what products you will put inside them, how many styles you will offer, and how you will price them. Or, if you want to start a mail order business, will you offer overnight delivery, allow customers to pay with credit cards, or offer money-back guarantees? Get the idea?

Putting everything on paper is a good start. Write a full description of your product or service. This will help you immensely later, when you are creating advertising campaigns and sales presentations. The better you know your product or service, the better you can sell it.

Defining Your Market

Unless you know who will buy your product or service, any marketing attempts will backfire. Mailing out thousands of beautifully designed, cleverly written brochures will do no good if you mail them to people who don't want your product or service.

Identifying your target market will give you a better chance that your advertising and promotional efforts will pay off. It will also help you determine your pricing strategy.

To discover who your ideal customer is, you should determine the following: customers' age range, gender, type of work they do, where they live, what their buying habits are, what they normally spend on your type of product or service, where they buy it, and how often they buy it.

Using this information, your task is to determine how big your target market is and what share of that market you can capture.

Analyzing Customer Motivation

Once you've identified who your customers are, you must figure out what motivates these customers to buy a particular product or service: price, quality, impulse, speed of delivery, or other factors. Create a questionnaire asking customers what makes them want a product or service such as yours. You can either list all the potential problems associated with a product or service and ask your survey subjects to rate them according to the level of importance they attach to each problem, or you can ask users to point out the benefits of the product or service and rate them in terms of importance. In this way, you'll learn which factors are more important than others to your customers.

Pricing Your Product or Service

Selling is never easy, but if your prices are too high compared to the competition, making a sale could become impossible. On the other hand, offering bargain basement prices could pose an equally serious problem. If you price your product or service so low that you don't leave yourself an adequate profit margin, your business won't survive.

There are other factors to determine as well. Are you going to set prices on the high side and then allow your customers to bargain with you? Or are your prices going to be set in stone? Will you offer discounted prices if a customer buys in bulk? Consider these options before slapping a price tag on a product or typing in fees on sales presentation materials.

To determine the best selling price for your product, factor in: your costs, your competition's prices, your customers, and the economy.

- Look at your costs (materials, supplies, overhead, your time) before setting a price. Make sure the price you set will leave you an adequate profit margin.
- Examine your competition to see what prices they are charging. Do you want to charge more, less, or the same as your competition? Your decision will depend on how you want to position your company. (Positioning your company is a later topic in this chapter.)

- Determine how much your customers are willing to pay.
- Is the economy weak or strong? Are people looking for a bargain or ready to spend? Price your product accordingly.

(See Chapter 8, "The Price is Right," for more details on finding the best price for your product or service.)

Reaching Your Customers

Determining how you will connect with your customers is one of the most important aspects of marketing. Among the possibilities, be sure to include:

- Trade publications, consumer magazines, and periodicals your customers read.
- Trade shows your customers attend.
- Directories or mailing lists of your target market that already exist.
- Organizations, clubs, or associations your customers belong to.

Once you know what networks exist, you can use them to reach your customers with advertising and promotions. Next, decide what methods you will use to reach customers. Here are some methods you may want to consider:

- Exhibiting at trade shows.
- Mailing out fliers.
- Advertising in local newspapers or magazines or in trade publications.
- Advertising on cable television or local radio.
- Telemarketing.
- Networking.
- Word-of-mouth.
- Customer referrals.
- Cross-marketing with a company that provides similar, yet noncompetitive products or services.

Analyzing the Competition

Know your competitors. In business, it's critical to know what you're up against, so you'd better take a good look at your competition. If you are going to succeed in taking away a share of their market, you'll have to find out a few things first:

- Who their customers are.
- How they reach those customers.
- What percentage of the total target market they are reaching.
- What products and services they offer.
- How much they charge.
- What their revenues are.
- What sales and marketing techniques they use.
- Where they advertise.
- How customers perceive your competitors.

From this investigation, you may discover that your competitors are not reaching a particular segment of your target market. If you can discover a way to reach that niche, you've got yourself a business. An examination of how competitors are reaching their customers may reveal better ways to get the word out about your business to those same customers. And you may be able to get a selling advantage by pricing your product competitively.

Positioning Your Business in the Marketplace

Positioning your company is similar to creating its image. It revolves around how you want customers to perceive your business. Do you want your company to be viewed as having the finest quality (and, therefore, higher prices)? Do you want customers to know that you will go the extra mile for them when other businesses won't? Do you want to be known as the company with the quickest turnaround on projects? Or do you want to have a reputation for the lowest prices in town? It's up to you to decide what you want your company to be.

Once again, put your thoughts in writing. Write a short paragraph describing how you want to position your company in the marketplace.

Responding to Outside Forces That Affect Your Business

Determine how your company is linked to the economy. If the economy dips or rises, how will your business be affected? Some businesses, such as those that determine how companies can save money on phone and utility bills, fare well in a depressed economy. Other types of businesses depend on a strong economy.

Researching Your Industry

When researching your industry, be sure to compile the following vital information.

Actual and Potential Size of the Industry

Actual industry size can be estimated by referring to several research sources, such as the Census Bureau and the Department of Commerce, as well as trade associations for a particular industry. These sources often provide market information by charting sales according to product line, growth, geographic markets, and major players in the industry. To gauge the potential size of the industry, look closely at gaps within the industry. Such gaps may occur in the product line, distribution, usage, competitiveness, or any number of areas. Through research of your customers, competitors, and the industry as a whole, you're going to have to spot those gaps.

Industry Growth Prospects

To forecast industry growth, look at current trends and how they could affect your industry. Trade associations may have growth projections.

Structure of the Industry

Look at the companies currently in the industry, the threat to newcomers in the industry, the threat of competition from alternate products and technology, the buying power of customers, and the negotiating power of suppliers.

Distribution Channels

When researching distribution systems within an industry, ask yourself at least three strategic questions:

1. What are the current distribution channels and by whom are they controlled?
2. Are there any alternative distribution channels?
3. Have any new distribution channels emerged or are any likely to emerge?

Trends and Developments within the Industry

Spotting industry trends is a matter of asking yourself several questions concerning your customers, your competitors, and the industry or market in general. Here are some key questions:

1. What is important to customers?
2. Is product quality paramount?
3. Do customers want a service that is convenient first and inexpensive second?
4. What needs aren't being met? In other words, what gaps in the market are you going to fill?
5. What new strategies are your competitors starting to employ? They may be useful to you as well.
6. If yours is a market for products, what are the new trends in distribution?

To recognize the significant industry and market trends that will affect your future strategy, take a close look at your market analysis up to this point.

Keys to Success

Perhaps the most important result of your industry analysis will be to identify the key success factors of companies already in the industry. These factors may include name recognition, distribution channel power, financial resources, customer loyalty, purchasing procedures, and access to raw material. Learn from what these companies are doing right and capitalize on what they're doing wrong.

Evaluating Your Community

When launching a home-based business, there are important questions to consider:

- Is the population base large enough to support the home-based business?
- Does the community have a stable economic base that will promote a healthy environment for your business?
- Are the area's demographic characteristics compatible with the market you wish to serve?
- Is the market well-served or saturated by similar businesses?

Each year, the U.S. Bureau of the Census publishes *Economic Censuses*—comprehensive studies on the number of firms in different spheres of business, and the populations of the communities where they are located. For more information, write to: Customer Services, Bureau of the Census, Washington, DC 20233.

A community's economic base plays a significant role in determining opportunities. The wealth produced in or near the community greatly affects local employment, income, and population growth, each of which plays a role in the success or failure of your home-based venture.

To evaluate a community's economic base, research the following:

- Percentage of people employed full-time, and the trend in employment.
- Average family income.
- Per-capita total annual sales/revenues for your products/ services.

You can obtain this information by studying the census data and business statistics mentioned earlier. You can also learn a great deal about your prospective community just by observing. Some danger signals include:

- The necessity for high school and college graduates to leave town to find suitable employment.
- The inability of other residents to find local jobs.
- Declining retail sales and industrial production.
- Apathetic attitudes of local business owners, educational administrators, and other residents.

Favorable signs are:

- The opening of chain or department store branches.
- Branch plants of large industrial firms locating in the community.
- A progressive Chamber of Commerce and other civic organizations.
- Good schools and public services.
- Well-maintained business and residential premises.
- Good transportation facilities to other parts of the country.

- Construction activity accompanied by a minimal number of vacant buildings and unoccupied houses for sale.

You must know the demographic profile of your potential customers. To properly evaluate your community's demographic characteristics, look at the following:

- Purchasing power (degree of disposable income).
- Residences (rented or owned; houses, condos, or apartments).
- Places and kinds of work.
- Means of transportation.
- Age ranges.
- Family status.
- Leisure activities.

Detailed demographic information should be available from established businesses within your industry or from a trade association. In addition, the Bureau of Labor Statistics publishes the *Consumer Expenditure Survey (CES)*. The *CES* annually samples 5,000 households to learn how families and individuals spend their money. Unlike other surveys that might ask only how much people are spending on household expenses or home appliances, the *CES* questions participants about nearly every expense category, from alcoholic beverages and take-out food to pensions and life insurance. Bureau of Labor Statistics analysts then sort the information and group consumers by income, household size, race, and other factors.

MARKET RESEARCH SOURCES

In conducting your market research, you'll be gathering two types of data: *primary* information that you will compile yourself, and *secondary* (information that is already compiled and organized—reports and studies published by government agencies, trade associations, or other businesses in your industry.

Primary Research

If you are going to conduct primary research, you will have to decide how you will question your target group of individuals. The most commonly used avenues are direct mail, telemarketing, and personal interviews.

Direct Mail Questionnaires

If you choose to circulate a direct mail questionnaire, these guidelines will increase your response rate:

- Keep your questions short and succinct. Because most people don't like to be bothered with questionnaires, your chances for a high response rate will diminish if the items are too cumbersome.
- Make sure your questionnaires are addressed to specific individuals and that they are of interest to the respondent.
- Limit the questionnaire's length to two pages.
- Enclose a professionally prepared cover letter that adequately explains what you need.
- Include a postage-paid self-addressed envelope, and use a special reply permit indicia. Postage-paid envelopes are available at your local post office.
- Send a reminder about two weeks after the initial mailing.

Be aware that mail response will be low, perhaps less than 5%.

Telephone Interviews

Mail questions can be moderately complex; telephone questions should be kept simple. Telephone surveys are generally the most cost-effective method, considering overall response rates; they're three times less costly than personal interviews, which yield an average response rate only 10% higher. Following are some phone survey guidelines:

- At the beginning of the conversation, confirm the name of the respondent if calling a home, or give the appropriate name to the switchboard operator if calling a business.
- Avoid pauses; respondent interest can quickly be lost.
- Confirm that a follow-up call can be made if additional information is required.
- Make sure you don't divulge details about the poll until the respondent is reached.

As mentioned, phone interviews are cost-effective. Speed is another big advantage. You may be able to perform five or six interviews per hour. Phone interviews also cover a wide geographical range at a relatively low cost. Phone charges can be reduced by taking advantage of cheaper rates during certain hours—for example, if on the West Coast, call the East Coast from 5 A.M. to 8 A.M.; if on the East Coast, call the West Coast from 5 P.M. to 8 P.M.

Face-to-Face Interviews

One of the most effective forms of marketing research is the face-to-face or personal interview. The primary advantages over telephone and mail surveys are: a low respondent-refusal rate, a less distorted sample—telephone availability and erratic postal response rates are not factors—and a wider range of subjects covered.

There are two main types of personal interviews:

1. *The group survey.* Used mostly by larger businesses, group interviews can be a useful brainstorming method resulting in enlightening information about product modification, new product ideas, buying preferences, and purchasing decisions among certain populations. In most cases, groups should be kept to four or fewer; otherwise, some respondents tend to dominate while others sit back and contribute nothing. Your role is to make sure the group doesn't stray from the subject, which is briefly introduced at the beginning.

2. *The depth interview.* In this one-on-one interview, you use a small checklist and basic common sense. Depth interviews are either nondirective or focused. Nondirective interviews encourage respondents to address certain topics with minimal questioning. The respondent, in essence, leads the interview. The focused interview, on the other hand, is based on a preset checklist. The choice and timing of questions are left to you, depending on how the interview goes.

Typical Costs of Market Surveys

When considering which type of survey to use, keep certain cost factors in mind:

- *Mail.* Most of the costs here concern the purchase of envelopes and postage, printing of questionnaires and a cover letter, time spent on analysis and presentation, your time, and any incentives used.
- *Telephone.* The main costs, in addition to the analysis and presentation, are the phone charges, preparation of the questionnaire, and your time.
- *Personal interviews.* Costs include the printing of questionnaires and prompt cards (if needed), the incentives used, your time, and analysis and presentation.
- *Group discussions.* Main costs are expenses in recruiting and assembling the groups, renting the conference room or other

facility, your time, any incentives used, analysis and presentation, and the cost of recording media, such as tapes, if used.

The questions a home-based entrepreneur asks are not markedly different from the kinds of questions asked by businesses operating from traditional locations. They should be designed, at least in part, to gauge public opinion of home-based businesses—whether people feel they are as professional as other businesses. These days, most consumers care less about where a company is located and more about the quality and value of that business's products or services.

Secondary Research

Secondary data consist of outside information assembled by government agencies, industry and trade associations, labor unions, media sources, Chambers of Commerce, and so on. These data are found in pamphlets, newsletters, trade and other magazines, and newspapers. The information has been gathered by another, or secondary, source. The benefits are obvious: time and money are saved because you don't have to develop survey methods or conduct the interviews.

Secondary sources are divided into three main categories: public, commercial, and educational.

Public

Public sources are the most economical because they're usually free and can offer a wealth of useful information. These sources are most typically governmental departments and the business departments of public libraries.

Government statistics are among the most plentiful and wide-ranging public sources. They cover virtually every aspect of American life, from census tracts to business trends from a variety of perspectives—commerce, agriculture, investment, and so on. Among other things, government data can help you:

- Track existing and emerging markets.
- Analyze your company's market share using updated, industrywide revenue data.
- Compare regional trends.
- Estimate the size and characteristics of a certain market, including customers' spending habits.
- Monitor distribution channels.

- Track changing retail, wholesale, and agricultural prices.
- Track stock movement and retail sales in preparing short- and long-term industry/economic forecasts.
- Assess foreign competition in domestic markets.
- Analyze world markets.
- Use regional statistics to establish quotas for sales reps.
- Track labor costs in a variety of industries.

One indispensable public source is the business section of most public libraries. The services provided vary from city to city, but libraries usually offer a wide range of government and market statistics, a large collection of directories with information on domestic and foreign businesses, and a wide selection of magazines, newspapers, newsletters, and journals.

Almost every county government publishes population density and distribution figures in widely available census tracts. These will show you the number of people living in specific areas: precincts, water districts, or even 10-block neighborhoods. Some counties publish reports that indicate population trends by showing the population 10 years ago, 5 years ago, and currently.

Declining, static, or extremely small populations typically do not support a wealth of commerce in a given area. (If any business is capable of flourishing in an uncertain area, however, it would be a low-overhead home-based operation.) The ideal is an expanding population in which you can stimulate a desire for your products or services. To judge whether they are potential customers, you must study the lifestyle of the community.

Maps of major trading areas in counties and states are also available from Chambers of Commerce, industrial development boards, trade development commissions, and city newspaper offices. These maps show the major areas of commerce, and reflect the population's spending habits.

Look at road maps of any area for information on the ease of access to specific sites. Access is an important consideration in determining market area limits.

Major cities have Chambers of Commerce or business development departments that encourage new businesses in their communities. They will supply you with information (usually free of charge) such as:

- Demographic reports on the local, regional, and state level.
- Seminars on networking, managing, financing, or developing a marketing plan.

- Directories that can help entrepreneurs get in touch with the decision makers within large local corporations (for distribution opportunities).

This information will help you to develop your market survey so you can partially gauge your likelihood of success. The bottom line: you'll run your business better.

Commercial

Commercial sources are equally valuable, but usually impose subscription and association fees. The money spent, however, is far less than if a research team collects the data firsthand. As mentioned earlier, commercial sources typically consist of research and trade associations and banks.

Ask the sales departments of local newspapers and magazines for copies of the business profiles used in their sales efforts. They will help determine the financial situation of potential customers/clients in your target market(s). Advertising managers are another source of information regarding a community's spending patterns.

Check with managers of local broadcasting stations as well. The research they routinely conduct can help you determine whether there is a valid market for your product or service.

Study local Yellow Pages directories to see how many potential competitors are currently in operation and where they work. (Also count how many of them are home-based and how many have commercial facilities.) This information is also available from Dun & Bradstreet.

Educational

Educational institutions are frequently overlooked as viable information sources, yet more research is conducted in colleges, universities, and polytechnic institutes than in virtually any sector of the business community.

Local colleges and universities are also valuable sources of information. Over 650 colleges and universities have branches of the Small Business Administration's Small Business Development Centers (SBDC). SBDCs offer a variety of information about the marketing, legal, financial, and accounting aspects of home-based business ownership, as well as state and federal business assistance programs. The centers will also help you prepare business plans and financial statements.

Help from a local college may be available if there is no SBDC near you. Many college business departments are eager to have their students work in the "real world" gathering information and doing research for a nominal salary or for college credit.

DO YOU NEED A CONSULTANT?

When you have a medical problem, you go to a doctor. When you have a legal question, you see an attorney. But whom do you see when you want to start a business? Business consultants exist in a number of fields—from franchising to start-up, production, finance, marketing, even home-based. If you think you don't have the money to hire a business consultant, remember that a consultant doesn't have to cost you an arm and a leg; you can hire consultants on a temporary basis. Hourly rates from $75 to $150 are common; daily rates for a specialized consultant can jump to more than $1,000.

If you are just getting your business off the ground, you may think your home-based company isn't significant enough to hire a consultant. But because the start-up period is the most precarious for a small business, this is actually the best time to let a professional evaluate your business plan.

After reviewing your business plan, the consultant can offer suggestions to make sure your business avoids any pitfalls and gets off on the right foot. If you don't have a business plan, the consultant can help you create a plan that will keep your business on track. For instance, if you are launching a pool cleaning business, a consultant may be able to help you with pricing questions, how to deal with seasonal ups and downs, deciding whether to lease or purchase equipment, how to advertise your service, working with subcontractors, and setting up your account books.

Finding a Qualified Consultant

Business and management consultants are not licensed like doctors and lawyers. Anyone can hang out a shingle and claim to be a consultant.

For this reason, demand proof of a consultant's expertise before retaining his or her services. Request professional and bank references, and confirm them. Make sure the consultant can prove practical experience in managing and operating businesses, especially home-based ventures. The more varied the consultant's experience, the better.

Although highly paid consultants are available in many specific areas affecting your business, the "consultant" best able to advise you is someone who is already successful at the same level of business. In another part of town or in a nearby city, find a successful business that will not be in direct competition with you, and ask the owner or manager to analyze your plans.

Because poor location and ineffective advertising are among the most common reasons for business failure, you will want these aspects of your plans examined with particular care.

If your start-up capital is limited, and you can't afford the high cost of a consultant, consider hiring an MBA student. You won't be buying the practical expertise of highly paid professionals, but a person with this background can easily research your competition, run a cash-flow projection, or perform other basic preparations.

Ideally, your consultant should be someone who understands your goals and is willing to work toward them—not someone who tries to force your company into a preconceived mold. The right consultant won't drive you to greater success but can provide a road map.

Ask for proposals from a few consultants. Make sure that (1) they understand what you want them to accomplish and (2) you understand their fee structure.

Let the consultant know that you will listen to any criticism or suggestions without getting defensive. A consultant may show an import/export entrepreneur that he or she has been spending too much money on travel, not spending enough on marketing, and overstocking inventory. By following the consultant's guidelines, the entrepreneur can shift funds where needed, lighten inventory, and ultimately improve efficiency.

Don't expect a consultant to put these ideas and suggestions into use. That's your job. Before hiring a consultant, be sure you are willing to take action on your consultant's suggestions.

4

START-UP FINANCING

You don't need to be a millionaire to start a business from home. In fact, many entrepreneurs have launched their companies with as little as a few thousand dollars. Starting a business from home significantly reduces the amount of start-up capital you'll need in the beginning, but you will still need a substantial amount to pay for sales materials, production materials, office supplies, phone usage, and other necessities.

Raising the money you need can be a real challenge, but it isn't impossible. In fact, there are many ways to finance your business:

- Tap your own savings.
- Borrow from friends and family.
- Borrow from banks.
- Take out an SBA guaranteed loan.
- Get help from a finance company.
- Use your suppliers as loan sources.
- Obtain capital from private investors.
- Use your credit cards.

Entrepreneurs may need to tap more than one source when seeking financing for a new venture.

Before asking anyone for money, make a careful assessment of the proposed value of your business, the amount of capital you need, the amount you will have to borrow, and the length of time it will take you to pay back the loan.

No matter which sources you decide to solicit, you're going to need a business plan that will explain your business to potential investors. A business plan enhances your credibility and your determination to actually launch the business.

TAP YOURSELF FIRST

The best source of financing is your own money. It is immediately available capital, there is no interest to be paid back, and you don't have to give any investors a piece of your business in exchange for funding. But getting a venture off the ground can be a very costly proposition—the investment may be beyond your immediate cash reserves. If this is the case, there are several avenues you can explore in order to obtain the necessary capital.

BORROW FROM FAMILY AND FRIENDS

After your own money, your friends and relatives are the next best sources. In fact, after personal savings, friends and family are the second most popular source for business start-up capital. After all, friends and family know you're trustworthy and competent, so lending money to you doesn't seem so risky.

However, borrowing money from people you know has its own risks. The relationship can be threatened if your business fails and you can't repay the loan. Mixing money with friendship or love creates a potentially explosive combination. Some entrepreneurs assume that receiving a personal loan from a friend or relative means they can take their time paying it back. And some people are willing to put up money to get your business going, but they regard their investment as a free license to meddle in your affairs.

But don't despair. There are ways to tiptoe through the delicate process without stepping on anybody's toes.

Before taking any money from acquaintances or family members, meet with them to discuss your business plan and explain the risks involved. Let them know how much, if any, control you are giving them in your business. Are they going to be silent investors or will you be including them in planning meetings? Whatever you decide, make sure you spell it out in writing.

In general, you should treat personal loans from friends and family like any other loan. Draw up loan papers for each friend or relative who contributes money to your venture.

When friends and relatives who lend you money sign loan papers, two purposes are served: (1) their loan is protected and (2) they are prevented from gaining equity in your business, unless you default on the loan.

BORROWING FROM BANKS

Banks are probably the most visible source of ready financing, and you should already have contact with a few through your personal accounts. Although banks are logical places to go in order to raise capital, they are notoriously conservative, especially where start-up home-based ventures are concerned.

Most banks will require some sort of collateral as security for a loan. Banks will also want to know the purpose of the loan, so be prepared to show them your business plan. Your personal background will have a direct bearing on how your loan applications are treated.

Finding the right bank and banker is key to securing a loan. Look for a bank and banker that know your industry and have done business with companies like yours. Talk to people in your industry and ask whom they would recommend.

One of the most common mistakes start-up entrepreneurs make is going into a bank without being prepared. Your business plan should help you explain your business concept, projections, and needs to a banker, but you need more. You should be able to answer—in detail—these seven questions from your banker:

1. *How much money do you want?* Be as exact as possible, and don't forget to add a little extra for oversights and contingencies.
2. *What are you going to do with the money?* Explain exactly what you will do with the money, such as buy new equipment.
3. *Why is this loan good for your business?* Be prepared to be specific about what the bank's money will do for your business and why your company is a good risk.
4. *Why do you need our depositors' money to do it?* The thinly veiled question here is "Why don't you have enough money of your own to do this?" Don't get flustered; have a well-thought-out answer.
5. *When will you pay back the loan?* This is where your cash flow projections come in. Knowing when you can expect to see the

fruits of the bank's cash injection helps you formulate a repayment time frame.

6. *How will you repay the loan?* This isn't the time to be vague. Using your financial projections and business plan, your job is to convince the banker of the long-term profitability of your business.

7. *What happens if your plans don't work out?* This is why you have collateral. Your mission is to reassure the banker of the value of your collateral in case your business doesn't work out.

Depending on the size of the loan you request, there are several bank loan and collateral possibilities. If you have a savings account at a bank, you can use this money as collateral for a short-term loan. This is actually a very good way to get financing, because it lowers your interest rate. For instance, if you take out a loan at 11%, and your savings account is earning 3%, the actual interest rate you'll be paying is 8%.

It may also be possible to use your life insurance policy as collateral if it has any cash value. Loans can usually be made for up to 95% of the policy's cash value. By borrowing against your life insurance policy, you don't have to actually repay the loan; all you need to do is pay the interest charges along with your premium. However, if you don't repay the amount at some time, your policy will decrease that much in value.

Signature (personal) loans are a possibility if your credit is good. You can usually take out a loan of this type for several thousand dollars—even more, if you have a good relationship with the bank. These loans are usually short-term and have very high interest rates.

Another short-term loan is a commercial loan. This type of loan is usually issued for a six-month period and can be paid in installments during that time or in one lump sum. Stocks and bonds, your life insurance policy, or your personal guarantee can be used as collateral. If the loan is exceptionally large compared to your assets, the bank may require that you post a cash reserve equal to 20% of the loan amount.

You can also use any real estate you own as collateral. Loans of this nature can be secured for up to 75% of the real estate's value and can be set up for a term of 20 years if necessary.

If you own your home, you may want to consider a home equity loan. However, there are two valid and opposing points of view about using home equity as a money source. On the positive side, if you have equity in your home, you can take it out and invest it in a business and make it work for you. On the flip side, if you have equity in your home but you don't own it free and clear, and something happens so you aren't able to make payments, you can lose your home and your equity. The decision is up to you.

Other loan possibilities include inventory, equipment, or accounts receivable financing. These types of loans use the value of your inventory, equipment, or accounts receivable as security for a loan. Using your inventory as collateral, a bank will usually lend up to 50% of its value. Equipment and accounts receivable loans will cover 80% of their value. However, during start-up, these options may not be available to you.

FINANCE COMPANIES

Finance companies will take greater risks than banks, but they charge a higher interest rate. Generally, finance companies will be more interested in your collateral, your past track record, and the potential of your new business than in the strength of your credit.

GETTING A LOAN FROM THE SBA

The Small Business Administration (SBA) was created in 1953 to "help small businesses start, grow, and prosper." Included in that pledge was a loan program to make low-interest, long-term loans available to businesses that would otherwise have a hard time finding capital. Today, the SBA has a multibillion-dollar loan fund that is distributed both as direct loans and as trough guarantees made on loans issued through local banks. In its 40-plus years, the SBA loan program has effectively helped nearly 1 million small business owners get the money they need to develop products, hire employees, and purchase equipment.

Many borrowers get SBA funding after they've been rejected by other lending institutions. And rejections from banks are currently running rampant.

The SBA makes several different types of loans. Understanding the different programs before you start your search, and preparing your applications properly, puts you that much closer to getting the money you need.

Most people think of SBA loans as money going straight from the government's coffers into an entrepreneur's hands. This is true only in some rare cases. Direct loans account for only a tiny percentage of the SBA loan program. Guaranteed loans, made through local banks and other lending institutions, make up the bulk of SBA loans.

The SBA will guarantee loans of up to $750,000. But borrowing $750,000 to start a business is like using a sledgehammer to drive in a thumbtack. Very small sums of money, or microloans, were created to fill the gap between low-investment start-ups and businesses with much greater capital needs.

There are a number of SBA-backed microlenders nationwide, offering loans of $25,000 or less. Your state or regional SBA office can tell you what SBA microloan programs are available, and may even have information about non-SBA microloan programs.

Although loans are available for as short a term as 1 to 2 years and as long as 25 years (for construction and real estate purposes), the vast majority of loans run for 5 to 8 years.

In general, the SBA focuses less on a business owner's collateral and more on his or her repayment ability. Nevertheless, you will need some collateral for an SBA loan. You can use certain assets as security:

- Land and/or buildings.
- Machinery and/or equipment.
- Real estate and/or chattel mortgages.
- Warehouse receipts for marketable merchandise.
- Personal endorsement of a guarantor (someone who is able and willing to pay off the loan if you fail).

If you're seeking a guaranteed loan from the SBA, be prepared to prove that your proposed company has the ability to compete successfully in its field. Whether you're seeking a loan for a new concept or an established one, don't underestimate the importance of the category into which the SBA assigns it. The success or failure of your application may rest on this classification. Decide which field your business can best compete in, state this on your application, and be prepared to back it up.

To help you prepare for this question, you should know how the SBA formulates its guidelines. A key publication it relies on is the *Standard Industrial Classification (SIC) Manual*, published by the Bureau of the Budget, Washington, DC. The SBA also uses published information concerning the nature of similar companies, as well as your description of the proposed business. The SBA will not intentionally work against you, but it is up to you to steer the agency in the direction that is best for you.

USING SUPPLIERS AS LOAN SOURCES

Although you won't be able to finance your complete start-up through suppliers, you may be able to offset the cost of the supplies and/or merchandise during your start-up period by obtaining a lengthy payment period, or trade credit (see Chapter 9, "Financial Management"). When you first start your business, suppliers usually will not extend trade credit. One of the things you can do to get credit is to have a properly prepared financial plan and negotiate with the owner of the business or the chief financial officer.

If you're successful, you may be able to defer payment for supplies from the time of delivery to 30, 60, or even 90 days interest-free. Although this is not specifically a loan, you still have those supplies during the crucial start-up period.

"ANGEL" INVESTORS

Raising start-up capital may require giving up a portion of your business to private investors, called "angels." Such money is called equity capital. Equity financing means dividing your business ownership among investors who contribute capital but may or may not participate in the operation of the business. There aren't any loans associated with equity capital, and there isn't any legal obligation placed on you to pay back the amount invested. All the investor gets is a percentage of the business, and the losses or profits associated with it.

Equity capital may, at first glance, seem like the best way to raise start-up capital, but there are many drawbacks. First, you give up a portion of your business and, with it, some control. That means you have to share your profits with your new partners, and, depending on how you set up the company—partnership, limited partnership, or corporation—you could become responsible for the actions of your partner(s). If the partners go into debt, you and your company may also.

Second, with some types of equity financing, you might relinquish control of your company. Have your lawyer draw up documents for equity investors to sign, stating the amount and value of the equity being offered. The individual with the idea will usually retain 50% of the equity in the company; the other 50% will be sold to investors. While the 50–50 rule is fairly common, everything is negotiable in a deal such as this.

Private investors, referred to as "angels," are called the "invisible" segment of the financing industry because they are so difficult to find. For entrepreneurs who need help locating individuals who want to invest in new companies, here are some guidelines from William Wetzel, a leading expert on angel financing and professor of management at the University of New Hampshire in Durham:

- Start early. Finding investors takes longer than you think.
- Look close to home. Target investors who are within a half-day's drive from your business.
- Look for individuals who have a high net worth and a knowledge of your market or technology.

- Seek out wealthy individuals in philanthropic organizations, Chambers of Commerce, local advisory boards, and non-profit organizations. Investors are often involved in such organizations.
- Network, network, network.
- Have your business plan in order. Investors are very concerned about their return on investment and want to see evidence that you will provide it.
- Get references from professional contacts, such as lawyers and accountants. Being referred to an investor is always better than a cold contact.

USING YOUR CREDIT CARDS

One of the most overlooked avenues of obtaining start-up capital is credit cards. This option used to be used solely as a last resort because most credit cards charged extremely high interest rates, but that is changing. Many credit cards are lowering their interest rates to make this a more viable option. This is a way to get several thousand dollars quickly without dealing with paperwork, as long as you don't exceed your credit limit.

One home-based entrepreneur had three credit cards with a $3,000 credit line on each. He needed approximately $8,000 to start a financial aid service. Using his credit cards, he cashed each in for the full amount and started his company. Within 6 months, he had built up a very good business and approached his bank for a loan of $10,000. He received the loan for a 3-year term at 12%. With the $10,000, he paid off his credit card balances, which were incurring a 20% annual rate. After another 6 months, he paid off the bank loan of $10,000.

5

LEGAL ISSUES

You decide to start a courier service from your home. Your plan is to cover a 30-mile radius. To operate legally, you must decide on a form of operation for your company that meets local, state, and/or federal regulations.

Wait a minute—already? You've barely started this business. Can't the legal considerations wait until you're actually making some real money?

No, you really shouldn't wait. To grow your business effectively and avoid tax or other legal problems, you should tackle legal issues early and consult an attorney about your needs and options. Establishing a relationship with an attorney in the early stages will significantly benefit you and your company over time.

CHOOSING A LEGAL FORM OF OPERATION

Many people ask: "Aren't attorneys awfully expensive for a small-time entrepreneur?" The answer is "Sometimes." Shop around first, and do much of the up-front homework on business formation yourself. In this way, you will make effective use of your time with the attorney and still benefit from the early relationship and his or her experience.

For example, you may have assumed that your small, home-based courier service would run best as a sole proprietorship. After all, it's just you—the sole proprietor—running the show, with some occasional help from your spouse and your 17-year-old nephew. You've gotten all the initial financing on your own, and you plan to simply work and work, grow the business, and take your income from the profits. Sole proprietors don't need to file separate business tax forms, they have complete control over their business bank accounts (including ATM access to funds), and they don't have to hassle with a lot of legal paperwork. They simply get a business license, file a fictitious name with the county clerk (i.e., "Doing Business As" or "DBA") and add on a Schedule C (or C-EZ) tax form to their regular Form 1040 filing. (Schedule C, shown on page 110, is used when gross receipts exceed $25,000 and expenses exceed $2,000. Schedule C-EZ, a much simpler three-line reporting form, can be used when gross receipts are below $25,000, expenses are below $2,000, your business has no inventory during the filing period, and you do not have a net loss to report. You must also have used the cash-accounting method for recording transactions. (See Chapter 10, "Record Keeping and Taxes.")

You do, of course, have the option of operating your business under your own name—though this is generally not a good idea. Naming your business after yourself, unless you are an expert in the chosen industry, does not lend any authority to the company's name and puts your name (i.e., reputation) at risk if the business encounters problems. Instead, it is recommended that you file a fictitious name statement, or "DBA" (mentioned above), and operate under a creative identity. To do so, simply inquire about your state's regulations at the county clerk's office. In many instances, a local newspaper that publishes DBA announcements will also file the necessary paperwork for you as part of its fee. You can also check with your attorney or banker; some banks have their own requirements about fictitious name filing statements.

A sole proprietorship is the most popular modus operandi for a new business, but being a sole proprietor is not the only way to go. For one thing, a sole proprietorship is financially attached to the owner in every way. If someone decides to sue your company, he or she can sue you personally. If vendors decide to press your business for overdue accounts payable, they can go after your home or other assets to make you pay your business bills. Your personal credit and reputation—and name—can be damaged by your sole proprietorship even though your only "crime" is falling victim to a poor economy or other business risk.

Therefore, you might want to look into forming a *corporation* or, if your state permits it, a *subchapter S corporation.*

SCHEDULE C (Form 1040) Department of the Treasury Internal Revenue Service (O)	**Profit or Loss From Business** (Sole Proprietorship) ▶ **Partnerships, joint ventures, etc., must file Form 1065.** ▶ **Attach to Form 1040 or Form 1041.** ▶ **See Instructions for Schedule C (Form 1040).**	OMB No. 1545-0074 19**93** Attachment Sequence No. **09**

Name of proprietor	Social security number (SSN)

A	Principal business or profession, including product or service (see page C-1)	**B** Enter principal business code (see page C-6) ▶

C	Business name. If no separate business name, leave blank.	**D** Employer ID number (EIN), if any

E Business address (including suite or room no.) ▶ ....
      City, town or post office, state, and ZIP code

F Accounting method: **(1)** ☐ Cash   **(2)** ☐ Accrual   **(3)** ☐ Other (specify) ▶ ....

G	Method(s) used to value closing inventory:	**(1)** ☐ Cost	**(2)** ☐ Lower of cost or market	**(3)** ☐ Other (attach explanation)	**(4)** ☐ Does not apply (if checked, skip line H)	Yes	No

H Was there any change in determining quantities, costs, or valuations between opening and closing inventory? If "Yes," attach
      explanation . . . .

I Did you "materially participate" in the operation of this business during 1993? If "No," see page C-2 for limit on losses. . .

J If you started or acquired this business during 1993, check here . . . . ▶ ☐

Part I   Income

1	Gross receipts or sales. **Caution:** *If this income was reported to you on Form W-2 and the "Statutory employee" box on that form was checked, see page C-2 and check here* . . . . ▶ ☐	**1**	
2	Returns and allowances	**2**	
3	Subtract line 2 from line 1	**3**	
4	Cost of goods sold (from line 40 on page 2)	**4**	
5	**Gross profit.** Subtract line 4 from line 3	**5**	
6	Other income, including Federal and state gasoline or fuel tax credit or refund (see page C-2) . . .	**6**	
7	**Gross income.** Add lines 5 and 6 . . . . ▶	**7**	

Part II   Expenses. Caution: *Do not enter expenses for business use of your home on lines 8–27. Instead, see line 30.*

8	Advertising	**8**		**19** Pension and profit-sharing plans	**19**
9	Bad debts from sales or services (see page C-3) .	**9**		**20** Rent or lease (see page C-4):	
				a Vehicles, machinery, and equipment .	**20a**
10	Car and truck expenses (see page C-3)	**10**		**b** Other business property .	**20b**
11	Commissions and fees. . .	**11**		**21** Repairs and maintenance . .	**21**
12	Depletion.	**12**		**22** Supplies (not included in Part III) .	**22**
13	Depreciation and section 179 expense deduction (not included in Part III) (see page C-3) .	**13**		**23** Taxes and licenses	**23**
				24 Travel, meals, and entertainment:	
14	Employee benefit programs (other than on line 19) . . .	**14**		**a** Travel	**24a**
15	Insurance (other than health) .	**15**		**b** Meals and en- tertainment .	
16	Interest:			**c** Enter 20% of line 24b subject to limitations (see page C-4) .	
a	Mortgage (paid to banks, etc.) .	**16a**			
b	Other	**16b**		**d** Subtract line 24c from line 24b .	**24d**
17	Legal and professional services	**17**		**25** Utilities	**25**
				26 Wages (less jobs credit) . .	**26**
18	Office expense	**18**		**27** Other expenses (from line 46 on page 2)	**27**

28	**Total expenses** before expenses for business use of home. Add lines 8 through 27 in columns. . ▶	**28**	
29	Tentative profit (loss). Subtract line 28 from line 7	**29**	
30	Expenses for business use of your home. Attach **Form 8829**	**30**	
31	**Net profit or (loss).** Subtract line 30 from line 29.		
	• If a profit, enter on **Form 1040, line 12,** and ALSO on **Schedule SE, line 2** (statutory employees, see page C-5). Fiduciaries, enter on Form 1041, line 3.	**31**	
	• If a loss, you MUST go on to line 32.		
32	If you have a loss, check the box that describes your investment in this activity (see page C-5).		
	• If you checked 32a, enter the loss on **Form 1040, line 12,** and ALSO on **Schedule SE, line 2** (statutory employees, see page C-5). Fiduciaries, enter on Form 1041, line 3.	**32a** ☐ All investment is at risk.	
	• If you checked 32b, you MUST attach **Form 6198.**	**32b** ☐ Some investment is not at risk.	

For Paperwork Reduction Act Notice, see Form 1040 instructions.   Cat. No. 11334P   **Schedule C (Form 1040) 1993**

Incorporating

Although most people think of huge entities like Mattel or Microsoft when they picture "a corporation," this is not necessarily the case. Owners of small businesses also form corporations, for several reasons:

- To protect their personal finances and assets from business creditors.
- To protect themselves personally from actions of the business.
- To take advantage of "executive privileges" afforded to the corporation's employees.
- To begin business operations with a setup that provides for future growth through investors/shareholders.

In both standard corporations and subchapter S corporations, you, the owner, are merely an employee of the corporation who owns some or all of the corporation's stock. All financial transactions from your home-based business belong to the corporation, and you are paid a salary from the business, plus a share of any corporate profits due to you as a shareholder.

Forming a corporation entails filing "articles of incorporation" or other required documents with the proper official for your state (usually the secretary of state). Getting the aid of an attorney is important when incorporating. Although some states only require that a simple form be filled out, there are other considerations. If you omit operational language regarding shareholder rights and voting in the articles of incorporation, for example, your corporation must automatically, by default, employ the statutory provisions of your state on these matters.

The articles of incorporation generally include the name and address of the corporation, names of the incorporators, and shares to be disbursed. Corporations also create bylaws to govern business operations. It is wise to address carefully all shareholder provisions, such as what will happen to a shareholder's shares upon his or her death. (Provisions that you adopt can allow the other shareholders to purchase the shares at a set rate, or at least to have first right of refusal, for example.) Records of all corporate business are recorded in a corporate minute book.

Most states require only one incorporator, although a handful require at least two. There is one drawback to incorporating: double taxation. A corporation is subject to corporate taxes, then each shareholder is taxed on his or her personal income (the income derived from salaries and corporate dividends). One way to offset this double taxation is to increase the salaries of corporate employees—such as yourself—to eliminate any corporate profits. For example, suppose the corporation pays you, the owner, $2,500 per month, and at year-end the business will show a profit of $3,000. Increasing your salary by $250 per month will wipe out corporate profits, and you will end up owing taxes only once—on your income.

Another way to prevent double taxation is to form a subchapter S corporation. In states that allow subchapter S filings to be recognized at tax time, the election serves to funnel profits directly to shareholders instead of having to record corporate profits (or losses) individually. Shareholders then claim their portion of the corporation's profits/losses on their individual taxes, and—in the case of losses—if the shareholders have had other income, they can sometimes deduct these losses against their income for an additional tax benefit.

Only domestic companies with 35 (or fewer) shareholders can qualify as subchapter S corporations. They must not include any group shareholders (only estates or individuals are allowed) nor any nonresident aliens. Only one class of stock can be issued to shareholders.

The Subchapter S Revisions Act of 1982 made forming a subchapter S corporation easier. Still, to be sure that you and your business (and partners/shareholders) will best benefit from this business formation, check with an attorney.

Naming your corporation is different from naming a sole proprietorship. By law, your corporation cannot have a name that is the same as any other business incorporated in that state—nor can the name be so similar as to be considered "deceptive" to consumers. You must check with state authorities to find out the availability of your selected name *prior to incorporating*, because the name is part of the articles of incorporation.

Adding a Partner

Let's say you've been operating your home-based courier service for about eight months, and you've developed some steady clients. Three of them are large retail pharmacies with stores across the state. You consider hiring employees in various cities to expand your business. As a new entrepreneur, however, you're hesitant to have too many people dependent on you for their incomes. You also worry that you won't be able to manage them well, because you would hire them to serve areas where you don't want to have to drive yourself.

At this stage, it may be a good idea for you to bring in a partner. Partnerships can be tricky ventures (some people compare them to marriages *without* the bond of love) but under the right circumstances they can be a good idea for small business owners who want to expand—geographically or financially—but are not ready to jump into full-blown employee expansion or incorporation.

Partnerships are similar to sole proprietorships in that the two of you will now work to grow the business and will take your separate incomes from the profits. In most cases, a partnership requires no additional paperwork beyond that filed for a sole proprietorship (i.e., "Doing Business As," etc.). However, your licenses and insurance papers will need revisions. The most important step is to draft *in writing* a partnership agreement that spells out how profits and losses will be shared, what the partners' individual responsibilities are to the company (including management authority), whether or how other partners can be added, and similar terms. A sample agreement is shown on page 114. Outline how each partner's share of the business will be handled upon his or her death, how one partner can buy out another if the need arises, and how operational or other disagreements will be resolved. By law, a partnership dissolves automatically upon the death of one partner, unless a buy–sell agreement has been implemented. This agreement is crucial in the event of not only death but divorce, disability, or unplanned retirement. Choosing the *right* partner is crucial.

Both partners named in a *general partnership* are financially attached to the business in every way, on the same terms as a single owner is with a sole proprietorship. The difference with a general partnership is that your personal credit, reputation, and name are dependent on the actions of your partner as well as yourself, and vice versa. Banking arrangements will require both partners' signatures to be on file (though, generally, only one signature is required to sign checks). You also will not be given an ATM card (at least not one that permits withdrawals of cash) if you form a partnership.

As an alternative, you can look into forming a *limited partnership.* Commonly used in real estate ventures, a limited partnership has a general partner that assumes all personal liability for the business. A limited partner (or partners) is simply an investor in the business, with no personal financial obligations or liabilities. In "silent partner" setups, the general partner has control over operating the business, and the limited partners simply provide financial backing. Either way, if someone sues the partnership, only the general partner's personal assets can be touched.

In some states, limited partnerships are subject to securities regulations. Depending on the type of business you operate, there may also be various tax liabilities to consider. Partnerships remain popular, and they serve some home-based business ventures well. Form a partnership carefully and thoughtfully, if at all. As always, legal advice should be solicited.

PARTNERSHIP AGREEMENT

DATE _____

COMMENCES_____

EXPIRES _____

LOCATION_____

THIS PARTNERSHIP AGREEMENT is made on
this _____ day of _____ , 19 ____ ,
between the individuals listed below:

_____

_____

_____

The partners listed above hereby agree that they shall be considered partners in business upon the commencement date of this PARTNERSHIP AGREEMENT for the following purpose:

_____

_____

The terms and conditions of this partnership are as follows:

1. The **NAME** of the partnership shall be: _____

2. The **PRINCIPAL PLACE OF BUSINESS** of the partnership shall be: _____

3. The **CAPITAL CONTRIBUTION** of each partner to the partnership shall consist of the following property, services, or cash which each partner agrees to contribute:

Name of Partner	Capital Contribution	Agreed-Upon Cash	% Share

Furthermore, the **PROFITS AND LOSSES** of the partnership shall be divided by the partners according to a mutually agreeable schedule and at the end of each calendar year according to the proportions listed above.

4. Each partner shall have equal rights to **MANAGE AND CONTROL** the partnership and its business. Should there be differences between the partners concerning ordinary business matters, a decision shall be made by unanimous vote. It is understood that the partners may elect one of the partners to conduct day-to-day business of the partnership; however, no partner shall be able to bind the partnership by act or contract to any liability exceeding $_____ without the prior written consent of each partner.

5. In the event a partner **WITHDRAWS** from the partnership for any reason, including death, the remaining partners may continue to operate the partnership using the same name. The withdrawing partner shall be obligated to sell their interest in the partnership. No partner shall **TRANSFER** interest in the partnership to any other party without the written consent of each partner.

6. Should the partnership be **TERMINATED** by unanimous vote, the assets and cash of the partnership shall be used to pay all creditors, with the remaining amounts to be distributed to the partners according to their proportionate share.

7. Any **DISPUTES** arising between the partners as a result of this agreement shall be settled by voluntary mediation. Should mediation fail to resolve the dispute, it shall be settled by binding arbitration.

In witness whereof, this **PARTNERSHIP AGREEMENT** has been signed by the partners on the day and year listed above.

_____   _____
PARTNER   PARTNER

                                                            _____
                                                            PARTNER

Although partnerships, like subchapter S corporations, allow each partner to file his or her earnings just once for taxation purposes, there is specific legal paperwork that must be completed. First, a federal employee identification number (or tax ID number) must be secured from the IRS. Then, each year, the partnership completes Form 1065 (see pages 116–117) and Schedule K-1 (page 118), to be sent to the IRS and each partner. Profits and losses are decided by preset terms for each partner. With your courier service, for example, you may choose to split profits and losses on all jobs or simply accrue profits and losses based on geographical definitions (i.e., one partner gets counties A, B, and C jobs, and the other gets counties D, E, and F jobs).

A new, popular form of business being used by partnerships is the limited liability company (LLC). It is similar to a subchapter S corporation in that partners receive profits or losses directly and are still protected from personal liability, but it has other regulations that make it generally unsuitable for home-based businesses—primarily, size restrictions. If you want to find out more about LLCs, check with your attorney.

YOUR BUSINESS AS PART OF THE NEIGHBORHOOD: ZONING LAWS

When operating a home-based business, remember that you are a residential neighbor first and a business owner second. At least, that's likely to be how your city, county, and state will see your situation when they review your application for a permit (see page 119).

City and county zoning requirements exist because people want the quality of life around their home to be optimal. The requirements have been around forever; some are actively enforced and others are enforced only when neighbors file complaints. You can check into zoning regulations yourself, or you may find out about them when you go to obtain your business license. (There is no *guarantee* that if it is not mentioned during filing, your area permits home-based businesses.) Some people are surprised to find out just how many areas in their city or county prohibit operating businesses from home—or how precisely their city or county lists which types of businesses *will* be allowed. A sample business license application is shown on pages 120 and 121.

For example, you may be allowed to run a computer repair business but not a dance class. Or, you may be permitted to bake and sell your special-recipe chili from home, but only if your home can meet stringent county health department requirements (generally, no small feat). Some entrepreneurs who are denied the right to run their business venture from home will appeal to their city by filing for a zoning

Form **1065**		**U.S. Partnership Return of Income**		OMB No. 1545-0099
Department of the Treasury Internal Revenue Service		For calendar year 1993, or tax year beginning .... , 1993, and ending .... , 19 .... . ▶ **See separate instructions.**		**1993**

A Principal business activity	**Use the IRS label.**	Name of partnership	D Employer identification number
B Principal product or service	**Otherwise, please print or type.**	Number, street, and room or suite no. (If a P.O. box, see page 9 of the instructions.)	E Date business started
C Business code number		City or town, state, and ZIP code	F Total assets (see **Specific Instructions**) $

G   Check applicable boxes: **(1)** ☐ Initial return   **(2)** ☐ Final return   **(3)** ☐ Change in address   **(4)** ☐ Amended return
H   Check accounting method: **(1)** ☐ Cash   **(2)** ☐ Accrual   **(3)** ☐ Other (specify) ▶ ....
I   Number of Schedules K-1. Attach one for each person who was a partner at any time during the tax year ▶ ....

Caution: *Include only trade or business income and expenses on lines 1a through 22 below. See the instructions for more information.*

Income	**1a** Gross receipts or sales	**1a**		
	b Less returns and allowances	**1b**	**1c**	
	2 Cost of goods sold (Schedule A, line 8)		**2**	
	3 Gross profit. Subtract line 2 from line 1c		**3**	
	4 Ordinary income (loss) from other partnerships and fiduciaries *(attach schedule)*		**4**	
	5 Net farm profit (loss) *(attach Schedule F (Form 1040))*		**5**	
	6 Net gain (loss) from Form 4797, Part II, line 20		**6**	
	7 Other income (loss) (see instructions) *(attach schedule)*		**7**	
	8 **Total income (loss).** Combine lines 3 through 7		**8**	

Deductions (see instructions for limitations)	**9a** Salaries and wages (other than to partners)	**9a**		
	b Less employment credits	**9b**	**9c**	
	10 Guaranteed payments to partners		**10**	
	11 Repairs and maintenance		**11**	
	12 Bad debts		**12**	
	13 Rent		**13**	
	14 Taxes and licenses		**14**	
	15 Interest		**15**	
	16a Depreciation (see instructions)	**16a**		
	b Less depreciation reported on Schedule A and elsewhere on return	**16b**	**16c**	
	17 Depletion **(Do not deduct oil and gas depletion.)**		**17**	
	18 Retirement plans, etc.		**18**	
	19 Employee benefit programs		**19**	
	20 Other deductions *(attach schedule)*		**20**	
	21 **Total deductions.** Add the amounts shown in the far right column for lines 9c through 20		**21**	

22 **Ordinary income (loss)** from trade or business activities. Subtract line 21 from line 8		**22**	

Please Sign Here	Under penalties of perjury, I declare that I have examined this return, including accompanying schedules and statements, and to the best of my knowledge and belief, it is true, correct, and complete. Declaration of preparer (other than general partner) is based on all information of which preparer has any knowledge.		
	▶ Signature of general partner	▶ Date	

Paid Preparer's Use Only	Preparer's signature ▶	Date	Check if self-employed ▶ ☐	Preparer's social security no.
	Firm's name (or yours if self-employed) and address ▶		E.I. No. ▶ ZIP code ▶	

For Paperwork Reduction Act Notice, see page 1 of separate instructions.   Cat. No. 11390Z   Form **1065** (1993)

Form 1065 (1993) Page **2**

Schedule A   **Cost of Goods Sold**

1 Inventory at beginning of year	**1**	
2 Purchases less cost of items withdrawn for personal use	**2**	
3 Cost of labor	**3**	
4 Additional section 263A costs (see instructions) *(attach schedule)*	**4**	
5 Other costs *(attach schedule)*	**5**	
6 **Total.** Add lines 1 through 5	**6**	
7 Inventory at end of year	**7**	
8 **Cost of goods sold.** Subtract line 7 from line 6. Enter here and on page 1, line 2	**8**	

9a Check all methods used for valuing closing inventory:

    (i) ☐ Cost

    (ii) ☐ Lower of cost or market as described in Regulations section 1.471-4

    (iii) ☐ Writedown of "subnormal" goods as described in Regulations section 1.471-2(c)

    (iv) ☐ Other (specify method used and attach explanation) ▶ ....

  b Check this box if the LIFO inventory method was adopted this tax year for any goods *(if checked, attach Form 970)* . . ▶ ☐

  c Do the rules of section 263A (for property produced or acquired for resale) apply to the partnership? . . ☐**Yes** ☐**No**

  d Was there any change in determining quantities, cost, or valuations between opening and closing inventory? ☐**Yes** ☐**No**

    If "Yes," attach explanation.

Schedule B   **Other Information**

	Yes	No
1 What type of entity is filing this return?		
Check the applicable box ▶ ☐ General partnership ☐ Limited partnership ☐ Limited liability company		
2 Are any partners in this partnership also partnerships?		
3 Is this partnership a partner in another partnership?		
4 Is this partnership subject to the consolidated audit procedures of sections 6221 through 6233? If "Yes," see **Designation of Tax Matters Partner** below		
5 Does this partnership meet **ALL THREE** of the following requirements?		
a The partnership's total receipts for the tax year were less than $250,000;		
b The partnership's total assets at the end of the tax year were less than $600,000; **AND**		
c Schedules K-1 are filed with the return and furnished to the partners on or before the due date (including extensions) for the partnership return.		
If "Yes," the partnership is not required to complete Schedules L, M-1, and M-2; Item F on page 1 of Form 1065; or Item J on Schedule K-1		
6 Does this partnership have any foreign partners?		
7 Is this partnership a publicly traded partnership as defined in section 469(k)(2)?		
8 Has this partnership filed, or is it required to file, **Form 8264,** Application for Registration of a Tax Shelter? . .		
9 At any time during calendar year 1993, did the partnership have an interest in or a signature or other authority over a financial account in a foreign country (such as a bank account, securities account, or other financial account)? (See the instructions for exceptions and filing requirements for form TD F 90-22.1.) If "Yes," enter the name of the foreign country. ▶		
10 Was the partnership the grantor of, or transferor to, a foreign trust that existed during the current tax year, whether or not the partnership or any partner has any beneficial interest in it? If "Yes," you may have to file Forms 3520, 3520-A, or 926		
11 Was there a distribution of property or a transfer (e.g., by sale or death) of a partnership interest during the tax year? If "Yes," you may elect to adjust the basis of the partnership's assets under section 754 by attaching the statement described on page 5 of the instructions under **Elections Made By the Partnership**		

Designation of Tax Matters Partner (See instructions.)

Enter below the general partner designated as the tax matters partner (TMP) for the tax year of this return:

Name of designated TMP ▶		Identifying number of TMP ▶	
Address of designated TMP ▶			

Schedule K   Partners' Shares of Income, Credits, Deductions, etc.

	(a) Distributive share items		(b) Total amount
Income (Loss)	**1** Ordinary income (loss) from trade or business activities (page 1, line 22)	**1**	
	2 Net income (loss) from rental real estate activities *(attach Form 8825)*	**2**	
	3a Gross income from other rental activities **3a**		
	b Expenses from other rental activities *(attach schedule)* **3b**		
	c Net income (loss) from other rental activities. Subtract line 3b from line 3a	**3c**	
	4 Portfolio income (loss) (see instructions): **a** Interest income	**4a**	
	b Dividend income	**4b**	
	c Royalty income	**4c**	
	d Net short-term capital gain (loss) *(attach Schedule D (Form 1065))*	**4d**	
	e Net long-term capital gain (loss) *(attach Schedule D (Form 1065))*	**4e**	
	f Other portfolio income (loss) *(attach schedule)*	**4f**	
	5 Guaranteed payments to partners	**5**	
	6 Net gain (loss) under section 1231 (other than due to casualty or theft) *(attach Form 4797)*	**6**	
	7 Other income (loss) *(attach schedule)*	**7**	
Deductions	**8** Charitable contributions (see instructions) *(attach schedule)*	**8**	
	9 Section 179 expense deduction *(attach Form 4562)* .	**9**	
	10 Deductions related to portfolio income (see instructions) (itemize)	**10**	
	11 Other deductions *(attach schedule)*	**11**	
Investment Interest	**12a** Interest expense on investment debts	**12a**	
	b **(1)** Investment income included on lines 4a, 4b, 4c, and 4f above	**12b(1)**	
	(2) Investment expenses included on line 10 above.	**12b(2)**	
Credits	**13a** Credit for income tax withheld	**13a**	
	b Low-income housing credit (see instructions):		
	(1) From partnerships to which section 42(j)(5) applies for property placed in service before 1990	**13b(1)**	
	(2) Other than on line 13b(1) for property placed in service before 1990	**13b(2)**	
	(3) From partnerships to which section 42(j)(5) applies for property placed in service after 1989	**13b(3)**	
	(4) Other than on line 13b(3) for property placed in service after 1989	**13b(4)**	
	c Qualified rehabilitation expenditures related to rental real estate activities *(attach Form 3468)*	**13c**	
	d Credits (other than credits shown on lines 13b and 13c) related to rental real estate activities (see instructions)	**13d**	
	e Credits related to other rental activities (see instructions)	**13e**	
	14 Other credits (see instructions)	**14**	
Self-Employment	**15a** Net earnings (loss) from self-employment	**15a**	
	b Gross farming or fishing income	**15b**	
	c Gross nonfarm income	**15c**	
Adjustments and Tax Preference Items	**16a** Depreciation adjustment on property placed in service after 1986	**16a**	
	b Adjusted gain or loss	**16b**	
	c Depletion (other than oil and gas)	**16c**	
	d **(1)** Gross income from oil, gas, and geothermal properties	**16d(1)**	
	(2) Deductions allocable to oil, gas, and geothermal properties	**16d(2)**	
	e Other adjustments and tax preference items *(attach schedule)*	**16e**	
Foreign Taxes	**17a** Type of income ▶ .... **b** Foreign country or U.S. possession ▶		
	c Total gross income from sources outside the United States *(attach schedule)*.	**17c**	
	d Total applicable deductions and losses *(attach schedule)*	**17d**	
	e Total foreign taxes (check one): ▶ ☐ Paid ☐ Accrued	**17e**	
	f Reduction in taxes available for credit *(attach schedule)*	**17f**	
	g Other foreign tax information *(attach schedule)*	**17g**	
Other	**18a** Total expenditures to which a section 59(e) election may apply	**18a**	
	b Type of expenditures ▶............................		
	19 Tax-exempt interest income	**19**	
	20 Other tax-exempt income	**20**	
	21 Nondeductible expenses	**21**	
	22 Other items and amounts required to be reported separately to partners (see instructions) *(attach schedule)*		

Analysis	**23a** Income (loss). Combine lines 1 through 7 in column (b). From the result, subtract the sum of lines 8 through 12a, 17e, and 18a	**23a**			

			(b) Individual			(d) Exempt	
b Analysis by type of partner:	(a) Corporate	i. Active	ii. Passive	(c) Partnership	organization	(e) Nominee/Other
(1) General partners						
(2) Limited partners						

CITY OF IRVINE

APPLICATION FOR HOME OCCUPATION PERMIT*

PLEASE PRINT

BUSINESS NAME _____

ADDRESS _____
(NOTE: Street address only. DO NOT enter mail box address.)
SPECIFIC TYPE OF BUSINESS/PRODUCT(S): _____

_____

		YES	NO

1. Will the house/home be the point of customer pickup or delivery? ___ ___

2. Will the business cause an increase in traffic in the neighborhood? ___ ___

3. Will the business be conducted in an enclosed structure? ___ ___

4. Will you have any signs? ___ ___

5. Will you be using the garage for business? ___ ___

6. Will you have any employees besides residents of the home? ___ ___

7. Will you be operating any electrical or mechanical equipment at the house? ___ ___

8. Will the home occupation create any noise or odors? ___ ___

If you have answered yes to any of the above questions, please explain:_____

_____

_____   _____
SIGNATURE OF APPLICANT   DATE

COMMUNITY DEVELOPMENT DEPARTMENT
LAND USE RECOMMENDATION: _____ _____
                                                  APPROVE   DENY

_____   _____
(SIGNATURE OF C.D. DEPT.)   DATE

* to be filed with Business Permit application

nwl/hopt

Form 40-27 Rev 11/89

License No. _____

BUSINESS LICENSE APPLICATION

Please return to:

Business License: $50.00   City of Irvine Business Licenses
One Civic Center Plaza • P.O. Box 19575 • Irvine, CA 92713
(714) 724-6310

Business Name _____

Business Name (other) _____

Street Address _____ Suite _____
                        (May not be a P.O. Box)

City _____ State _____ Zip _____

Mailing Address _____ City _____ State _____ Zip _____

Business Phone ( ) _____ State Sales Tax No. _____

State Employer ID (SEIN) _____ Federal Employer ID (FEIN) _____

Social Security No. 1 _____   2 _____
                    (List only if your business does not have a State or Federal Employer ID No.)

State Professional License No. _____ Class _____ Expiration _____

State Contractors License No. _____ Class _____ Expiration _____

Please describe the exact nature of business activity to be conducted _____

_____

Indicate ownership type   ☐ Sole Proprietorship .... ☐ Partnership .... ☐ Corporation .... ☐ Trust

Is your business   ☐ Local .... ☐ Regional .... ☐ National .... ☐ International

Indicate type of business   ☐ Retail .... ☐ Wholesale .... ☐ MFG .... ☐ Service .... ☐ _____
                                                                                                    (explain)

Do you sell Alcoholic Beverages?   ☐ No .... ☐ Yes, if yes: ☐ Beer/Wine and/or ☐ Liquor

Alcohol Beverage License No. _____   Expiration _____

List principal's residence, address, phone, title (Owner, Partner, President, CEO, CFO, etc.) and driver's license number:

1 _____   _____   _____   ____ ____
        name   residence address   city   state   zip

( ) _____   _____   _____   ____ ____
        phone   title   driver's license   issuing state

2 _____   _____   _____   ____ ____
        name   residence address   city   state   zip

( ) _____   _____   _____   ____ ____
        phone   title   driver's license   issuing state

Please indicate the number of people involved in your business   _____

On what date will/did your business begin operating in Irvine?   _____

PLEASE COMPLETE THE OTHER SIDE

*** For Official Use Only ***

Public Works	Community Development	Building & Safety	Public Safety

Form 22-05, Rev. 5-93

Indicate security arrangements on premises: ☐ Audible .... ☐ Silent .... ☐ Other .... ☐ None

Alarm Service _____ (   ) _____

                   name   phone

Security Patrol _____ (   ) _____

                   name   phone

Please indicate who the City should contact in the event of an emergency:

1 _____ _____ (   ) _____

             name   tittle   phone

2 _____ _____ (   ) _____

             name   tittle   phone

Please list other business locations in Irvine:

1 _____ _____ _____

             name   address   function

2 _____ _____ _____

             name   address   function

Does your business use outside agencies or independent contractors to provide services for your company? ☐ No .... ☐ Yes

Does your business create, store, generate, or use hazardous substances or any products that are considered to be corrosive, reactive, ignitable, toxic, and/or ozone depleters?   ☐ No .... ☐ Yes

Is this business conducted from your home?   ☐ No .... ☐ Yes

Does your business collect Sales Tax?   ☐ No .... ☐ Yes

Did you purchase this business?   ☐ No .... ☐ Yes, if yes, what was the date of purchase?_____

Do you rent or lease your business location?   ☐ No .... ☐ Yes, if yes, who is your Rentor/Lessor?

_____ _____ (   ) _____

      Lessor's name   Lessor's address   Lessor's phone

Annual Gross Receipts $ _____   Annual Payroll $ _____

Please help us track the number of commuters in our City. Indicate the number of people involved in your business that live in:

     Irvine _____   Other Orange County Cities _____   Outside of Orange County _____

Please <u>print</u> the Owner or Principal's name that should appear on the license

_____ _____

                         name   title

The business for which this license is requested intends to occupy space at the stated location. The approximate square footage of the premise is _____ . There: (check one) ☐ HAS ... ☐ HAS NOT been any physical changes to the premises. I will not make any future modifications to the building without notifying the City of Irvine. I am aware of the requirement to obtain an approved Building Permit from the City prior to making any physical modifications to the premises. If you have made or intend to make physical changes to the premises, please indicate the Building Permit or Plan Check number here _____

Please indicate the prior type of business at this location (if known) _____

Please indicate the date that you first occupied your current location _____

     If you have any questions about building modifications contact the Building and Safety Division at (714) 724-6520.

I hereby certify, under penalty of perjury, that the information provided on this application is true and correct.

_____ _____ _____

          applicant's signature   print applicant's name and title   date

Form 22-05, Rev. 5-93

variance or conditional-use permit application. Many factors are considered when local government officials evaluate such requests:

- Will the business create excessive noise, odor, or traffic?
- Will it require business operations at all hours, or only general business hours (i.e., 8 A.M. to 5 P.M.)?
- Is employee or customer parking going to be a problem?
- Will huge trucks be coming by on a regular basis to make deliveries? Are these trucks even allowed on this street (i.e., are there weight restrictions on the kinds of vehicles that can drive on it)?
- Will the business's numerous phone lines or hefty electronic needs put neighbors at risk of undue interference?
- How many employees will this business require, and how many are permitted to work from a person's home under city and county ordinances? Under state laws? (Note: The federal Fair Labor Standards Act prohibits home-based businesses from employing others to manufacture jewelry, buttons, gloves, mittens, buckles, handkerchiefs, and other knitted or embroidered goods without a special certificate of authorization. Call the U.S. Department of Labor for information.)
- Can the business, if permitted to operate, use a sign? A showroom?

If you live far from other neighbors, or you know of neighbors who are also operating—or would like to operate—home-based businesses, you may want to file a zone change application. Unlike a zoning variance or conditional-use permit, an official "zone change" is permanent and reclassifies the affected neighborhood. Where zoning variances can take 90 days or more, zone changes can take six months to a year. The outcome depends on your city and county regulations and your neighbors' wants and needs.

Take a good look at the impact your business will have on your home and/or neighborhood. If you are planning to cultivate and sell bonsai trees or rose bushes, find out whether you need any environmental permits. If you will be repairing cars or boat engines, you may need a fire department permit (since gasoline is flammable); you may even require one if your home will be open to the public during business hours. If you will be spray-painting and decorating ceramic pots and wicker furniture, you may need a special permit from local air and water pollution control agencies. And don't forget about the state; many states require special licensing for building contractors, painters, electricians, auto mechanics, real estate agents, beauticians, and others (not to mention lawyers, doctors, dentists, and nurses). The list goes on and on.

Don't take chances and wait for someone to complain or to fine you. You may be risking having your entire business closed down. Instead, do your homework up front and ask questions. Cities and counties must think of their general citizenry, but many will be supportive of your entrepreneurial venture and will help you operate safely and legally. They can also point you in the right direction for finding state and other agencies that produce written guidelines, forms, and permits for home-based businesses.

LEGISLATION AFFECTING ALL BUSINESSES

Home-based or not, there are some laws that affect every company. Most are common-sense "good guy" regulations, such as laws against "bait-and-switch" tactics or misrepresenting guarantees, warranties, quality standards, or other product/service characteristics. You cannot, for example, keep client deposits against fair refund practices. You cannot keep someone's original property unless an "exchange" is part of the agreed-on terms of sale (i.e., if you do computer repair, you cannot keep someone's old monitor even if you replace it with a new monitor, unless the customer has agreed to give you the old monitor in exchange for a lower price on the new monitor).

There are also laws that exist to (ideally) facilitate a market economy. Antitrust laws, for example, exist to encourage competition among businesses by prohibiting actions or contracts that unfairly restrain trade (including pricing a product or service severely below market, to damage your competition). "Deceptive practice" laws forbid slandering your competition or marketing a product that simulates a competitor's product and marketing; they also make false advertising a crime.

Look into Federal Trade Commission (FTC) regulations if you will be operating a business that crosses state lines. For example, if you operate a gift basket company that advertises across the country, the FTC has jurisdiction over your business since you are advertising in more than one state. If, however, you advertise your gift baskets only locally, but clients have them sent across the country, this does not make you automatically subject to FTC rules.

THE INSURANCE GAME

You need insurance for your business—period. There are so few home-based businesses that do not require some sort of business insurance that you should simply assume you need it. Why? Because if you are a sole proprietorship or partnership, you can be personally sued for business actions. If you are a corporation, your entire operation can become extinct—and your shareholders *very* upset—should a lawsuit or other problem call for huge sums of money that the corporation cannot produce.

Especially when working out of your home, you need to be realistic about the risks you place on yourself (and on your home and your family) if you do not have adequate coverage. If a fire, earthquake, tornado, flood, or theft severely damages your residence, you will not only suffer a great personal loss but you will find yourself with many customers who—while sympathetic to your loss—will want their products, services, or money back when your business is temporarily or permanently shut down. For example, if you provide business consulting services, your clients can sue you for loss of their files and other important documents if they are burned in a fire in your home.

A courier service, or other business that requires operating a vehicle, presents a whole new set of risks. Many business owners require drivers to have a clean driving record and proof of insurance, but only an attorney can tell you how to properly cover yourself and your business if motor vehicle operation is involved.

Don't automatically assume that your homeowner's or renter's insurance covers business-related equipment or losses, or that it will be sufficient for your business needs. For one thing, it won't protect you if someone is injured on your property or injured by one of your products or services. This type of claim requires liability insurance—personal, product, general, or comprehensive. Depending on the type of business you have, the products or services you sell, and the type of work required, this insurance could run you as little as $100 per year or as much as $2,000 per year—and more—for a $1 million policy.

Again, examine your business closely. Will people visit your home on business? Will they work there? Will anyone operate heavy or complex machinery? Are you selling a product with an expiration date (e.g., food, chemicals)? Are you helping to type or file legal documents that could land someone in hot water if they are done incorrectly? Come up with a complete list of all potential liabilities. Then, check with a reputable insurance agent on how best to cover your business in this manner. Generally, a standard, comprehensive liability policy (with auto liability and workers' compensation, when necessary) can serve your needs.

Liability insurance doesn't protect your business equipment or inventory, however; nor does it protect you under a partnership gone sour. To cover equipment, ask about special home-based business coverages that often come as riders to general homeowner policies. Ask about ceilings or other limits that make additional insurance (fire, theft, earthquake) necessary for adequate coverage. Make sure that the policy you purchase covers the replacement cost of the items being insured. For example, if your $3,500 computer is insured today, what amount will your insurance company give you to replace it if it is stolen five years from now?

Every partnership *needs* a partnership insurance policy. As mentioned above, partnerships automatically dissolve upon the death of one partner, unless a buy–sell agreement has been entered into. The big question then becomes: If your partner passes away, gets divorced, or becomes severely disabled and the buy–sell agreement goes into effect, will you have the money to buy that partner's stake in the business per the agreement?

Similar in some ways to a life insurance policy, a partnership policy basically is taken out on each partner by the other, and the policy kicks in should the partnership dissolve due to a death or other delineated mishap. It is up to the partners how the insurance is paid for; some partners split the costs, others pay the premium that covers the other partner, or arrange for the firm to pay the cost of the insurance as an overhead expense. Be sure to have a professional business planner, attorney, arbitrator, or other experienced person help you to set the value of these policies. Potential business growth and other future economic factors must be considered.

Numerous other types of insurance are available, from plate glass insurance to fraud insurance or malpractice coverage. In some lines of work, such as painting or landscaping, a fidelity bond is needed to cover potential employee theft at a client's home or business. And don't forget about life and health insurance coverage. As an entrepreneur, you're no longer automatically covered by "the company"; if you don't have coverage by some other means, you need to get it. The last thing your new business needs is to have you struck down by a virus or an accident with no financial means to get back in shape quickly.

Luckily, many health insurance plans now cover very small businesses, and some national, entrepreneurial groups have formed cooperatives to buy insurance at a reduced rate (the way larger companies buy it). Look into all kinds of plans, and learn what their differences are: HMOs, PPOs, point-of-service plans, indemnity plans, and universal coverages (which include both basic medical and workers' compensation claims).

As home-based businesses have become more prevalent, many insurance firms have diversified to meet the specific needs of home-based entrepreneurs. These special policies, however, can be expensive, so you should definitely invest some time in shopping around. The more agents you approach, the better you'll get at asking questions and determining exactly what type of coverage you will need. More importantly, follow the references of other entrepreneurs or professionals whom you trust (your attorney, banker, partner). Getting the best coverage possible for your business takes someone who knows small business and is willing to work hard to meet your complete and specific needs.

KNOWING YOUR RIGHTS

Freelance writers who make their living from home likely will be the first to tell you how important original works protection is to your livelihood. Your business is never too small to benefit from proper legal protection guaranteeing that you receive earnings from any original, creative products, ideas, or inventions.

The easiest form of protection to obtain is a "copyright"; designated as ©. Applied to any desired original work of authorship or other "creative" expression (i.e., paintings, sculptures, sound recordings, maps, globes, drawings, and so on), copyright protection can be given to your work from the moment of its completion in a tangible, recognizable form. To affix the copyright, simply place onto the work the word or the © symbol followed by your name and date: © Jane Roberts, 1995.

If a manuscript you submit for publication is purchased by a magazine, newspaper, or other publication, be sure to inquire as to what rights the publisher is buying. Some publishers buy all rights, others buy first-time rights or first North American serial rights (so they have the first right to publish your work in the United States, Canada, and Mexico). Some publications will buy only one-time rights or simultaneous publication rights. Generally, you will be paid more for your work when more rights are purchased. What is important to understand is that, although you automatically hold a copyright on authorship, you forfeit those rights by agreeing to sell your manuscript to a publisher or other entity that buys the work plus all (or delineated) rights.

To ensure that any work is copyrighted, your best bet is to file with the U.S. Copyright Office at the Library of Congress in Washington, DC. Filing requires filling out a simple form, attaching a copy of the original work, and mailing it all to the Copyright Office—an added protection should your copyright ever be called into question. There are four main classes of copyright protection, plus the renewal class (Class RE). The four main classes are:

1. *Class type: TX.* Nondramatic literary works (fiction, nonfiction, advertising copy, and similar pieces—published or unpublished).
2. *Class type: PA.* Works of the performing arts (choreography, motion pictures, musical works, and so on).
3. *Class type: VA.* Works of the visual arts (sculptures, globes, models, maps, and so on).
4. *Class type: SR.* Sound recordings (either the recording itself or the recording plus the written lyrics or other musical/dramatic qualities in the recording).

The renewal class, RE, is for extending copyrights on original works first copyrighted before January 1, 1978. It extends the rights by 47 years.

A copyright is good for your lifetime plus 50 years, so that your family or heirs may benefit from your work. It is advisable to register your copyright even though a work is automatically copyrighted upon creation. In cases of infringement, it is always good to have a public record of your copyright and the date it went into effect. In fact, in order for an infringement suit to go to court, it is generally necessary to have your copyright registered with the Copyright Office. Contact this office at the Library of Congress, Washington, DC 20559; (202) 707-3000. To request forms, call (202) 707-9100.

Intellectual Property: Protecting Your Inventions and Ideas

If you're an inventor, you need more than copyright protection. In fact, copyrights only protect actual works in their unique form; they do not protect the ideas behind the work.

What you need is patent protection. Patents available to you will vary, based on the type of invention you have and the length of time your invention will be covered. For example, two main patents—plant patents and utility patents—protect your invention for 17 years, at which point they become open for use or reproduction in the public domain. (Actually, an act of Congress can extend a plant patent, but such acts are rare.) Design patents—the most common type—range in protection length from 3 to 14 years (generally, 3, 7, or 14 years).

Any person who "invents or discovers any new and usable process, machine, manufacture, or composition of matter, or any new and useful improvements thereof, may obtain a patent." Your specific type of patent will depend on your invention. The following descriptions of the three types of patents discussed above pertain only to U.S. patents.

- *Design patents.* This patent is the most common because it protects the way something looks as opposed to the way it operates. For example, if you designed a tissue-box holder that looks like a volcano, you may be able to get a design patent (you don't claim to have invented tissue-box holders, just the look of the tissue-box holder you designed).
- *Utility patents.* Now, let's say your volcano tissue-box holder spritzes an almost invisible layer of soothing cream onto the tissue as it "erupts" from the holder, keeping the tissues beneath it dry and sanitized. For this invention, you may be able to get a

utility patent. Utility patents protect the actual mechanical, chemical, computer, or process design of an invention. (When applying, you must include these design specifications with your application.)

- *Plant patents.* This type of patent covers new strains of plants created by engineered, asexual production. To receive patent protection, the plant you invent must be original and "useful" in some manner. It cannot be an obvious strain that could easily be created by anyone with a knowledge of plant reproduction.

Applying for patent protection is easy, but requires great attention to detail. Design patents need every possible view of your creation drawn or photographed clearly for all identifying characteristics. Utility patents need the same documentation, along with official specifications of the item's function and, when necessary, a flowchart showing each step in the function. The specifications provided in your application should include:

- What the invention is called.
- Related applications.
- Its nature and substance.
- Descriptions of the drawings or photographs (keep them brief).
- A detailed utility description.

A plant patent will also require a specification and drawings, as well as a declaration and your signature.

Beyond these details, you must send a transmittal letter, your application filing fee, a self-addressed receipt postcard, and any forms specifically required for the desired patent. The U.S. Patent and Trademark Office address is simply: U.S. Patent and Trademark Office, Washington, DC 20231. A patent agent or patent attorney can help you with any complex aspects of patent filing (such as helping you conduct a patent search to see whether your application efforts will be worthwhile or whether someone has beat you to your idea).

One final important note: a patent is only granted to inventions that have not been sold or "publicly known" for more than one calendar year. The minute your invention is talked about on public airwaves or written about in either U.S. or foreign publications, it is considered to be "publicly known."

If you are going into business because of a new invention and you want to protect the idea even before you have it finished, you can apply for the Disclosure Document Program—a two-year temporary protection plan that covers your invention. (You must apply for a patent by the end of the two years, or your file will be destroyed.) To apply, send a signed document (or "disclosure") describing your invention in detail—especially how it differs from other similar items—as well as drawings or signed photographs (submitted in duplicate) to the Commissioner of Patents and Trademarks at the U.S. Patent and Trademark Office. Number your pages, make two signed and dated copies of the document, and have two witnesses sign both of them. (You should also make a third copy for yourself—as with all documents sent into the Copyright or Patent and Trademark offices.)

Trademarks: Protecting Your Name

Kleenex® tissues and Coca-Cola® got to be household words through trademark protections. For your business itself or for a product you make, the only way to keep your original and unique name original and unique is to apply for a registered trademark.

It's not always easy to get a trademark. There are literally thousands of trademarked names in existence, and you should save yourself time and heartache by conducting a trademark search prior to using a name you've grown attached to. This can be done in several ways; new trademark-listing CD-ROMs allow you to search for names and products by subject or use, and online search services are available through various carrier services.

Make sure that you don't try to trademark a name that has general acceptance for public usage—such as Car Phone or Lawn Care. While CarFone Company may have a chance, it will create other problems for you by making it hard for people to find your business in telephone directories or business listings, should it get trademark protection. Only you know for sure which image is most important for your company and products.

Trademarks can also be applied to slogans, mascots, or symbols of your business, as long as they are unique and original. If your courier service, "On-Time Delivery Couriers" always advertises as "On-Time Delivery Couriers—Where Every Package Is Treated Like a Crystal Chandelier," you may be able to get your slogan, "Where Every Package Is Treated Like a Crystal Chandelier" trademarked. Likewise, if you design a sign bearing a specially drawn courier, this sign and mascot may be able to receive trademark protection.

Unlike copyrights, which exist upon creation of an original work, a trademark will not be granted until a name, slogan, mascot, or other "mark" is used in conjunction with a business or product. To protect your mark during the development process, you must use a "trade secret." This means that you place the trademark symbol "TM" following the mark during its usage; for example, CarFone™ Company. Once a trademark has been officially registered with the Patent and Trademark Office, it receives the ® symbol (CarFone® Company).

As with patents, you must submit a trademark application containing:

- The filing fee.
- Your name, address, proof of the mark being used with your product/business, product/business description, your citizenship status, and the class of merchandising under which your product/business falls.
- A drawing or typewritten copy of the mark (symbol, name, or mascot).
- Five copies of your mark (either exact duplicates of the mark, or photographs of the mark if the mark is three-dimensional).

The Patent and Trademark Office will send you free information regarding trademarks. Request a copy of *General Information Concerning Trademarks; Trademarks; Trademark Laws;* or the *U.S. Patent Gazette* weekly newspaper. The office will not, however, provide legal advice regarding trademarks.

6

SETTING UP YOUR HOME OFFICE

Even if your business will require you to spend 95% of your time out in the field—visiting customers, embarking on aggressive marketing campaigns, or traveling to trade shows and expositions—your home is still the center of your business. Your office environment needs to be well-planned and well-equipped.

Setting up an office at home poses challenges you wouldn't face if you were moving into a commercial facility. In a commercial office building, phone lines are already in place and areas are designed specifically with business in mind. Homes, on the other hand, are not designed with business in mind, so you'll have to do some creative thinking to make your office work.

If you're not careful, your home-based business could easily take over your entire home—files in the den, products in the garage, desk in the spare bedroom—and this encroachment can lead to problems with your business and your family. The first step in creating an efficient home office is choosing a space for it and keeping the business contained within that space.

The area you choose should provide these basic requirements:

- Adequate space for a desk, chair, computer and/or typewriter, and file cabinet.

- Adequate storage space for files, supplies, and other equipment.
- Adequate shelf space for books, magazines, and shipping supplies, and incidental equipment.

If clients will be visiting your home office, you'll also need space for a couch or chairs for meetings.

If your business involves any manufacturing or assembly of products, you'll also need space for a large table for production.

Converting a spare bedroom or den into an office provides the best home-based operation because it isolates your business structurally from the rest of the house and you can close the door while you're doing business. If you don't have a spare room available, however, a corner of the garage, the basement, or even the kitchen will suffice. Take note, however, that, in the latter, cases, you may not be eligible to take a home-based office deduction on your taxes.

It doesn't really make any difference whether you choose to set up your work space in a corner of your dining room or in a spare bedroom, unless you are going to have clients visiting your home office. In that case, you may want to set up in an area that has a separate entrance, or is near your front door, so clients don't have to be escorted through the entire house to get to your office. Keeping an air of professionalism is key, and you risk losing that image if clients have to step over children's toys or walk through your entire house to get to your office.

FURNISHING YOUR HOME OFFICE

When setting up your home office, keep it simple. One of the main reasons for starting a business from home is saving money on start-up, so don't go overboard buying new furniture and equipment. Many businesses can be started with no more than a desk, a file cabinet, and a phone. Once your business gets rolling, you can start to invest in some other equipment that will make your day-to-day activities more efficient.

Before heading to the nearest office supply store to furnish your new home office, look around your home. Do you already have anything you can use for your business—a table, desk, or chair? If so, use it. However, if you are going to be spending several hours a day at your desk, make sure that your desk and chair fit your needs. Is there enough drawer space? Is the desktop big enough? Does the chair fit with the table ergonomically?

If you do need to buy furniture, think about how you will use it. Will you work at a computer? Will you conduct most of your business over the phone? Will you need a typewriter? Will you need a work table to create a product? Will you do any design work? Answers to these questions will help you select the right furnishings.

There is nothing wrong with using a scratched table or a chair that's missing an arm, if no one will see your office. However, if clients will be visiting you, your home office will need to convey a more professional image. You will also have to outfit your office appropriately, allowing for a comfortable space (perhaps a sofa and coffee table) where you can meet to talk business. If you can't fit that much furniture in your office space, use your living room or dining room for client meetings, or hold off-premises meetings at restaurants or the clients' offices.

Before extending an invitation to a client, make sure you have adequate seating, enough table space for you to spread out files or other presentation materials, and sufficient lighting.

The same advice applies to filing cabinets. To save on initial expenses, you can convert a bookcase or a spare closet into an efficient storage area. With a bookcase, simply arrange your files and materials on the shelves in a way that allows easy retrieval. Your home office may gain a more cluttered look, but the space usage can work. A closet or cupboard is adequate for storage. You can even use a cardboard box to store files if you don't want to spend money on file cabinets. These options may not be the most efficient or stylish, but they certainly can work during start-up.

If you opt to purchase a file cabinet, you can find one for as little as $30. (Prices can go as high as several hundred dollars for the sturdier products.) The lower-priced models may not hold as much, they may not open and close as smoothly, and they may even tip over when you open full drawers. If you purchase a file cabinet, you'll have your choice of letter-size or legal-size, and two, three, or four drawers. Opt for a letter-size cabinet (unless your business is in the legal field) with two drawers. If you run out of space, you can purchase another one. To increase efficiency and make it easier to locate files, make sure your file cabinet comes with racks for hanging file folders.

You may be able to get by with the lighting you already have. Your existing overhead lighting or natural lighting may be sufficient for your needs, but if you set up your office in a basement or if you don't have overhead lighting and you will be working at night, you may have to buy some table lamps.

Different types of lighting are available. The most popular are fluorescent and incandescent. Each has its own distinct qualities and is effective for certain types of activities. If, for instance, you will do a lot of paperwork or sit in front of a computer most of the time, incandescent light is probably your best choice because it puts less strain on the eyes. Most industrial plants, large offices, garages, and other work facilities use fluorescent light because it is more cost-efficient, energy-efficient, and practical than incandescent, though not necessarily better for the people working under it.

As with every other facet of the home working environment, the best lighting offers maximum usefulness and minimum cost. Your layout will determine what kind of lamps you should use. For heavy office work (the kind that will keep you at your desk for hours on end), small desk lamps can add a perfect degree of extra light without taking much space. Adjustable clamp-on lights have the same space-saving advantages, and add light exactly where it is needed. Track lighting, which you might install along the ceiling or the walls of your work area, can also improve light conditions.

Proper lighting, especially when heavy computer use is involved, is a must in order to reduce eyestrain and allow you to work productively. This advice may seem rather trite, but lighting is one of the most overlooked aspects of the home-based workplace. Spending hours at a desk reading or doing computer work in a poorly lit office is like skiing on a bright clear day without sunglasses—it's something you definitely want to avoid. For a nominal investment, you can give yourself the lighting you need for your kind of work.

We advise you to contact your local General Electric Co. sales office and request literature and the advice of their experts on lighting a store or workplace. Several publications are available from: General Electric Co., Lighting Business Group, Nela Park, Cleveland, OH 44112.

Guest Furniture

Before extending an invitation to a client to come to your home office, take a look at your hospitality area. Does it have adequate seating? Is there enough space for you to spread out files or other presentation materials? Is the lighting adequate? At the very least, you will need a couple of comfortable armchairs, good lighting, and a table of some sort. If you will need to access your computer during the meeting, plan your route beforehand and decide whether the client will accompany you to the monitor or will wait in the hospitality area while you pull up the necessary data.

Where to Buy

If you don't have the furniture necessary to start your business, you have several options on where to buy. Traditional office furniture stores are probably out of your price range, but there are several ways to get quality furnishings without breaking the bank. With a little effort, you can find great buys on new and used desks, chairs, file cabinets, and lighting.

Office and furniture warehouses offer low-cost, functional products. If you don't mind buying used furnishings, you can really save a bundle. Check out flea markets, garage sales, auctions, estate sales, and second-hand stores. This method may require a lot more time, but it can pay off.

EQUIPPING YOUR HOME OFFICE

With the right equipment, your home office can be just as productive as a commercial office. By using advanced telecommunications and computer technology, your home-based business can compete with the big guns in your industry.

Does equipping your office seem to be an intimidating and costly endeavor? It doesn't have to be. If you take the time to figure out exactly what you need and to search out good deals, you can set up a first-rate office without spending beyond your budget.

Depending on the kind of business you are starting, you may need some or all of the following office basics:

- Typewriter.
- Computer.
- Fax machine.
- Copier.
- Telephone.
- Cellular phone.
- Answering machine.
- Filing (record keeping) system.
- Standard office supplies.

Typewriter

While it is true that computers have revolutionized the way the world does business, typewriters still have their place in the office environment. Most businesses that use standardized applications, government paperwork, official forms, and other preprinted documents could not survive without typewriters. For ease of use and size of investment, typewriters are hard to beat.

You can find a good electric typewriter for $100 to $200, or lease one for about $50 per month. Don't go overboard—as long as the machine produces crisp letters that look attractive and professional, it's fulfilling its purpose. If, however, you'll be using your typewriter for more complex word-processing tasks than just typing letters, but aren't ready to make the switch to full-scale computerization, companies like Brother, Smith-Corona, Xerox, Panasonic, and others have full lines of sophisticated machines that combine the memory and word-processing features of a computer with the simplicity of a typewriter. Look for such features as: memory (internal or diskette), liquid crystal display, print speed, correction capabilities, a spell-check function, and automatic style features. These high-end typewriters range from $200 to $800.

Computerization

An inevitable move for any successful business is a computerized record-keeping system. Computers can help you manage complex bookkeeping and inventory control and make keeping customer records and files a snap, but they cost several thousand dollars. Consider the long term when you computerize. It is much easier to pick the right hardware and software when you know your growth plans. The difference between an adequate system for a new home-based business and a system for a thriving three-year-old company can be $15,000 or more.

Though not a cure-all for every business dilemma, personal computers can make life easier and businesses more profitable. Desktop computers are great "special purpose" problem solvers. You type more quickly and professionally, speed your billing process, track your growth more accurately, and plan with greater efficiency. If, however, you wish to create an integrated solution to all of your business problems, you are in for a longer and riskier haul, particularly in a home-based business, where the economics of computerization can be prohibitive.

For a personal computer system to be cost-effective, it should give you at least one, and preferably several, of the following benefits:

1. Help you supply your customers or clients with a product or service not otherwise possible.
2. Provide a measurable decrease in labor costs.
3. Give you a clear competitive edge your customers or clients understand and benefit from.
4. Give you better profit control and useful management information.

5. Help you prospect new clients or customers and keep existing ones satisfied.

Despite popular myth, a new computer system is no longer extraordinarily expensive. Minimum cost is usually about $4,420. That may seem excessive, but the cost accounts for the hardware as well as the software needed to run the system. Although newspapers advertise PCs for less than $1,000, most of these computers are extremely limited and cannot run many of the programs you will want to use.

To get the most out of your computer and its compatible software, purchase a PC based on 486/DX technology, with 4 megabytes RAM, a 120-megabyte hard drive, and high-density 5¼-inch and 3½-inch floppy drives. Couple those specifications with a Super Video Graphics Array (SVGA) monitor, an SVGA graphics board, a 9600-baud modem, a laser printer, and a mouse controller. This system will run all the latest, most powerful software, and give you enough room for more software and technology in the future. For a complete breakdown of computer-related costs, see the computer equipment table shown below.

COMPUTER EQUIPMENT TABLE	
HARDWARE	
486 DX/33 Computer	$1,295
SVGA Monitor	320
SVGA Graphics Board	120
Modem-9600 bps/software	350
Laser Printer	810
Mouse	70
Surge Protector	15
Printer Stand	45
Total Hardware	**$3,025**
SOFTWARE	
Windows	$90
Word Processing	295
Spreadsheet	295
Database	470
Total Software	**$1,150**
MISCELLANEOUS	
Miscellaneous Supplies	$200
Magazine Subscriptions	45
Total Miscellaneous	**$245**
TOTAL	**$4,420**

Service contracts, if you decide to purchase them, usually run 10% to 20% of the hardware cost per year. If you use a reputable consultant for help with the selection, installation, testing, and training process, this could cost an additional 5% to 20% of the total system price.

Training is one of the most time-consuming aspects of computerizing. The duration of your training will depend on your previous exposure to computer systems. There are user-friendly systems on the market that are easy to learn. Apple Computer's Macintosh uses a standard graphics interface for all of its programs, so you don't have to spend countless hours memorizing the proper commands and learning the quirks of each program.

The disadvantage to the Macintosh is the expense. Although Apple has taken steps to reduce the cost to the end user, a Mac with features comparable to those of the PC outlined in the computer equipment table costs almost twice as much. Furthermore, you will not have access to the wider universe of software available to PCs. However, less expensive Mac clones are now becoming available.

To make the PC more user-friendly, Microsoft introduced Windows in the late 1980s. Toward the beginning of the 1990s, it introduced Windows 3.0, an operating system similar to the Macintosh, that runs on top of DOS, the standard PC operating system. The recently released Windows 3.1 addresses some of the shortcomings of its predecessor, such as limited file management capabilities and frequent system crashes. All software written for Windows uses the Windows interface, so they all look and feel the same. Training time, when compared to DOS-based programs, is reduced considerably.

The drawbacks to Windows 3.1 are its comparatively slow operating speed and the space required to install it on a hard drive—approximately 8 MB. A good alternative to Windows 3.1 is Desqview 2.3 from Quarterdeck Office Systems. Although it handles DOS programs the best, it is able to handle Windows 3.1 and its compatible software efficiently if combined with Quarterdeck's Expanded Memory Manager (QEMM) 5.1.

Whether you choose a Macintosh or a PC running Desqview 2.3, Windows 3.1, or a combination of both, you will need to purchase stand-alone software (programs dedicated to doing a single task). For DOS, Windows, and Macintosh systems, examples of powerful stand-alone software are:

- For word processing, Microsoft Word 6.0 for DOS, 2.0 for Windows, and 5.1 for Macintosh.
- For spreadsheet functions, Microsoft Excel 4.0 for Windows and Macintosh.

- For database files and records, Microsoft FoxPro 2.5 for DOS and Windows, and Microsoft FoxBASE+ 2.01 for Macintosh.
- For accounting and bookkeeping, Intuit's Quicken 7.0 for DOS, 3.0 for Windows, and 4.0 for Macintosh.

In addition to these programs, you may need telecommunication software for sending and receiving electronic information. In many cases, software will come packaged with a modem; if it doesn't, Data Storm produces an excellent package called PROCOMM Plus, available in DOS and Windows versions.

Once you have decided to purchase a computer, consider the following guidelines for using your computer effectively.

Take Time to Learn

Many people purchase computers without learning how to use them. Most of today's new software comes with self-paced, on-screen tutorials and printed documentation. Spend time exploring these aids.

Establish Standards and Procedures

Failing to establish computer standards, policies, and procedures creates problems. You need policies regarding the use of virus protection software, backup, and software piracy. Keep these policies updated.

Make Backups

Don't get stuck spending days or even months trying to restore information that was lost or destroyed. If you don't make regular back-ups, you're destined to learn the hard way.

Plan for Expansion

Find out what's involved in moving from single-user to multi-user versions of your software and hardware. Make sure your computers and printers can be easily networked.

Quit "Frittering"

Today's computers give us fun ways to turn out impressive documents, tempting you and your employees to add artwork, color, and even motion to your documents. Nip that tendency in the bud if it starts to get out of control.

Train Employees on Your Computer System

Computer ignorance is a time-waster. Encourage employees to learn how to use their computers and software efficiently.

Protect against Viruses

Never insert disks that have been in someone else's computer. Virus protection software is a necessity that must be updated regularly.

Keep It Simple

Overcomputerizing is a mistake. It's much easier to set up a huge database than it is to maintain one. Don't waste time collecting unnecessary information that makes your system overly complex.

Stay Honest

Software piracy can be expensive. Software makers are cracking down, taking even fairly small companies to court if they think software has been copied illegally.

As mentioned earlier, you may not want to computerize during start-up because you're keeping capital expenditures down, but once your business is on its feet and running, you should seriously consider computerizing.

Facsimile (Fax) Machine

Fax machines have become standard for the transmission of handwritten or graphic information such as maps, drawings, or signatures over telephone lines. Fax machines provide an efficient way to communicate any information rapidly between you and your clients, prospective clients, or business associates anywhere in the world. The number of fax transmissions that occur worldwide each business day reaches well into the hundreds of millions.

Fax machines now range from small units that can plug into any outlet and send documents over phone wires for reception by any other fax, to the larger floor-standing models that many offices use. The "personal fax" machines usually offer a built-in telephone and a photocopier that comes with automatic feed capabilities. Some models even serve as answering machines and flatbed copiers. Priced as low as $400, personal fax machines are well worth the cost, especially for home-based entrepreneurs. Faxes are one of the easiest and most inexpensive ways to lend your business a professional appearance; in fact, it has reached a point where a business—any business—is at a potential loss if it does not have the ability to transmit information via fax machine.

Check your local Brother, Canon, Sharp, Toshiba, or Xerox dealer for more information on their lines of personal fax machines.

On the high end of the scale are the large floor-standing models that transmit information using both public and private digital networks at the incredible speed of 3 seconds per page. Standard models of these machines usually come with automatic document feeders, one-touch or coded speed dialing, and sequential broadcasting and polling to and from multiple locations. Some employ state-of-the-art laser printer technology that allows transmission of documents with a resolution of 400 × 400 dots per inch. This is especially useful if you plan to send graphics-oriented documents. These machines, however, cost about $8,500.

New facsimile boards added to an open slot within your computer and coupled with the right software can turn your personal computer into a fax machine that will be able to transmit and receive documents from other fax-outfitted machines. These add-on cards allow the user to send either a computer file or a scanned image, and to view and edit incoming documents on the computer monitor. Many of these cards come with an integral modem that provides high-speed transmission up to 9600 baud. As an add-on to your personal computer, these facsimile boards are very reasonable (about $250).

Yet, if you receive faxes via a fax board, you live with a major limitation of the technology: the incoming fax is a graphics file that can only be viewed or printed and not used with a word processor. If you want to enter text into your word processor, you have to type it in by hand. Look into Calera Recognition Systems' *FaxGrabber,* a Windows-based utility that converts incoming faxes into text neatly and efficiently. *FaxGrabber* can automatically poll your fax board for incoming faxes and convert them into text files. For more information, call Calera Recognition Systems at (800) 544-7051.

With all communication taking place through the phone wire, you should consider whether to install a second phone line. The fax machine can be hooked up to any phone jack, so you could, in practice, get away with using one phone line for your phone and fax. However, a shared line means you can't use the phone while sending or receiving a document—which may annoy customers or clients trying to call you. They will get either a busy signal or the shriek of a fax machine in their ear. Ideally, a business fax machine should be hooked up to a second phone line.

An alternative is to invest in an automatic voice/data switch. Plugged into a fax machine, this device can instantly tell the difference between a data and voice call, and adjusts the machine accordingly. Some fax machines include an automatic switch, as well as a telephone and answering machine.

Another big decision is what kind of paper you want. Thermal-paper fax machines are less expensive, as is the paper supply. The drawbacks are that thermal paper is flimsy, has an irritating tendency to curl, and fades after a while. Plain-paper machines, especially laser models, cost more, but the output quality is much better. Think about who will see your faxes, how often you'll end up copying them onto plain paper anyway, and the kind of data you'll be receiving.

Here are some other points to consider:

- *Memory.* This feature is needed for saving transmissions if you run out of paper, sending batch transmissions at a later time, and saving and accessing confidential faxes. Low-end models usually carry enough memory to store up to 30 pages.
- *Transmission speed.* This determines how long it takes to transmit one page. Average transmission speeds range from 10 to 20 seconds per page—longer, if there are photographs or illustrations.
- *Document feeder.* With a feeder, you can transmit multipage documents without having to feed the paper through the machine page by page.
- *Delayed transmission.* The fax machine can be programmed to send a document at another time, such as during off-peak hours when long-distance rates are lower.
- *Polling/Broadcasting.* The fax machine automatically calls a group of selected fax machines and either receives documents from them, or sends a document stored in memory.
- *Automatic redial/Alternate number redial.* These features allow your machine to redial a number after receiving a busy signal, or to dial a different assigned number.

Before you buy a fax, give this purchase some thought. Fax machines vary in features, price, speed, and image quality. Do a little investigating—and a lot of comparison shopping. You'll not only make a better choice, but you'll also learn how to get the most from the fax machine you finally select.

Copiers

A copier is a fixture of the modern office. Some copiers offer features such as automatic document feeders; collating for multipage documents, with sorting by both group and mode; color reproduction; paper cassette choices that range from the standard 8½ × 11 format to ledger-size options; reduction and enlargement—all within a compact unit that can be placed on its own stand or on a desktop.

While not every business needs a copier, office-oriented home-based businesses often require one because of the volume of documents that must be reproduced. If you don't expect to do a tremendous amount of copying or you feel it will be cheaper to use a print shop when large copy jobs arise, you can avoid this substantial equipment cost.

Some important features to look for when purchasing a copier are the copies-per-minute rate, reduction and enlargement capabilities, collating and sorting capabilities, paper tray size and capacity, and two-sided copying. A copier will improve your efficiency and increase your staff's productivity, particularly if there isn't a copying service nearby, but it only makes sense to lease or buy a machine if you're going to use it.

A basic copier with multiple paper trays will handle different sizes of documents, but one with most of the features listed above may be more appropriate. A basic copier is suitable for simple reproduction of one-page documents such as invoices and correspondence; the high-end machines are most appropriate for lengthy documents and the presentation of materials that require color reproduction.

Basic copiers with a minimum of features can be purchased for around $600; high-end office copiers can cost close to $8,000. Copiers can also be leased on a monthly basis for $300 to $500 with a $150 installation/removal charge. Call your local Xerox, Canon, Sharp, or 3-M dealer for more information.

On-Line Services

One of the most significant technological breakthroughs in personal computing has been the birth of on-line communications. Their ability to link together millions (and potentially billions) of computers allows individuals and businesses to communicate in ways never before possible, and to gain access to more information than they could use in several lifetimes.

The advent of the fax machine and personal computer brought a whole new dimension to the age of information. Electronic mail (e-mail; messages sent electronically through a telephone line) reaches someone in another country in less than 10 minutes.

If you're a newcomer to the information highway, you may ask, "What are on-line services and how are they useful for home-based entrepreneurs?" On-line services are electronic networks that connect an infinite number of local computer terminals to each other. This allows rapid transmission of large amounts of information at the wink of an eye and a touch of a keyboard.

By logging onto an on-line service using a local access telephone number and a modem hooked up to a personal computer, a person can perform a variety of functions that will allow access to many different types of information: local, national, and global news; reference materials such as those provided in a well-stocked collegiate library; professional and financial data; entertainment; and personal interests and hobbies.

Bulletin board services, commonly referred to as BBSs, were mentioned earlier. A BBS is a message board in electronic format, where people can write, post, and reply to messages from other BBS members. Bulletin board services also contain library databases, from which members can download any kind of PC file—a text file, graphic image, or executable application.

On-line services are large BBSs. The most popular commercial on-line services among people who compute at home are Prodigy, CompuServe, and America OnLine (AOL). Each of these services has its own assortment of news information, message boards, file databases, and conference or "chat" capabilities, in which users can hold live (referred to as "real time") conversations with other people located anywhere in the world.

Many commercial on-line services offer a means to connect, known as a "gateway," to the Internet, which is a giant international network made up of smaller networks, each with bulletin boards, file databases, and other information resources. Gateways serve to transfer data between separate networks or applications not normally connected to each other. For example, the on-line service America OnLine is a separate network outside of the Internet. However, AOL offers gateways through which subscribers can send and receive e-mail from the Internet, as well as access certain parts of the Internet.

For more information about the Internet—what it is and how to access and use it—see *The Whole Internet User's Guide and Catalog* by Ed Kroll, published by O'Reilly & Associates, Inc., 1992.

For information about the CompuServe Information Service, write to CompuServe Member Services, 5000 Arlington Centre Boulevard, Columbus, OH 43220; (800) 848-8990.

To find out about the Prodigy service, contact Prodigy Services Company, 445 Hamilton Avenue, White Plains, NY 10601; (800) 776-0845.

To learn more about America OnLine, call America OnLine, 8619 Westwood Center Drive, Vienna, VA 22182; (800) 827-6364.

You can use on-line services for research, whether for your own business or for a client, and you can network with other entrepreneurs in your field or in other industries. On-line services are also good for making contact with consultants and other individuals who can offer valuable advice. You can even conduct business on-line with clients in other parts of the world if necessary. This part of the information highway can be very beneficial for home-based entrepreneurs.

See Appendix D for a complete list of the most useful on-line services for home-based entrepreneurs.

If for no other reason than to have the *possibility* of reaching valuable information sources, no matter how frequently they are contacted, entrepreneurs who subscribe to one or more on-line services have a distinct advantage over those who do not.

TELECOMMUNICATIONS

Telephone and utility companies usually require deposits before they initiate service, be it for a home-based office or a sprawling commercial office. A deposit may not be required if you own your home or have established a payment record with the utility company in the past.

Telephone deposits are determined by the number of phones and the type of service required. Unless you need a large number of phones and lines, the deposit will probably range from $50 to $250.

Most small businesses find a single-line phone system (plus a separate fax line) adequate. However, if you reach a point where a single line cannot handle the volume of business you're doing, you will want to invest the extra money and install a multiline (push-button) phone system, allowing you to switch back and forth between lines while on one phone. You may also want to think about buying a cordless phone, which offers the advantage of freedom of movement. These phones vary widely in quality; research the latest models before buying. A speaker phone also allows you to move around and offers hands-free communication, which means you can continue working while talking.

Whether you choose a single-line or multiline system, there are some features you may want to consider when deciding which phone to buy.

If you want clients to be able to reach you while you are at a job site or in your car, you may want to get call forwarding. Calls arriving at your home office can then be transferred to another phone number where you can be reached. Another way to increase your accessibility to clients is to purchase call waiting, which signals you if someone is trying to reach you while you are on the phone. You can then take the incoming call while holding the original call.

To save time and avoid looking up numbers you dial often, you may want a phone that offers automatic redial and programmable memory. With redial, the phone calls back the last number called, or it may redial a number at regular intervals until the call gets through. Programmable memory lets you store numbers and call them by entering a code or pushing a single button. If you call long-distance numbers frequently, this feature is especially helpful.

Some telephones are voice-activated. They let you dial a number by speaking a code name. Such phones can also help you save time. Your local phone company's business sales rep should have the answers to your specific needs.

One caution involves your phone cables, electric wiring, heating/air conditioning, and plumbing. If any intended equipment or fixtures might put an unusual demand on the present installations, *always* check with a contractor to be sure you're not exceeding capacity.

Voice Mail

Any business owner—or customer, for that matter—knows the one essential ingredient in running a successful business: customer service. You can be hard-working and dedicated, have a flawless business plan and a bottomless source of financing, but if you don't keep customers satisfied—and coming back—your business will never succeed. Customers' primary complaints regarding the response they've received often center around phone service; they've called repeatedly and heard only a busy signal, or a phone that rings nonstop, or they've been made to wait on hold indefinitely.

A voice-mail system answers and directs incoming calls, takes messages, and costs less than hiring more employees. Formerly available only to large corporations, voice mail is now possible for small and even home-based businesses. For less than the cost of a cup of coffee a day, you can receive customer orders and inquiries professionally without having extraneous equipment to buy, operate, or repair.

You can put your voice mail number on your letterhead, business cards, and advertisements. You can also forward your phone to your voice mail box, creating an answering service on your live line or lines when you are either swamped or out of the office. In that way, you can conduct sensitive calls on the same phone line without interruption or fear of losing messages. Dozens of published articles and studies have shown the dramatic dollar and time savings afforded by voice mail to both large and small businesses.

Long-Distance Carriers

Since deregulation, the competition in the telecommunications industry has grown fierce among the primary contenders: AT&T, MCI, and U.S. Sprint. Buying long-distance services from one of the Big Three means buying years of research and development, millions of miles of telephone lines, and the assurance of a well-established company that stands behind its product. Brand-awareness is a big factor in purchasing long-distance services, and many business owners prefer to stick with what they know.

Your next option is regional carriers—companies that have their own facilities and switching equipment, but usually cover only a limited region: a tristate area, or the Southwest, for example. They are sometimes called switch-based resellers because they augment their own lines with time purchased from the big carriers.

Among the regional carriers, ITT, Metromedia Long Distance, Cable and Wireless Communications, and Allnet Communications Services are gaining popularity with small businesses that place the bulk of their calls to very specific areas. For example, if 80% of your customers are within a 100-mile radius, you could negotiate a good deal with a regional carrier covering that area. On the other hand, if your customers are all over the map, it might not be worth the inconvenience of using several different regional carriers.

Some business owners find it advantageous to sign with the smaller long-distance companies; they claim that they often respond more quickly to customers' problems. But not all regional carriers are created equal; some of them may not offer all the amenities you want, like calling cards or dedicated data lines.

Most cities are served by numerous regional carriers. Look in the telephone directory under "Telecommunications" or "Telephone" for representatives, and ask for a consultation.

Another option is to go through switchless resellers, a small but growing group of competitors out to get a piece of the long-distance pie. Their edge? Same service—for less money.

Switchless resellers are companies that buy long-distance time in bulk, then resell it to individuals or small businesses. Because they buy in bulk, resellers receive a substantial discount, part of which they pass on to their customers. One reseller in Illinois says that about 95% of his customers are small and medium-sized businesses.

Before making the switch, however, research the reseller. Some fraudulent companies are making promises of big discounts, then reneging. Call the Telecommunications Resellers Association to get a list of qualified resellers in the area, or to verify the reliability of a company that may be soliciting you. When you call the resellers, ask to be put in touch with one or two of their customers, whom you can ask about service, billing, and any problems they may have had.

When choosing a long-distance carrier, keep in mind that the major network providers, like AT&T, offer direct-line service; a host of national and regional carriers beneath the majors lease their lines from them and offer long-distance service; or they, in turn, act as "fiber carriers" and sublease those lines to yet another carrier.

Your choice of carrier obviously depends on a number of factors. Analyze the calling patterns of your business and consider what will best satisfy them:

- Which area(s) do you call most frequently (regional, national, worldwide)?
- At what time of day will you be making most of your long-distance calls?
- How much do you anticipate spending on long-distance calls each month?
- Do you foresee a seasonal trend in your calling patterns?
- Can a particular company customize its services to fit your business needs?
- Can it provide all the services you need: calling cards, conference calling, data services, 800 numbers?
- How responsive is the company; that is, how willing and/or able is the company to solve your problems quickly?
- What billing increments does the company use? Does it offer "first dollar" discounts, or is there a minimum threshold you must cross before a discount kicks in?
- Is billing customized? Can it reflect specific reporting information such as length of call, time of day and area codes called?
- How many carriers does the company contract with? If it uses more than one, does it consolidate everything for you on one bill?
- Will the company act as a consultant if you need specialized help, such as installing dedicated data lines or linking two office buildings?
- Most carriers offer specialized services structured for both small and large businesses. If your business deals only with customers or clients within your state, a regional dedicated WATS line could be the most cost-efficient option.

Be sure to read the fine print in telephone company brochures. Some carriers charge installation and/or start-up fees for their services. Others charge minimum monthly usage or flat monthly fees. Make sure you can meet any minimum usage requirements, or that the discount or service you receive warrants the flat monthly charge. If you require computer telecommunication services, find out if this option is available.

You should be familiar with the following terms when choosing a long-distance carrier:

- *Accounting codes.* Special codes entered directly into the telephone which allow the caller to charge the call to a specific account. This can be helpful when reconciling phone bills.
- *Billing unit.* Measure of calling time by which calls are billed. Long-distance carriers usually bill in one-minute or six-second increments.
- *Calling card.* Plastic card containing the caller's account number. Enables calls to be placed through the caller's long-distance carrier from any phone and charged to a home or business number.
- *Dedicated access/Dedicated line.* Allows the caller "exclusive" use of a portion of a line that leads to the telecommunications network.
- *Hotline connection.* Enables users to pick up a phone and have a dedicated number dialed automatically.
- *Local access and transportation area (LATA).* The geographical area in which a local telephone company will transmit calls. There are two types of LATA calls. INTRALATA calls (calls within a LATA) are carried by a local telephone company. INTERLATA calls (also known as toll calls) are transmitted by a long-distance carrier. INTRALATA toll calls are short-distance calls that are outside of a LATA but are still transmitted by and billed by a local telephone company. The regulations that determine which toll calls will be carried by local telephone companies and which will be awarded to long-distance carriers vary from state to state.
- *Least cost billing.* Every call is automatically billed at the lowest rate.
- *Magnetic tape.* Service offered by some long-distance carriers. Summarizes monthly activity in detail, call by call.
- *Mileage sensitive/Distance sensitive.* Mileage or distance from a call's point-of-origin determines cost per call.
- *Time of day sensitive.* Time of day determines cost per call.
- *Retail billing.* Service that enables a mark-up of phone charges. Would be used for hotels, hospitals, and universities.
- *Speed dialing.* Feature that enables callers to reach frequently called numbers by dialing a three- or four-digit code number.
- *Volume discounts.* Savings acquired as a result of a predetermined amount of money or hours spent on long-distance calls. Usually calculated as a percentage of the total amount spent on long-distance calls.
- *WATS.* Wide Area Telecommunication Service. WATS was the name given to AT&T's first-generation long-distance service.

Since deregulation, the term has been adopted by more than 100 telephone companies that offer this service. INWATS, or 800 service, refers to inward or incoming calls from any phone in a specified geographical area or band. OUTWATS refers to dialing to any phone in a specified geographical area from a specific phone. Traditional banded WATS lines are charged by minutes of usage in a certain region or band. WATS lines are cheaper than direct dial. Callers receive a discount because of the higher volume of calls to a specified geographical region.

The 800 Telephone Number

The 800 number exploded in the early 1970s as a national and regional marketing tool. Previously, consumers who wanted to reach a company located across the country had to place a long-distance toll call. This was a strong deterrent; many potential customers weren't (and still aren't) willing to spend extra money to find out what companies elsewhere had to offer. With the advent of the 800 number, consumers were able to make long-distance calls without spending an extra cent.

So common are 800 numbers these days that businesses marketing and selling throughout a wide territory are at a competitive disadvantage if they don't have one. The opposing argument is that an 800 number, if not handled right, encourages a certain number of "shoppers"—unqualified leads—on whom sellers' time and money are largely wasted. It is now often possible to have an 800 number that covers only a small geographical area, thus saving companies from paying for service to people who probably will never become customers or clients.

The installation, monthly service charges, and usage rates can add up to a substantial sum, so weigh the costs against the value of the service. A home-based business that relies on telephone inquiries and ordering for most of its business can anticipate substantial rewards from an 800 number service. This is another relatively inexpensive way to dissolve the "small-time" image of your home-based business.

Toll-Free Answering Services

A lot of retail, mail order, and other product-oriented businesses use toll-free answering services that will take orders for their products over the phone. Usually, customers can dial an 800 number 24 hours a day. For a per-order fee of about 25 cents to one dollar, the service's operator will take the name, address, credit card number, and product-ordered information from each caller.

Hiring a service does cut into your profit, but if you wanted to install your own inbound WATS line, hire operators, and do the paperwork, it could cost you several thousand dollars each month. Answering service companies will give you access to that service without taking money directly from your pocket.

Cellular Phone

As a home-based business owner, you need to keep in touch with your clients and company at all times during the day. Once considered a luxury, cellular phones have dropped considerably in price over the past few years, to the point where they are becoming standard equipment for many entrepreneurs.

There are four different types of cellular phones, all of which can be used inside a car:

1. *Mobile cellular phones.* These units are permanently installed in the car and are powered by the car's battery.
2. *Transmobile cellular phones.* Designed for in-car use, these phones plug into the vehicle's cigarette lighter outlet, but are not permanently installed. Instead, they can be removed and reinstalled in other vehicles.
3. *Transportable cellular phones.* These units can be plugged into a car's cigarette lighter outlet, but they have their own rechargeable batteries and can be used outside the car. Transportable phones come with a carrying case, which houses a battery, and they are somewhat bulkier than other types of cellular phones.
4. *Portable cellular phones.* Designed to be carried in the caller's hand or pocket, portable cellular phones contain small, lightweight batteries, and can be mounted in cars.

Many cellular phones can be mounted in more than one way. (You can buy a mobile phone, for instance, and convert it to a transportable.) The complete price for a cellular phone will often depend on the mounting option; however, prices for just the phone will usually range between $200 and $600.

Don't forget about the other costs involved with purchasing a cellular phone. These costs usually include a fixed monthly service charge plus "airtime" charges and any "roaming" fees for calls outside the local cellular service area.

Car phones are available with a number of special features designed to make them safe and easy to use. Many come with speakers built into the handset. The caller can keep both hands on the wheel and carry on a conversation without lifting the phone off the hook. Many models can be set to answer automatically after a specific number of rings. Others allow continuing a conversation after the ignition is turned off, thanks to the call-in-progress protection feature that is standard on most phones.

Some other useful features are standard on most cellular phones. A caller can use a mute feature in order to speak privately to a passenger in the car, but maintain contact with a caller on the cellular phone. When dialing a number yields a busy signal, the automatic retry will keep dialing the number until the call gets through. Call timers are handy for keeping track of phone usage.

Perhaps the most important standard feature is memory, which allows the caller to scroll through stored phone numbers until a particular number is found. Once it is found, the caller usually need only hit the "send" key on the phone to dial the number. A two-digit speed-dial code can be assigned to important numbers. Phones with *numeric* memory store only phone numbers; those with *alphanumeric* memory store both numbers and names. Pause dialing allows access to important number sequences, such as a calling card number, from memory and appends them to the phone number being dialed. "Scratch pad" memory, another convenient feature, allows input of numbers into memory while the caller is speaking on the phone. Speed dialing and scratch pad memory are especially useful when business people are on the road; they don't distract any attention from driving.

Cellular phones also offer a number of options to make in-car use even more convenient. Voice recognition systems let the caller "dial" a number by saying it, instead of having to punch buttons. Another option, automatic radio mute, turns off a car's audio equipment whenever a call is made or received. If a caller is often outside the car but still near it (for instance, while visiting construction sites), the caller can take advantage of the optional horn-alert feature, which signals incoming calls by sounding the car's horn.

Answering Machine

You may want to purchase an answering machine to receive calls while you're away from the office. These machines come with a variety of features. Basically, all you'll need is a simple machine that will record messages and play them back. Make sure your message is professional and gives your name as well as the name of your company. Ask callers to leave their name, number, and a brief message. In this way, if a client or prospective client has a specific question, you can research it and have the answer ready when you call them back. For a suitable answering machine, you should expect to pay between $80 and $200.

If you will be out of the office, or if you will be spending a great deal of time on other lines, consider installing a voice-mail system as well.

BUYING OR LEASING A COMPANY VEHICLE

You may need a vehicle of some kind in order to operate your home-based business successfully. If your business involves a great deal of travel and client interaction, you may want a nice four-door sedan that is comfortable and will make a good impression on your clients. On the other hand, if you need to haul equipment and supplies to a site where you will perform a service such as pool cleaning, you are going to need a light truck or van. If your own vehicle is in good working condition, use it. If you don't have a vehicle or if the one you have is unreliable, you will have to acquire one that will meet your needs. You have two options: leasing and buying. Both offer certain advantages.

If you need to curb start-up costs, leasing may be the way to go because you don't need a substantial down payment. You may be able to get away with no down payment at all or a minimal down payment. There are two major kinds of leases: open-end, where you pay low installments with an option to buy at the end, and closed-end, where you pay fixed installments for a defined period and give up the car at the end. The disadvantage of an open-end lease is that if the vehicle depreciates more than expected (and is therefore worth less at the end of the lease), you will pay the difference between the expected price and the actual price. The disadvantage of the closed-end lease, of course, is that you are usually not given the option to buy the vehicle at the end of the term. Keep in mind that while leasing usually doesn't require a lot of money up front, it is considered a liability when it comes to borrowing money. The main drawback to leasing is that, in most cases, you make monthly payments as you would in a financing plan but own nothing in the end. Also, if the car is totaled or stolen, the leasing company may charge you a substantial penalty for "early termination."

Buying a car requires a substantial initial outlay of cash—possibly several thousand dollars. Most start-up home-based entrepreneurs don't have that kind of capital available. Keep in mind that, like leasing, financing the vehicle will place a liability on your books until it is paid off. If you purchase outright, you will have acquired an asset for your business that will look good on your financial statement should you need to borrow money.

When deciding which option to choose, consider the cash flow of your business. If you can handle the cost of the outright purchase of a vehicle, this is the best route. If you don't have the money to buy a vehicle or to make a down payment for a financing plan, consider leasing. This gives you great tax breaks even though you don't own the vehicle. The least expensive route is to use your own vehicle, at least at first.

Either way, your automobile expenses can be used as a tax deduction to lower your reported income. Any mileage you put on your vehicle for business-related activities is deductible. Driving from your home office to a client's location or to the office supply store for business supplies counts; driving to the grocery store or a friend's house doesn't.

Currently, business mileage is deductible at 28¢ a mile for the first 15,000 miles. If you surpass 15,000 miles, the deduction is 11¢ a mile. You can calculate deductions based on either a straight mileage method or by totaling the actual operating expenses.

As your business expands, you may need to hire employees who will also need vehicles to perform their work. You don't need to purchase vehicles for employees; it is much more economical to have them use their own cars. You can either reimburse them for mileage, or they can deduct business mileage on their personal taxes.

HOME OFFICE SUPPLIES

When you shop for your business stationery, check stationers and office supply stores as well as printers. Many of these outlets provide business start-up packages that include letterhead, business cards, and envelopes for about $300 or $400. If you already have art ready for reproduction, the price could be less. For the best results and the lowest possible cost, you should have your stationery printed at a local quick-print shop. Get several estimates before placing your order, and always insist on getting the quality you've asked for (or that has been promised). Your business materials are a reflection of your company's image and should be of the highest possible quality.

Local stationers and office supply stores will have most or all of your miscellaneous operations materials. A few hundred dollars should buy you a good supply of blank stationery and envelopes, record-keeping equipment (files, ledgers, and index cards), sales slips, invoices, bags, boxes, labels, tagging guns, and other paraphernalia you need. (Sales receipts can be specially printed, but keep costs down in the beginning by buying standard two-copy receipt books.)

Ask for referrals from other local businesspeople you may know, or check the Yellow Pages under "Paper Products—Wholesale," "Office Supplies," and "Stationers—Retail."

LAYOUT

Needless to say, there are probably as many ways to design home offices as there are home-based businesses to occupy them. Whether your home office is set up in a separate room, a portion of your den, or a corner of your kitchen, maximize the efficiency of the space you have. Put a walk-around cord on your telephone (or buy a portable phone) if you will need to access files or your computer while you're making or taking a call. Look for sturdy stackables that use vertical space well and require minimal floor space. Allow enough room to move between and around your furniture and equipment, and don't block any natural light or air flow just to fit everything in one area. You'll be spending many hours every day in your office. It has to be a place where you can work comfortably day in and day out.

The square footage required by a home-based business depends on what will take place there on a daily basis. Business owners who currently work from home usually utilize an average floor area of 250 square feet to 500 square feet. Available space is usually subdivided into work space and storage space. Depending on the original floor plan and individual design, storage space can occupy up to 25% of the total. If you plan to do assembly or light manufacturing work, you will need even more square footage (probably garage or work room space).

The less storage space you have, the more room you have to conduct your business. However, storage space is an important part of the floor plan for any home-based business, especially if you are product-oriented. Shipping and receiving and related chores; paperwork, and storage of extra supplies and inventory all need attention during your planning stage.

PURCHASING EQUIPMENT AND SUPPLIES

Once in business, entrepreneurs tend to neglect the area of purchasing. They continue to purchase materials or supplies, but, because of their busy schedule, they don't take measures to control the amount of money spent to keep their business going. Entrepreneurs tend to think of purchasing as merely placing orders. They don't ask questions of equipment dealers and supplies vendors concerning level of service, quality of material, or costs associated with the purchase. They merely keep placing orders.

Unfortunately, their cost of doing business then rises to a point where it cannot be justified. As operating expenses increase, profit margins shrink, and they face the dilemma of either living with reduced profits or raising their prices, neither of which is very appealing.

Perhaps the significance of purchasing can best be seen in the amount of money companies spend on purchases as compared to revenue. According to the Small Business Administration (SBA), approximately 50% of the average manufacturing firm's sales dollar goes to pay for purchases of materials or services, about 15% goes to administration, and 25% is spent on labor. For retail establishments, purchases account for 70 cents of every sales dollar. Service businesses are perennially the cheapest firms to run with regard to equipment and supplies purchases.

Don't underestimate the importance any purchase—a chair for your desk or a ton of new paper stock for your desktop publishing business. It is a major cost center of your enterprise and, like everything else, can benefit from proper procedures and control systems. By keeping your costs under control, you will be able to maintain your prices at very competitive levels while still realizing a desirable profit.

Used Equipment

You can buy second-hand equipment for almost any type of business for a fraction of its retail cost. Other businesses that have failed, merged, or outgrown their existing equipment are often good sources of used furniture, business machines, and related equipment that looks and functions as well as it did the day it was first purchased.

Careful shopping will turn up some excellent bargains. You will find a host of used furniture and equipment bargains in the classified sections of most large city newspapers. Also check the "Business Opportunities" category. Businesses that are being liquidated or sold may have furniture or equipment for sale at substantial savings.

Don't overlook suppliers of new equipment when looking for used equipment. Ask them if they have good used items or discounted demonstration models. They frequently have trade-ins or repossessions for as little as 50% of the new price. You can save hundreds of dollars by shopping wisely for second-hand items.

Lease or Buy?

If your equipment investment will be large, compare the potential tax savings available if you lease rather than buy. See your accountant for current rulings. Ask whether your potential leases are suitable for write-offs.

Limited start-up capital can often be stretched with leasing because it significantly lowers the initial cash outlay. However, if you have a legitimate tax-deductible lease, you do not acquire equity in your equipment and therefore do not build up your balance sheet.

A financial statement showing a strong net worth is important to any business, especially one that is home-based, because it lends an added degree of legitimacy. In addition, the total cost of leasing over a period of years is higher than if the same items were purchased. Consult your accountant about the wiser choice for you.

The tax laws generally make the *purchase* of equipment, whether new or used, more attractive than leasing. Some financing sources offer no-money-down options for equipment purchases or leases. No-money-down leases enable you to own the equipment when the term of the lease is completed.

Purchase Contracts

Two types of credit contracts are commonly used to finance equipment purchases: (1) the conditional sales contract, in which the purchaser does not receive title to the equipment until it is fully paid for; and (2) the chattel mortgage contract, in which the equipment becomes the property of the purchaser on delivery, but the seller holds a mortgage claim against it until the amount specified in the contract is paid.

Dealing with Suppliers

Reliable suppliers are an asset, especially to businesses that require a great deal of supplies or are involved in the distribution of products. Suppliers can bail you out when customers make difficult demands on you or when business becomes unexpectedly strong, but they will do so only as long as dealing with you is profitable to them. Suppliers, like you, are in business to make money. If you go to the mat with them on every bill, ask them to shave prices on everything they sell you, or fail to pay their bills promptly, don't be surprised when they stop calling.

Your industry will no doubt be competitive, and you must look for the best deal you can get on a consistent basis from your suppliers.

Remember, however, that no worthwhile business arrangement can continue for long unless something of value is rendered and received by all those involved.

Don't expect at first to receive the same kind of attention a long-standing customer gets, but over time you can develop excellent working relationships that will be profitable for you and your suppliers. Be open, courteous, and firm with your suppliers, and they will respond in kind. Tell them what you need and when you need it. Have a specific understanding about the total cost, and expect delivery on schedule. In other words, expect from your suppliers what your customers or clients demand from you.

DEPRECIATION

Depreciation can be either cash-value or tax-related. Cash-value depreciation is based on the difference between the initial cost of the equipment and its current fair market value. If a piece of equipment that cost $15,000 in January had a market value of $11,000 in December of the same year, the cash-value depreciation would be $4,000. In other words, your actual expense of owning the equipment would have been $4,000 for that year, or $333 per month.

Tax-related depreciation is purely an accounting device to take advantage of the maximum deduction permitted by law when figuring your annual net taxable income. Tax-related depreciation is determined by a formula laid down in the Internal Revenue Code. It has nothing to do with the actual condition of your equipment or its loss in value at the end of each year's use.

The Tax Reform Act of 1986 created a new form of accelerated depreciation. In general, for any equipment purchased throughout the year, a half-year of accelerated depreciation is allowed, regardless of whether the equipment was purchased in January or December. The remaining half-year of depreciation is recognized in the year the equipment is sold or abandoned.

There is a critical exception to this "half-year convention." If more than 40% of your equipment is purchased in the last three months of the year, all your asset purchases for the year are subject to the "midquarter convention," which weighs depreciation substantially more for assets purchased in January through March and correspondingly less for equipment bought in October through December.

Many entrepreneurs wait until the end of the year, see how much money they have left, then buy their equipment. This approach, however, may throw you into the midquarter convention instead of the half-year convention for depreciation. If you recognize in September that you need to buy equipment, make your purchase before October to qualify for the extra depreciation.

Cash-Value Depreciation

If you buy a piece of equipment, depreciation of its cash value should be included as an expense on your monthly operating statement. If you lease a piece of equipment, the monthly lease payment will be a part of your monthly operating expenses. (Cash-value depreciation is frequently figured into the cost of an equipment lease and need not necessarily be figured separately by you.)

Many equipment-leasing agreements have a clause providing for a *depreciation reserve.* This consists of money set aside to correspond with the declining value of the vehicle. When the lease is up, the equipment will be sold either to the lessee or to a third party. If it sells for more than its depreciated value, the difference can be refunded to the lessee. If, however, the equipment is sold for less than its depreciated value, the lessee must pay the difference to the lessor. This is where the depreciation reserve comes into play. It is usually a part of the lease and should be considered a monthly expense of running the business.

Straight-line or uniform depreciation is the most frequently used method of depreciating new equipment. In straight-line depreciation, the equipment loses an equal part of its total value in every year of its life.

Suppose you buy a $15,000 computer system with a 10-year useful life, according to your accountant's schedule. The straight-line depreciation rate would be calculated by dividing the price by the useful life ($15,000 ÷ 10 = $1,500 a year). If you are in the 28% tax bracket, $1,500 in depreciation will save you $420. Suppose you need only 20% down to buy a $15,000 machine and you finance your purchase on an installment plan. The interest you pay on any amount owed is going to be another deduction for you. So, if you have a $12,000 loan that costs you $1,200 in interest, you will wind up with savings of another $336 if you are in the 28% bracket (or $600 if you are in the 50% bracket). This means that your cash savings of $3,000 will take care of that down payment.

Depreciation for Taxes

The depreciation method used on financial statements is often different from that used on your tax return. For your tax return, your accountant will usually use a tax-approved depreciation table that will reduce your taxes as much as is allowed.

The Tax Reform Act of 1986 revised the depreciation rates that may be used for federal income tax purposes on all equipment, real estate, and so on, purchased after December 31, 1986. These new methods are often referred to as "MACRS" (standing for Modified Accelerated Cost Recovery System), whereas the method used for assets acquired before December 31 1986, is called "ACRS" (Accelerated Cost Recovery System).

Assets used in your trade or business that were purchased before that cut off date are depreciated using methods different from those discussed here. Those earlier methods generally yielded a larger depreciation deduction than the current rates. Keep in mind that, in many states, an entirely different set of rules is used.

Section 179 of the Internal Revenue Code gives a tax break for small businesses. It allows you to deduct up to $10,000 for equipment each year. Entrepreneurs cannot take the Section 179 deduction if it created a loss; the unused portion of the deduction may, however, be carried to future tax years.

You can learn the rules for depreciation of assets used in your business by ordering Publication 17 (entitled *Your Federal Income Tax*) and Form 4562, with the accompanying instructions, from the Internal Revenue Service.

Depreciation Schedules

If you are depreciating real estate for investment, the time period over which residential real property is depreciated is 27.5 years, using the straight-line method. (Commercial real property, to compare, is depreciated over 31.5 years using the straight-line method.)

Several different depreciable lives are possible for depreciable personal property used in your trade or business. Those lives include periods of 3, 5, 7, 10, 15, and 20 years. Almost all equipment, such as automobiles, trucks, typewriters, desks, and machines, will be depreciated using either a 5-year or a 7-year life. Consult IRS publications to determine which types of assets use other lives.

Equipment that fits into the 5- or 7-year life classes can be depreciated using the 200% declining balance rate. This means that the equipment is depreciated using twice the straight-line rate. However, in the years of acquisition and disposition of the property, you can only take half of a full year's depreciation, no matter in which month of the year the property was purchased.

Some of the items included in the 5-year depreciation class under MACRS are:

1. Automobiles and light trucks.
2. Typewriters, computers, calculators, copiers, and computer-based telephone-switching equipment.
3. Research and experimentation property.

The 7-year MACRS depreciable life property accounts for most forms of office furniture used in business (such as desks, chairs, and fixtures), and any other equipment that does not have a class life and is not otherwise classified.

Here's an example. If you purchase a $1,400 personal computer that has a 5-year MACRS depreciable life, the depreciation in the first year would be $1,400 ÷ 5 = $280. You can take twice this straight-line rate depreciation, or $560, but since you are limited to a half-year's worth of depreciation, you would claim $280 depreciation in the first year.

After the initial year's depreciation, you would calculate your depreciation for each subsequent year using the following formula:

$$\text{Initial cost} - \text{prior year's depreciation} \times [1 \div 5] \times 2$$

Certain properties, such as luxury automobiles used less than 50% of the time for business, are limited to straight-line depreciation.

Automobiles that are used for business and that cost more than $12,800 are limited to $2,560 depreciation in the first year, $4,100 in the second year, $2,450 in the third year, and $1,475 for all subsequent years.

Except for automobiles, under Section 179 of the Internal Revenue Code, you can immediately deduct up to the first $10,000 of equipment purchased for your business each year and avoid depreciating it over a period of time. However, if you place in service personal property in excess of $200,000 in any one year, the $10,000 is reduced, dollar-for-dollar for all property purchased in excess of the $200,000. In addition, the $10,000 deduction is limited to the taxable income of your trade or business before taking this deduction. If the equipment is sold, this deduction must be recaptured.

These points are current at the time of publication but *may change from year to year*. Make sure your financial adviser(s), particularly your tax adviser(s), are aware of any changes that may occur in tax-related depreciation guidelines. Your adviser(s) should pass all relevant information on to you.

SOURCES OF SUPPLY

The following are representative, but certainly not exclusive, suppliers of business machines and office equipment. New companies are coming into the market all the time, and you should watch for announcements of their development in trade magazines (listed in Appendix C). To find equipment locally, look in your Business-to-Business Yellow Pages under headings such as "Office Furniture & Equipment—Dealers," "Office Furniture & Equipment—Used," "Office Supplies," and "Computers."

To find local offices of the companies listed below, write or call the national office at the address and telephone number provided, and ask to be directed to a local representative. If you write to the national office and receive no reply, spend the money for a phone call. The expense can be worth the information you might receive.

Photocopiers/Facsimile Machines

Canon U.S.A., Inc.
One Canon Plaza
Lake Success, NY 11042
(516) 488-6700

Sharp Electronics Corp.
Sharp Plaza
Mahwah, NJ 07430
(800) 237-4277

Xerox Corp.
Direct Marketing
300 Main St., Suite 27B
East Rochester, NY 14445
(716) 423-5090

NovAtel
3800 Sandshell
Ft. Worth, TX 76137
(800) 231-5100

Oki
437 Old Peachtree Rd.
Suwanee, GA 30174
(800) 342-5654

Panasonic Co.
One Panasonic Way
Secaucus, NJ 07094
(201) 348-9090

Uniden
4700 Amon Carter Blvd.
Ft. Worth, TX 76155
(800) 235-3874

Cellular Phones

Motorola
600 N. Highway. 45
Libertyville, IL 60048
(800) 331-6456

Computers

IBM
Old Orchard Rd.
Armonk, NY 10504
(914) 765-1900

Hewlett-Packard Co.
3000 Hanover St.
Palo Alto, CA 94304-1181
(415) 857-1501

Compaq Computer Corp.
P.O. Box 692000
Houston, TX 77269-2000
(713) 370-0670

Apple Computer, Inc.
20525 Mariani Ave.
Cupertino, CA 95014
(408) 996-1010

Software

Data Storm Technologies, Inc.
    (PROCOMM PLUS)
P.O. Box 1471
Columbia, MO 65205
(314) 443-3282

Intuit (Quicken)
155 Linfield Ave.
P.O. Box 3014
Menlo Park, CA 94026
(415) 322-0573

Microsoft
One Microsoft Way
Redmond, WA 98052-6399
(800) 227-4679 or (206) 882-8080

Quarterdeck Office Systems
150 Pico Blvd.
Santa Monica, CA 90405
(310) 392-9851

Symantec Corp.
10201 Torre Ave.
Cupertino, CA 95014-2132
(408) 253-96004

HOME OFFICE TAX DEDUCTION

Working in a home office allows you to take advantage of certain tax deductions. However, you must choose a room—not just a corner of a room—to be used solely as an office. If it also contains a television and stereo and is used as a den, your home office deduction probably won't hold up under an audit. Additionally, in January 1993, the Supreme Court ruled that you need to conduct the majority of your business in your home office space to qualify for a deduction. Under the ruling, unless business owners spend most of their work time within the home, and use it for visits from clients, customers, or patients, the IRS will not allow the deduction.

To qualify for deductions, the home office has to:

1. Be your principal place of business.
2. Be used as a place where clients, customers, or patients visit on a regular basis.

3. Be in connection with your trade if it is a separate place, i.e., the garage.
4. Be used exclusively and on a regular basis for business.

You cannot deduct your entire rent or mortgage payment for your home-based business. The amount you can deduct from your income taxes depends on the amount of space your home office occupies. Do you use one room for your office? What percentage of the total area of your home does that room represent? You can deduct as business expenses that portion of your rent/mortgage. For instance, if you have a six-room home and you use only the den for your office, you can deduct one-sixth of your rent/mortgage plus one-sixth of your utility bills. According to recent federal tax legislation, however, you cannot deduct any part of the base rate of the first telephone line into your residence, even if you use the telephone for business.

Before you begin your business in a home office, review all local zoning codes. Zoning ordinances that prohibit or restrict business operations in residential areas may directly affect your plan for a home-based business. (See Chapters 5 and 10 for additional information on zoning codes and home-office tax deductions.)

Contact your insurance broker to judge whether your homeowner's insurance adequately covers the added liability risks of operating your business from your home. (Insurance requirements have received a more thorough treatment in Chapter 5, "Legal Issues.")

You'll want to keep overhead as low as possible when you're just starting out. Don't invest too much in elegant office fixtures and decor that customers or clients will never see; that defeats the purpose of starting from home. Once the business is in full swing, you can always upgrade.

MANAGING INVENTORY

Many home-based business owners have to keep raw materials and products on hand to fulfill orders. If you create or distribute a product for sale, you may have to store that product at home or in a storage unit.

Product-oriented businesses aren't the only ones that have to deal with inventory management. Even if your business falls in the service category, you may have to keep certain items in stock. For example, a balloon delivery service fills orders constantly and has to have a stock of balloons ready to go when the next telephone call comes.

Storing your products at home may be the cheapest solution to your inventory problem—if you have the necessary space. Most often, home-based business owners use a garage or spare bedroom to house inventory, but any area will do if you are short on space: bedroom, kitchen, dining room, or all of the above. To convert a garage or den into an efficient storage area, you may need to make some alterations—build shelves, install storage cabinets, and so on.

If you don't have enough room to accommodate your company's wares in your home or apartment, you can rent a storage unit. The charge can run anywhere from $50 to a few hundred dollars per month, depending on the amount of space you need.

Even though you may not be storing thousands of items at home, learn some basic techniques of inventory control. Without that self-schooling, you could end up with a garage, living room, and den full of products you can't sell, or you may have a backlog of orders you can't fill because you don't have enough stock on hand. Your angry customers may then take their business elsewhere.

The following discussions will give you a quick rundown on how to keep your inventory from taking over your home and how to avoid being empty-handed when orders start rolling in.

Basic Stock

Your basic stock should provide you with enough products and/or raw materials to fulfill orders from customers. To accurately calculate basic stock, you must review actual sales during an appropriate time period, such as a full year of business. Because you will have no previous sales and stocking figures to guide you during start-up, you must project your first year's sales based on your business plan and maintain your stock accordingly.

Lead Times

If you purchase products from a supplier and then resell them to others, take the lead time into account when figuring out when to order more inventory. Lead time—the length of time between reorder of a product and delivery of that product—must be factored in when you calculate basic stock. For instance, assume you import jewelry and handbags from Asia. If your lead time is 4 weeks and you usually sell 20 handbags a week, then you must reorder before your handbag inventory falls below 80 units. If reorders are not made until you run out of handbags, you'll have a one-month back-order on sales.

Ordering late isn't the only reason your inventory may fall short at times. An incoming shipment may be delayed in customs or arriving late because of severe weather conditions in the country of origin. To avoid such shortfalls, you may want to pad your inventory a bit by ordering more handbags than you actually need. There is no magic formula to tell you exactly how many extra units of a product you should keep in stock; experience will be your best guide. In the meantime, you'll have to make an educated guess.

Hidden Costs of Overstocking

Excess inventory creates extra overhead, and that costs you money. Inventory that sits in your garage does not generate sales or profits; it generates losses that will shrink your bottom line in the form of:

- Debt service on loans to purchase the excess inventory.
- Additional personal property tax on unsold inventory.
- Increased insurance costs on the greater value of the inventory in stock.

To avoid accumulating excess inventory, establish a realistic safety margin and order only what you're sure you can sell.

Tracking Inventory

Many small business owners, especially those working from home, fail to realize the importance of inventory control. An adequate stock control system will tell you how much merchandise you have on hand, what is on order, when it will arrive, and what has been sold. With such a system, you can plan purchases and manufacturing intelligently, and you will quickly recognize fast-sellers and slow-moving items.

Suppose your product line allows you to offer both custom orders and ready-made styles. By tracking your inventory, you will soon discover which category sells best, when you should start making more of each type of product, and whether you should discount any slow-moving items. After you have been in business for a while, you will start to see sales patterns developing, and they will give you a better idea of how many of each type of product you should have on hand.

Entrepreneurs frequently devise their own inventory systems or adopt those recommended by accountants. A basic tracking method begins with sales receipts listing the product, quantity sold, and price. Eventually, you may want to computerize your inventory tracking. When you're ready, research software designed specifically for inventory control. Even if it's too detailed for your operation, you can imitate the approach when you set up your own tracking system.

7

MARKETING, ADVERTISING, AND SELLING

For the home-based entrepreneur in particular, marketing and promotion take on extra significance. Because you don't have a storefront or a commercial office location in which to present your business, it's up to you to get the word out that your company exists. All the things you do to publicize your business—direct mail advertising, fliers, promotions, networking—should be considered part of your overall marketing strategy. Using such techniques as direct-response advertising, personal sales, presentations, sales promotions, and, most importantly, creative thinking (all of which are highlighted in this chapter), even the smallest home-based business can thrive in markets dominated by large corporations.

There are at least three essential reasons for marketing your business:

1. To promote awareness of your business.
2. To directly stimulate sales and generate revenues.
3. To create a market niche for your business.

167

These goals can be accomplished through the aggressive but intelligent marketing practices described in this chapter. Before you start designing your ads or sending out fliers, however, you need to develop a detailed marketing plan that outlines the individual points of your overall strategy.

DEVELOPING A MARKETING PLAN

Using your market research, you should be able to devise a strong marketing plan that will help you sell your products or services successfully. Like a business plan, a marketing plan has no set formula. However, a complete marketing plan should include the following:

- *A summary of your products or services.* Describe what you will be selling to customers.
- *A list of the benefits your products or services provide.* Explain how customers will benefit from what you are selling.
- *The characteristics of your target market.* Include age, gender, income, buying habits, geographic location, and anything else you have learned from your market research.
- *An analysis of your competitors.* Examine how many companies already exist in your industry, their price points, the percentage of market share they hold, how they market to their customers, and any special features they offer, as revealed by your market research.
- *A plan for positioning your business within the marketplace.* Describe how you want customers to perceive your company in comparison with your competitors.
- *An explanation of how you plan to sell to your market.* Write down what your tactics will be: telemarketing, mail order, selling to wholesalers or retailers, marketing to a business clientele or consumer clientele, and so on.
- *The advertising and promotion methods you will use.* Include all the ways you will advertise your business: fliers, brochures, business cards, print ads, television commercials, radio spots, inperson contacts, and word-of-mouth.
- *Your advertising budget.* Calculate how much you are able to spend on advertising.
- *Your pricing policies.* Spell out how much you will charge, what prices are negotiable, any guarantees you will offer, your credit terms, shipping and handling costs, returns policy, discounts

for bulk and off-season purchases, and use of merchandise coupons that reduce ticketed prices.

- *Your strategy for coping with outside forces, such as the economy.* Describe how you will react if the economic picture changes, including what you will do to make sure your business survives any downward changes in the economy.

These are some of the issues that you should consider when devising your marketing plan, the map for your sales strategies. Depending on the type of business you start, you may need to include other items as well. Regardless of how little money you have at your disposal, with careful planning and some hard work, you will gain a clear idea of how to sell your products to your customers, and you'll learn exactly how to gain an advantage over your competitors. However small the advantage, gaining that edge over your competitors is what marketing is all about.

Your marketing plan must be flexible. In today's rapidly changing business environment, static companies get left behind. As your business grows, you will find yourself making minor and sometimes major adjustments in your marketing plan. Industries change, and you must be able to (1) adapt quickly in order to maintain your advantage over your competitors, and (2) find new ways in which you can strengthen your market success. Whether this occurs in the form of creative pricing brackets, using new technologies, or simply investing in greater customer service, you must maintain a marketing plan that can anticipate changes in the marketplace and position your company to capitalize on them.

LOW-COST MARKETING STRATEGIES

Like most start-up home-based business owners, you will not have a lot of money to spend on traditional advertising. There are other ways you can spread the word about your business without breaking the bank. Try some of the following tactics to jump-start your marketing efforts.

Give Free Samples

If you create a product, offering free samples to existing and potential customers can entice people to purchase more. For example, let's say you run a mail order cookie business from home. By sending a few cookies to potential clients, along with a brochure and order form, you can increase your chances of getting orders. A few bites of a delicious cookie can do more for your business than a dozen sales phone calls.

Ask for Referrals

Take advantage of your existing customers: ask them to refer others to your business. You might offer some kind of referral discount program, or start up a contest that awards a prize to the customer who sends you the most new business. Many entrepreneurs rely on word-of-mouth referrals as the basis of their marketing strategy. Positive word of mouth is the best type of advertising. And the best part is—it's free.

Join Forces with Other Entrepreneurs

Do you know any other entrepreneurs who offer complementary products or services? Ask them to advertise your business to their customers while you do the same for them. Teaming up with them to cross-market can cut advertising costs and increase your clientele.

Establish Yourself as an Expert in Your Field

Giving seminars or lectures about your industry can help establish or enhance your reputation as an authority on the subject and will increase listeners' awareness of your business. For example, if you sell vitamins and health products, you may want to conduct free lectures on nutrition at local gyms or health food stores. But don't make the mistake of approaching the presentation as a chance to make a direct sales pitch about your products or services in particular. If you're not careful, your attendees will feel that you are taking advantage of them, or that you are misleading them in some way. Instead, show and prove. That is, *show* the audience that you really are an authority on the subject, and *prove* through the quality of your presentation that you would be a good supplier for their health product needs. While you shouldn't make the presentation a live version of an infomercial, do bring literature about your business in case anyone in the audience requests it.

Write Articles about Your Industry

As an example, if you run a tax preparation service, you may want to submit an article on tax tips to the local newspaper. Call the paper and offer to write it for free. The time you take on the task will be well worth the new customers you'll attract.

ADVERTISING THAT WORKS

Advertising is a crucial element of any successful marketing program. It is a powerful tool that helps forge your business identity and provides a direct line of communication to current and prospective customers. A good advertising campaign performs the following functions:

- *Creates customer awareness of your product or service.* Quite simply, if prospective customers don't know you exist, they won't be able to order your products or hire your services.
- *Convinces customers that your company's product or service is top-quality.* If the quality of your product or service does not match or exceed that of your competition, you won't be able to survive in the marketplace.
- *Creates a unique identity for your company.* Not only are you selling a product or service, you are selling your company as well. Take care to avoid one of the cardinal mistakes of marketing: running an ad campaign that neglects to position the company in a positive light. Creating a positive public image is essential.
- *Creates and reinforces the desire for your service or product.* In essence, it helps generate demand, both new and continuing.
- *Publicizes new products or services.* Consumers cannot know about your company's products or services unless you inform them.

Before you plan your advertising program, you need to know who is most likely to buy from you. Ask yourself the following questions:

- Who will buy my product or service? Am I selling to individual consumers or to businesses?
- Why will they buy it?
- Where and how do my competitors advertise?
- Am I positioning my product or service correctly? (If you face a great deal of competition, you might want to look for a market niche.)

Keeping Costs Low

How can you cut costs wisely when advertising? To begin with, keep in mind that freelancers often cost much less than a professional full-service ad agency or marketing company. There are many sophisticated graphic designers, for example, who will create an ad or brochure for you at a fraction of the cost that a full-service ad agency would charge. These days, many designers advertise in the Yellow Pages or Business-to-Business telephone directories. If you do choose to hire an ad agency, consider using a smaller agency that will offer you the attention and services that you require while still staying within your budget.

Another avenue to consider is the business services centers of such value-oriented office supply retailers as Office Depot and Staples, or full-service printing shops such as Kinko's or Copy Mat. These discount retailers and service houses offer greatly discounted business services that range from printing custom business cards to helping you create your own flyers and brochures. Many even offer design services at very reasonable prices.

You also can cut costs by engaging the chosen media by yourself. In this way, you won't have to pay the standard ad placement commission to an advertising agency. The commission is often 15% of the total media time and space cost, and 17% of the production cost. Offer to exchange your products or services for air time or ad space. Your chances for success with such trade-offs are greater with smaller media, such as community-based radio and television stations, than with larger stations. As a small business owner, you have a wealth of advertising options available to you. The following sections describe some that you should consider.

Print Advertising

Local/Community/Weekly Newspapers

If your home-based business draws its clients primarily from the local community, you'll find newspaper advertising invaluable. A display ad (usually at least one square inch with a design, logo, or other art element in addition to the words) or classified ad is not expensive compared to the major dailies, and, in fact, may be much more effective for your purposes. An attractive, well-placed ad in community publications puts your sales pitch in the homes of people who can easily travel to your location or reach you with a local phone call.

Classified ads can be effective if you offer a service, such as kitchen cabinet refinishing or antiques restoration. However, these ads are often less effective for entrepreneurs selling a commodity, such as antiques. Classified ads work best if you draw your clientele from a specific region. For instance, if you run a lawn-care service, aim to attract only customers in your area; it makes little sense to advertise in a newspaper whose audience is spread out too broadly for you to service.

Although display ads are more expensive than classifieds, they can be more effective at addressing your needs. Remember, it's how many potential *customers* see your ad, not just how many *people*. Try a less expensive classified ad to begin with, just to test the waters, before investing fully in a display ad.

Magazines

Consider some major classifications of magazines: consumer-oriented, women's, food, travel, business, men's, automotive, and sports. Although *Reader's Digest* continues to thrive, the era of the general-interest magazine has passed. Most magazines on the newsstands are targeted toward a specialized sector of readers. You will be able to target your audience by using specific publications. Classified ads in national magazines may work best for entrepreneurs who sell a product or provide a service that doesn't require meeting clients in person.

"Penny-Saver" Magazines

Home-based business owners may find that advertising in these local weekly publications works well for them. Bargain hunters often scan these handouts looking for a good deal. Because you run your business from home and have less overhead than your competitors do, you may be able to offer those who respond to your ad a deal they can't refuse. These publications work best for businesses that are looking for a local or regional clientele.

Newsletters

For reaching specialized markets, newsletters are great print vehicles. Because circulations are typically small, rates for advertising in newsletters are often very reasonable. Their circulations also are very narrowly targeted to readers of their specialized editorial content. In terms of cost-effectiveness, this is one of the best types of print media a home-based business can purchase.

Trade Journals

Dollar for dollar, trade journals may be the most accurately targeted medium. They are particularly useful if you serve specific types of businesses. If you were a freelance legal assistant, for instance, you might advertise in a regional or state law journal.

Yellow Pages

Many local businesses advertise their goods and services in the Yellow Pages. The phone company has specific categories for classifying businesses. Be careful to choose the most appropriate one(s). It may be worthwhile to advertise in more than one category or to cross-reference your listing.

Broadcast Advertising

Radio

Advertising on small, regional stations that broadcast to local markets is fairly reasonably priced. When you buy time on a station that reaches a limited area, you're not paying for wasted circulation. Contact local radio stations for details.

Television

Advertising on television has a reputation for being expensive, but TV costs can be surprisingly affordable. The price of television time depends on several factors: the size of the market area, the length of the ad, the time of day (or night) the ad appears, the rating of the program, the quantity of advertising purchased, and a handful of other factors.

Keep in mind that you must budget not only for the cost of running the spot, but also for the cost of producing it. This can range from a low of $50 for a simple, station-produced announcement to a sum well into four or five figures for a professionally produced spot.

Cable Television

Perhaps the medium best attuned to small-business owners is a local cable television station. Cable stations are very flexible; ad spots range anywhere from 10 to 120 seconds. The prices are usually quite reasonable; they depend on the number of subscribers to the channel, so you should ask each station's ad department for its rate scale. Some very localized cable stations offer 60-second spots for as little as $5, but rates can go much higher. Keep in mind that you also can buy local spots on national channels like ESPN, MTV, and CNN—quality air time—at a fraction of the cost of regular television advertising.

Cable-TV advertising can be very effective for entrepreneurs who sell a product—just think of past infomercial successes TopsyTail and Juiceman, which have enjoyed sales in the millions.

Infomercials

In recent years, start-up entrepreneurs have discovered that infomercials—those half-hour or hour-long commercials on cable TV—can be a great way to sell a new product. Production costs of an infomercial can reach thousands of dollars, but the expense can be worth the sales realized. Infomercials work well for companies operated from the home because customers need only call to place an order. They don't have to travel to your place of business. Start watching infomercials to see what approaches you like and what might work for you.

Video Brochures

You don't have a national sales force, and you probably don't have a huge travel and entertainment budget, so video brochures may be the answer to selling on a national level. Create a 6- to 10-minute video about your business, and send it out to prospects you can't reach in person.

Direct Mail

Fliers and Mailers

Fliers and other mailers are an affordable way to get information to a selected audience. And they are by far the most popular form of advertising among home-based businesses. Suppose a lawn-care specialist wants to introduce his new service. He might send a flier to all the homes within a 10-mile radius of his home office announcing that "Larry The Lawn Man" is in business. Listing services offered—mowing, edging, seeding, and so on—and a special introductory offer could garner a host of new clients. And once he has clients, they will start referring their neighbors to him—if he does a good job, of course.

To generate an effective flier or mailer, start with straightforward, no-nonsense copy. Be specific and accurate. A clever, catchy phrase can help the customer remember your firm, but a clumsy slogan will just as quickly deter response.

Layout is important. Knowing that the reader's eye follows the page from top to bottom and left to right, you can plan to catch the reader's attention with pictures, charts, graphs, or any number of visual grabbers.

Coupon Mailers

Coupon mailers are an ideal advertising avenue for service businesses, such as carpet cleaning, mobile auto repair, and lawn care, that draw their clientele from the local community.

Coupon mailers are generally of two kinds: (1) an envelope containing loose coupons from several local merchants, and (2) a small booklet of 10 to 20 pages. The cost of advertising in these mailers is cheap compared to the return they can generate.

The coupon should give a simple, clear statement of the special promotion you are advertising. It should also include your company name, logo, and location, along with an expiration date. If you forget the expiration date, the coupon must be honored for the life of your business.

You can find companies specializing in coupon mailers by looking in your Business-to-Business Yellow Pages under "Distributing Service—Circular, Sample, Etc."

Brochures

A brochure can give the impression of a serious, established, high-quality business—even if you just opened. A brochure is an ideal companion for your direct-mail marketing efforts, as well as an excellent handout.

Catalogs

There's more than one way to make money from a catalog. You don't have to start your own catalog to cash in on the $243 billion mail order industry. If you have only a single product, try to place that product in someone else's catalog. This cuts down on the work you have to do. In this instance, you would supply the products to the catalog company and they would take care of order-taking, fulfillment, and returns.

Getting your product into someone else's catalog isn't always easy. If you have a specialized product, say, wooden jigsaw puzzles for children, you should target a specialized catalog, such as a children's catalog or a toy catalog. There are hundreds of specialized catalogs on the market—from antique furnishings to high-tech computer equipment, and everything in between. Find a couple of catalogs in which you think your product will fit.

Many major national catalogs accept products from new entrepreneurs. To get your product into a catalog, you need to send a brief description of the product, a color photo, a statement of its wholesale price, and a sample (if it isn't too expensive or bulky to send).

Note that many major catalog companies require that, before they'll list your products, you must give proof of product liability insurance.

If you want to create your own catalog, you don't need to have hundreds of products on hand. Most catalogs fall between 20 and 36 pages in length, but a catalog can be as small as a single sheet if the product selection is too small to fill more pages.

Using sketches or black-and-white photos of your products can save you money on production costs. You don't need coated or glossy paper to impress your clients. Ask your printer for recommendations.

Postcards

Postcards are effective because they get your message across quickly and efficiently. Postcards are also less expensive to create and more cost-effective to mail than brochures and catalogs.

Because mailing costs are minimal, postcards should be mailed frequently. A postcard mailer should be sent out about seven times over the course of an 18-month period. This frequency will work well for your business because, although a prospect may not need your product or service on a given occasion, one of your postcard mailings may strike a chord when the prospect does need you.

The All-Important Mailing List

For any kind of direct response advertising, you'll need to create a mailing list; that is, a list of persons to whom you will send your ad. Mailing lists can be rented from list brokers, but you can also create your own list. It won't cost as much, but it will take more time to develop.

To build your own mailing list, try the following techniques:

- *Collect names of friends, business acquaintances, and relatives who may have an interest in your product or service.* Ask these same people to supply you with the names of other prospective customers. Collect the names of anyone you meet through networking—at the grocery store, at a convention, or at a seminar.
- *Include the names of anyone who makes a purchase from you.* (Even if they've already bought from you, they may need a reminder from time to time.)
- *Sponsor a contest at a local business and ask entrants to include their name and address.* For example, if you are a personal fitness trainer who also sells a fitness product, you may offer a free training session or sample product through some local gyms. Anyone who enters can then be put on your mailing list.
- *Try to get membership lists of trade associations or industry organizations within your target market.*

In addition to compiling your own list of names, you may want to rent a mailing list. Most list rental companies won't rent fewer than 5,000 names, so this alternative may be well beyond the scope of your business. If you are targeting a large market, keep in mind that you want your list to be as specific as possible, and the more specific a list is, the more expensive it is. A generic list of names will cost you anywhere from $40 and up, per 1,000 names. For each "select," or specification (i.e., women under the age of 35 who live in California and have children), count on paying more.

You can find list rental firms in your Yellow Pages under "Advertising—Direct Mail." Today's highly sophisticated mailing lists are designed to fit just about any category you want. The one-time rental fee varies, depending on your market and the size of the list.

Other Advertising Avenues

Bus Benches

Advertising on a bus bench can be an excellent medium for any product or service, whether the business is home-based or not. Essentially, you have a huge captive audience—drivers and pedestrians waiting for the bus, or stuck at red lights and in slow-moving traffic. One account executive at a Los Angeles-based bus bench manufacturing company said that an advertisement on one bus bench at a busy Los Angeles intersection will typically be seen by 35,000 to 50,000 people per day.

Bus-bench ads usually consist of simple two-color artwork with a company's name, brief copy describing the service, the address, and the telephone number. Think of them as huge business cards that present a company to the public. Rates and terms will vary from city to city and location to location. Call your city's mass-transit department or local bus company to find out who manufactures and/or rents advertising space on their bus benches.

Online Advertising

With the increasing popularity of online computer services, new advertising opportunities are arising for home-based business owners. Consider that the major online services—CompuServe, America Online, and Prodigy—boast million-plus memberships, with hundreds of new subscribers joining daily. And we can only guess how many millions of people are hooked onto the Internet. Just think, you could potentially introduce your service or product to millions of prospective customers with the touch of a button.

Getting the word out online is easy. If you own a tax preparation service, you could search your online service's membership directory for small businesses, then e-mail a message to them announcing your service. Or, you could search for a small business forum on the Internet and log on to chat directly with small business owners.

Using the principles that drive a direct-mail campaign, you can also create a mailing list for your e-mail. And you can send a sales letter (e-mail message) to all those prospects at the same time. To get hooked up to an online service, you'll need a computer, a modem, and an account with an online service or a local provider for the Internet. Check with the various online services for information on their prices and the services they offer.

Specialty Ad Items

You can have your company name imprinted on any number of items, from calendars to T-shirts to pencils to caps. Giving away specialty advertising items such as these can be an affordable way to keep your name in the public eye.

Personal Sales Letters

You don't always need expensive ads or high-tech strategies to land a sale. Sometimes, a personal letter can do more for your business than a colorful brochure or display ad. When you meet a prospect, be sure to follow up with a sales letter. Nothing fancy; just a few words about your product or service and how that prospect would benefit from doing business with you. For instance, a resume writer could send out a quick letter detailing how a strong resume can make a big difference to a job seeker, and might include a few success stories of clients who have landed good jobs.

A sales letter may be sent under the guise of a simple thank-you note. After meeting with a prospect, shoot off a quick acknowledgment and reiterate the benefits of your business.

Sales Presentations

Ads and coupons can only do so much for your business. Nothing can represent your product or service better than you can. Making a face-to-face presentation can make the difference in turning a prospect into a customer. If you sell a computer-related product, for example, potential customers may not understand exactly what your product can do for them unless you show them on their own computer. Moreover, if your product fits in a particularly competitive niche, you may find that your personality and professionalism are what win the sale. An effective presentation will highlight not only the product, but the company as well.

Sales presentations don't have to involve charts, graphs, and slides. All you need is a healthy dose of confidence and a strong knowledge of and belief in your business.

Is It Working?

In appraising prospective advertising media, weigh their benefits against their costs. Take the following into account:

1. *Reach.* Refers to the number of people whom your advertising will contact in a specific period of time.
2. *Frequency.* When you use specific media, how many times, on average, should the individuals in your target audience be exposed to your advertising message? It takes an average of three

or more exposures to an advertising message before consumers take action—that is, buy your product or use your service.

3. *Cost per thousand (CPM).* This is a standard measure of the costs of advertising in print media. You can figure out a given publication's CPM by taking the cost of the ad space and dividing it by the circulation of the publication, expressed in thousands. Compare the CPMs of different publications before you select one in which to advertise.

4. *Impact.* Does the medium in question offer full opportunities for appealing to customers' senses of hearing and sight in presenting design, color, or sound?

5. *Selectivity.* How much control do you have in determining who sees your advertising message? In other words, will the selected medium convey your message to the people most likely to use your products or services?

CREATING YOUR AD

Regardless of which advertising medium you select, the words and images you use to deliver your message are critical. Your advertising response plays a dynamic role in your overall marketing plan. The primary goal of your message, its ultimate purpose, is to capture the public's attention. A creative, effective message can be instrumental in establishing your company's image, attracting customers who otherwise might not have known about your company or considered buying your product or service.

As a home-based entrepreneur, you will need to keep your costs down, so you should consider creating much of your marketing and ad program by yourself. One note of caution, however: know your limitations. If you're not a good writer, be ready to hire a freelance copywriter. If you don't have a good eye for artwork or graphic design, hire a freelance designer to create your brochure. Try to balance comfortably between what you require, what you want, and what you can afford.

PROMOTING YOUR HOME-BASED BUSINESS

A thoughtful and well-designed advertising program may be the most effective way to publicize your business. When you purchase advertising, you determine what your message is and how you convey it. An effective ad campaign, however, may end up costing you a lot of money. If you're not careful, that expense can break your budget much faster than you think.

Public relations can enhance your image and boost your sales while keeping your costs down. Public relations should be considered a key marketing tool. You should always be prepared for any opportunity to publicize your business.

A beginning entrepreneur might ask: Can my products or services generate public interest? Would the media really be interested in covering my business? You can gain the attention of the media if you know how to market your skills and your business. Every day, newspapers and radio shows, and even local evening newscasts, are filled with general-interest stories. Experts are cited, companies are profiled, and individuals are interviewed. In each case, free publicity is generated, both by the subjects of the stories and by the commentators.

Publicity

Keep in mind that the major task of newspaper and magazine editors is filling their publications with newsworthy items. Starting a new business, sponsoring a contest, contributing to charities, or being the beneficiary of an unusual occurrence—all are newsworthy items that you may be able to parlay into media coverage.

The principal advantages of media publicity are:

- A news story or magazine article takes more time to read and gives more information than an ad. The more time readers spend with your story, and the more they learn about your business, the more likely they will remember you and your product or service.
- Being mentioned in a publication or on a TV or radio show can provide you with additional publicity that you may not be able to afford through paid advertising.
- Because your appearance in print or on a TV or radio show occurs only if it meets the standards of the editor or programming director, your company will gain additional credibility and a more positive public image.

When you begin any publicity campaign, you must make the right media contacts. For newspapers, the most likely contact is the local edition editor or city editor; for radio or cable television, it's the programming director. Don't be afraid to call these contacts directly. Call the newspaper or broadcast station, and ask for the name and correct title of the appropriate person and the exact spelling of his or her name. Whenever you engage in professional correspondence, paying attention to details and conducting your affairs in a professional manner are essential. Taking the time to find and address the right people will pay off for you.

Keep alert to anything that can give you publicity. Whether you're sponsoring a charity function, celebrating a business anniversary, or introducing an unusual new product, you may be able to take advantage of the story or event by building a connection to your business. Not all of your communications will be accepted by the media, but you only need one positive mention in a column, show, or interview to publicize you and your company. And once you do get your name in circulation, be sure to reprint all your publicity stories and news releases. They can become highly credible handouts and mailers.

CREATING A PROFESSIONAL IMAGE

Home-based entrepreneurs have a much tougher road to success than traditional business owners do. Traditional storefronts or office-based businesses can promote themselves by putting up a catchy sign, hanging a bright banner, or even renting spotlights to criss-cross the night sky. You, however, can do none of these things. You will need to depend on your advertising materials to inform your customers of your business. And because this contact may be the best and sometimes the only opportunity you have to introduce your business to potential customers, you must be able to present your business in a dynamic and clear way, with a style and focus that make customers remember you and your business. One of the most powerful ways to create this positive customer perception is by using a well-conceived name and a clean, dynamic logo; these two closely related elements of your business identity are crucial to the success of your business.

8

THE PRICE
IS RIGHT

The price you charge for your product or service may have a direct impact on the ultimate success of your business. If your prices are too high, customers may go to a competitor who offers a better deal; if you offer bargain basement prices, you may cut into your profit margin and stall your business's growth. Finding a price that appeals to customers and still gives you an adequate profit margin is a key to success.

Pricing is often neglected by home-based entrepreneurs because they do not understand the concepts associated with this business function. Many small business owners tend to take the cost of making their product or providing their service and multiply that number by an arbitrary figure, reasoning that the end price will produce a sufficient profit.

That calculation may or may not be true. The costs of operating the business may not have been covered, and an appropriate profit may not be produced. When the pricing is arbitrarily figured, the results will be just as arbitrary.

Costs and desired profit are just a few factors that entrepreneurs fail to include in their pricing scheme. There is also little regard for the competition and for the image the end price will produce for your company. All of these elements should be considered in conjunction with your overall business or marketing plan.

This chapter is designed to familiarize you with the fundamentals involved in pricing and the various methods employed. Keep in mind as you read through this chapter, however, that pricing is very subjective. What works for one company may not be entirely correct for another. The important thing to remember is that some basic rules apply to all home-based businesses.

As a home-based business owner, you may have an advantage when it comes to pricing. Because your overhead costs are likely to be less than your competitors', you may be able to offer a lower price to consumers without sacrificing quality. This can be a very strong selling point. However, don't price your product or service so low that you undercut your profits. In your pricing, you must include overhead, labor costs, material costs, profit margin, and your own time.

YOUR TIME IS MONEY

Figuring out how much your overhead expenses are, or what you need to spend on materials, is relatively easy. You can look at your receipts and bills and add up the numbers. On the other hand, deciding how much your own time is worth is far more subjective. Whether you sell a product or a service, you must set a value on your time, that is, give a dollar value to the time it takes you to complete a project. This stated value is especially important for service businesses, which essentially sell time and expertise.

For example, if you are a personal fitness trainer, you are selling the time you spend with clients *and* your experience and knowledge. Only so many hours in a day can be spent training clients, so you have to find a price that makes that time worthwhile for you. Remember, training your clients isn't the only time you spend on your business. What about all the hours you spend seeking out new clients, doing paperwork, reading books or magazines to stay on top of new fitness techniques, and driving to and from the gym or your clients' homes? This time counts too. Your pricing will have to reflect these "nonbillable" hours too.

To set a value on your time, consider your education, expertise, and professional reputation, in addition to some intangible factors, such as confidence and aggressiveness.

Many employees-turned-entrepreneurs use their former salary as a basis for their billing. This may not be the best formula. Your former job may have included some perks: health insurance, vacation days, a company car, membership in a gym, and so on. You would have to add these costs to your former salary in order to come out even.

What's a Profit?

Many novice home-based entrepreneurs confuse wages and profit. Let's say you sell a product through mail order. If you deduct all your expenses and costs from the money you receive from the sale, that's your profit, right? Wrong. You must deduct your wages (the money you are going to live on) from the revenue as well. Then, what's left over is profit.

Including a profit margin in your pricing strategy is the only way to ensure that your company will actually produce a profit, rather than simply providing you with a wage. That means adding a percentage of your product's or service's price to cover profit.

If you forget to include a profit margin in your pricing strategy, how costly can it be? Let's say you run a mobile auto detailing company from your home and you have calculated that the cost of providing your service (your hourly wage, equipment, overhead, and so on) comes to $50. Adding a 20% profit margin will take your price to the customer to $60. That may not seem like such a big difference to your customers, but when you multiply that extra $10 by the number of jobs you do per year, it adds up. If you do 5 detailing jobs per day, 5 days a week, 52 weeks a year, that's a total of 1,300 jobs. Multiply that total by the additional $10, and your business earned $13,000 profit:

$$1,300 \times \$50 \quad = \$65,000$$
$$1,300 \times \$60 \quad = \$78,000$$
$$\$78,000 - \$65,000 = \$13,000$$

Working a profit margin into your price also protects your business from unforeseen setbacks or problems. With the extra financial padding, your business is far more likely to survive the ups and downs of start-up.

Image, Time Commitment, and Pricing

Your pricing strategy should reflect the image you want your home-based business to project, and it should fit with the amount of time you want to spend on your business: high-priced, exclusive service for a few customers, or discounts for hordes of bargain-hunters? Either way—with high prices or discounts—your business can make a profit. It is up to you to decide whether you would rather do a lot of jobs at a low price or a few jobs at a high price.

If you are a graphic designer working from home, you can choose to do a series of big projects for one large corporate client or turn your emphasis to smaller clients and more short-term projects. For example, working for a large corporation, you could do a series of six two-month-long projects at $6,000 per project, which would bring in a total of $36,000 that year. You can make that same amount of money by seeking out clients who pay you $750 per week-long project.

Note that working with smaller clients and lower prices will require you to seek out more new business, but closing a deal for a bigger project could take more time. The length of time you spend seeking out new business may actually equal out, whether you are working on two projects a year or 20 jobs a year. Remember to factor the time you spend looking for new clients—not just the time you spend on the actual project—into your prices as well.

BASIC PRICING GUIDELINES

Whether your home-based business sells a product or provides a service, the price you charge your customers or clients will have a direct effect on the success of your business. Pricing strategy and computations can be complex, but the basic rules of pricing are straightforward.

- All prices must cover costs.
- The best and most effective way of lowering your sales prices is to lower costs.
- Prices must be changed as needed, to ensure that they reflect the dynamics of cost, demand, changes in the market, and response to your competition.
- Prices must be established to ensure sales. Do not price against a competitive operation alone; rather, price to sell.
- Product utility, longevity, maintenance, and end use must be judged continually, and target prices should then be adjusted accordingly.
- Prices must be set to preserve order in the marketplace. If you increase your marketing budget and raise your prices to offset that increase, but the competition doesn't follow suit, your price will not be consistent with the market.

Many different methods are used to establish prices. The rules listed above are universal and should be adhered to when forming and maintaining pricing strategies. To understand these rules better, you should first become familiar with the basic structure of pricing.

Cost Versus Price

Before you can set a price for your product or service, you have to determine the costs involved in running your business. If the price you set for your product or service doesn't cover your costs, you will have to infuse more cash into the business until your resources are depleted and your business fails.

Exactly how much does it cost to run your business? You must add fixed costs—equipment leases, loan repayments, management costs (i.e., salaried employees), and depreciation—to the variable costs of raw materials, inventory, utilities, and hourly wages/commissions. You must also calculate the costs generated by markdowns, shortages, damaged merchandise, employee discounts, cost of goods sold, and desired profits, and add them to the operating expenses listed above. You can then arrive at an initial price for your product.

The most important aspect of cost versus price—a factor that you must grasp if you are to learn how to price correctly—is that, ultimately, the market dictates the price you may charge for your product or service. Your costs of providing customers and/or clients with that product or service simply establish a minimum or break-even point. The range within which you must work is between that break-even figure and the maximum price you could demand (and get) for your product or service.

The Economic Theory of Pricing

What is the relationship between the price you set and the quantity of goods you can sell at that price? According to general economic theory, the higher the price you establish, the lower the customer demand for that product at that price. You can visually depict this ratio as a graph, a table, or an algebraic equation. Among businesspeople, it is usually referred to as the *demand curve,* and it graphically represents how revenues (i.e., price × units sold) change as price changes.

Quite often, new entrepreneurs learn of the demand curve and automatically infer that the *only* way to stimulate higher sales volume is by lowering prices. This is not always the case. Changes in the market can also affect the demand curve. Occasionally, these changes may enable a particular company to charge more *and* sell more—which seems to violate the theory. Actually, it does not. If the public *perceives* that a particular product has a significant value, consumers are generally willing to pay more for that product. That's why people are willing to pay more for a name brand than good old Brand X, even though there may be absolutely no difference in the quality of the two products.

Pricing and Repricing Considerations

Don't make the mistake of thinking that your prices are set in concrete. They aren't. Just because you've established a price doesn't mean you can simply forget about it. That is a mistake that many first-time small business owners commit. Because pricing is so important, and can be so confusing, many entrepreneurs set prices once and "hope for the best." In reality, they are consigning themselves to lost profits. Or, in effect, they are putting profits directly into the pockets of their competitors. A smart small business owner checks pricing continuously, to make certain that his or her company always makes the best price available.

Certain circumstances warrant pricing or repricing consideration, such as:

1. When you introduce a new product or product line.
2. When you're testing for the best price.
3. When you decide to pursue a new market.
4. When your competitors change their prices.
5. During high inflation/recession.
6. When you plan to change your overall sales strategy.

As a rule of thumb, if the economic situation changes, your competition changes, your product mix changes, the market changes, or any other factor affecting your business experiences a change. You should then reconsider your previous pricing decisions in light of these new factors in the market.

Price should also reflect a good–better–best relationship among similar or competing products, if the market is to retain some semblance of order. Your creativity in merchandising, flair for the inventive, product selection, and motivating management style are all significant factors in this market balance. List the activities you perform that are designed to create customers and keep them. Monitor those activities against your actual costs and how they relate to price. It's vital to the success of your business for you to recognize that too high a price cannot compensate for overly high promotional costs. Simply raising your prices does not solve a cost problem—it only compounds it.

Covering your costs is important, but it is only one aspect of pricing. Overcompensating (by raising your prices) is quite another matter, and will ultimately upset the market balance. This is particularly dangerous for businesses that seem to be in noncompetitive markets. All too often, a company without competition will price its products or services so high that it creates the perfect environment for a new competitor to undercut it.

PRICING METHODS

Many methods of establishing prices are available. They include:

- Cost-plus pricing.
- Demand pricing.
- Competitive pricing.
- Markup pricing.

Cost-Plus Pricing

Cost-plus pricing is used by many manufacturers. The key to employing cost-plus pricing effectively is ensuring that the "plus" figure not only covers all overhead, but generates the required percentage of profit as well. The following sample calculation should help you grasp the concept of cost-plus pricing. Let's say you run a mail order operation from home, selling a single product. Here's how you would calculate your pricing:

Cost of materials	$20
Cost of labor	10
Overhead	10
Total Cost	40
Desired profit on sales (20%)	$10
Required sale price	$50

To calculate 20% profit on sales, multiply the total cost ($40) by 1.25, which equals the required sale price of $50.

If you decide to employ cost-plus pricing, you must ensure that *all* costs are accounted for in overhead. In this instance, a mail order operation would need to include freight, packing, and postage charges in addition to other costs of doing business. Should you fail to include a cost in the overhead category when calculating price, that cost will reduce profit.

Demand Pricing

Demand pricing is determined by the optimum combination of volume and profit. Products usually sold through a variety of sources at differing prices—such as those sold at retailers, discount retailers/chains, wholesalers, or direct mail marketers—are good examples of goods whose price is set based on demand. A wholesaler who buys significantly greater quantities than a retailer will purchase at a markedly lower unit price. The wholesaler will then seek to generate profit from a greater volume of sales because the product is priced lower than what the retailer will eventually charge customers. The retailer must pay more per unit because he or she is stocking (and selling) significantly fewer units than the wholesaler. The retailer cannot sell at the wholesaler's price and therefore must charge a higher price to retail customers. A direct mail company can charge even more for a product, but the higher price is offset by the firm's higher promotion cost.

Demand pricing is a difficult method to master because you must correctly calculate *beforehand* what price will generate the optimum ratio of profit to volume.

Competitive Pricing

Competitive pricing is generally used when there is an established market price for a particular product or service. If you do windshield repair and replacement and all your competitors are charging $100 for a replacement windshield, for example, that's what you should charge. Competitive pricing is used most often within markets where it is difficult to differentiate one product from another. If a major player in the market acts as the market leader, that company will often set the price that other, smaller companies within that same market will be compelled to follow.

To employ competitive pricing properly and effectively, it is *imperative* that you know exactly what prices each of your competitors has established. Call your competitors and ask for their pricing information. You don't have to tell them that you are starting a similar business; just say you're interested in their products and/or services. Determine what price you would like to set in an optimum situation. You must then gauge your prices against the market as a whole and decide, based on direct comparison, whether you can defend the prices you have set. If you wish to charge more than your competitors, you have to be able to make a case for the higher price, such as providing a superior product or offering additional services. For instance, if you run a windshield repair service and your competitors charge $100 for a replacement window, you can charge more if you offer something extra: window tinting at no extra cost, a money-back guarantee, or on-site replacement (meaning you go to your clients' home or place of business). In your marketing and advertising efforts, call attention to these extra services in order to justify the higher price.

Before making a final commitment to your prices, it is advisable to determine the level of price awareness within the market.

If you wish to use competitive pricing to set the fees for a service business, be aware that, unlike a situation in which several companies are selling essentially the same products, services vary widely from one firm to another. You could conceivably charge a higher price for better quality of service and still be considered competitive within your market.

For example, if you are a wedding coordinator, you may offer your clients more choices when it comes to hiring a photographer, florist, or caterer. Or, you may provide services such as honeymoon travel plans for the bride and groom, or travel planning for out-of-town wedding guests. Extras like these can give you a competitive edge even if your prices are higher.

Markup Pricing

Used by manufacturers, wholesalers, and retailers, markup is calculated by adding a set amount to the cost of a product, to arrive at the price to the customer. For example, if the cost of a product is $100 and your selling price is $140, the markup would be $40. To find the percentage of markup on *cost*, divide the dollar amount of markup by the dollar amount of product cost:

$$\$40 \div \$100 = 40\%$$

This pricing method often generates confusion—not to mention lost profits—among entrepreneurs, particularly first-time small business owners, because markup, expressed as a percentage of cost, is often confused with gross margin, expressed as a percentage of selling price. In the next section, we will discuss in greater depth the difference between markup and margin.

PRICING A PRODUCT VS. PRICING A SERVICE

Although most pricing methods can be used for either a product or a service, some factors differ. When you are selling a product, you will have to include manufacturing costs, material costs, packaging costs, and inventory costs, among others, to your price. Service providers may not need to include these factors in their pricing, but they have other considerations. Should they calculate a price per project? per hour? per day? per person? In the following sections, we will explore the differences in pricing a product and a service.

Pricing a Product

To price products, you must become completely familiar with pricing structures, including the difference between margin and markup. As mentioned already, every product should be priced to cover its production or wholesale cost, freight charges, a proportionate share of overhead (fixed and variable operating expenses), and a reasonable profit. Such factors as high overhead, unpredictable insurance rates, shrinkage (theft, shippers' mistakes), seasonality, shifts in wholesale or raw material product costs, freight expenses, and sales or discounts will all affect the final pricing.

Overhead Expenses
We use *overhead* here to refer to all nonlabor expenses required to operate a business. Expenses can be divided into fixed expenses and variable expenses.

- *Fixed expenses.* No matter what the volume of sales is, these costs must be met every month. Fixed expenses include: depreciation on fixed assets (such as cars and office equipment); liability and other insurance; utilities; membership dues and subscriptions (which can sometimes be affected by sales volume); and accounting and legal costs. All of these continue at the same rate with little or no relation to a firm's revenues.

- *Variable expenses.* Most so-called variable expenses are really semivariable. They will fluctuate from month to month in relation to sales and other factors, such as promotional efforts, seasons, and variations in the prices of suppliers' products and services. In this category are: phone calls, office supplies and business forms (the more business, the greater the use of these items), printing, packaging, mailing, and advertising and promotion. In estimating variable expenses, it is common to ignore month-to-month variations (unless they are large and can be accurately predicted in advance) and use an average figure based on an estimate of the yearly total.

Cost of Goods Sold

Cost of goods sold, also known as *cost of sales,* refers to your cost of purchasing products for resale, or your cost of manufacturing the products. Freight and delivery charges are customarily included in this figure. Accountants segregate cost of goods sold on an operating statement because it provides a measure of gross profit margin when compared with sales, an important yardstick for measuring a firm's profitability. Expressed as a percentage of total sales, cost of goods sold will vary greatly from one kind of business to another. But within a given line of business, it should fall within a relatively narrow range.

Normally, the cost of goods sold bears a close relationship to sales. It will vary, however, if increases in the prices paid for merchandise cannot be offset by increases in sales prices, or if special bargain purchases are made that increase profit margins. These situations seldom make a large percentage change in the relationship between cost of goods sold and sales. Therefore, the cost of goods sold is a semivariable expense.

Computing Margin

Margin, or gross margin, is the difference between total sales and the cost of those sales. For example:

Total sales	$1,000
Cost of sales	300
Margin	$ 700

Gross profit (GP) margin can be expressed in dollars or as a percentage. As a percentage, the GP margin is always stated as a percentage of net sales. The equation is:

(Total sales − Cost of sales) ÷ Net sales = GP margin

In the above example, the margin would be 70%:

($1,000 − $300) ÷ $1,000 = 70%

When all operating expenses (salaries, utilities, insurance, advertising, and so on) and other expenses are deducted from the GP margin, the remainder is the net profit before taxes. If the GP margin is not sufficiently large, there will be little or no net profit left.

Some businesses require a higher GP margin than others in order to be profitable, because the costs of operating different kinds of businesses vary tremendously. If the operating expenses in one line of business are comparatively low, then a lower GP margin will still yield the owners an acceptable profit.

The following comparison illustrates this point. Keep in mind that operating expenses and net profit are shown as the two components of GP margin, i.e., their combined percentages (of net sales) equal the GP margin.

	Business A	**Business B**
Net sales	100%	100%
Cost of sales	40%	65%
Gross profit margin	60%	35%
Operating expenses	43%	19%
Net profit	17%	16%

Computing Markup

Markup and (gross profit) margin on a single product, or group of products, are often confused. The reason for this confusion is that, when expressed a percentage, margin is always figured as a percentage of the *selling price*, while markup is traditionally figured as a percentage of the *seller's cost*. The equation is:

$$(\text{Total sales} - \text{Cost of sales}) \div \text{Cost of sales} = \text{Markup}$$

Using the numbers from the preceding example, if you purchase goods for $300 and price them for sale at $1,000, your markup *in dollars* will be $700. As a percentage, this markup comes to 233%.

$$(\$1,000 - \$300) \div \$300 = 233\%$$

In other words, if your business requires a 70% margin in order to show a profit, your average markup will have to be 233%.

You can see from the example that, although markup and margin may be the same in dollars ($700), they represent *two different things* as percentages (233% vs. 70%). More than a few new businesses have failed to make their expected profits because the owner assumed that if the markup is X%, the margin will also be X%. This is not the case.

The table on page 195 shows what the markup on cost must be in order to give the desired margin in a number of more common cases. To

Markup Table—Pricing a Product

Margin % of Selling Price	Markup % of Cost	Margin % of Selling Price	Markup % of Cost	Margin % of Selling Price	Markup % of Cost	Margin % of Selling Price	Markup % of Cost
4.8	5.01	18	22	32	47.1	50	100
5	5.3	18.5	22.7	33.3	50	52.4	110
6	6.4	19	23.5	34	51.5	54.5	120
7	7.5	20	25	35	53.9	56.5	130
8	8.7	21	26.6	35.5	55	58.3	140
9	10	22	28.2	36	56.3	60	150
10	11.1	22.5	29	37	58.8	61.5	160
10.7	12	23	29.9	37.5	60	63	170
11	12.4	23.1	30	38	61.3	64.2	180
11.1	12.5	24	31.6	39	64	65.5	190
12	13.6	25	33.3	39.5	65.5	66.7	200
12.5	14.3	26	35	40	66.7	69.2	225
13	15	27	37	41	70	71.4	250
14	16.3	27.3	37.5	42	72.4	73.3	275
15	17.7	28	39	42.8	75	75	300
16	19.1	28.5	40	44.4	80	76.4	325
16.7	20	29	40.9	46.1	85	77.8	350
17	20.5	30	42.9	47.5	90	78.9	375
17.5	21.2	31	45	48.7	95	80	400

use this table, find your margin or gross profit percentage in the left-hand column of each pair of columns. Multiply the cost of the article by the corresponding percentage in the markup column. Add this result to the cost to give you the correct selling price.

Pricing a Service

How should you set the price(s) for your service business? Procedures vary with the type of business, but the same three elements are present in every situation:

1. Labor and materials costs.
2. Overhead.
3. Profit.

These factors must be considered not only during your start-up phase, but also when you decide to increase the level of service-fee income in your business.

Labor and Materials

Labor costs include wages and benefits you pay the employees and/or subcontractors who perform, supervise, or manage your service business. If you as the owner are even partly involved in executing a job, then the cost of your labor, proportionate to your input, must be included in the total labor charge. This amount will be quite significant during the first year or so (at least).

Labor cost is usually expressed as an hourly rate. Check in your library's reference room for government publications that give national and state salary ranges for different occupations. The editors of trade publications might also have such information. Also check for current rates in classified newspaper ads and at your Chamber of Commerce.

Labor can be subcontracted. Under this system, you do not put a worker on the payroll as an employee. Thus, you eliminate the time and expense associated with timekeeping, payroll preparation, payroll taxes, and benefits. Also, when labor is purchased for each job on a contract basis, the full cost is agreed on in advance; you know exactly what your cost (for that particular project) will be.

Carefully estimate the labor time it will take to accomplish each job on which you bid. For example, if you estimate that your service contract will take 2 hours of labor during each 24-hour period of a 5-day week, plus 2 hours of supervision each month, you would compute your labor and materials cost for a month as follows:

	Hours/Month × Rate	= Cost
Labor	2 hrs. × 21 days × $4.50/hr.	= $189
Supervision	2 hrs. × $6.00/hr.	= 12
Total labor cost		= $201
Supplies (@ 6% of labor cost)		= 12
Total labor and materials		= $213

If you put people on payroll instead of subcontracting labor, add 10% to this total to cover payroll taxes, workers' compensation, and any other related costs.

Overhead

Overhead refers to all the indirect expenses required to operate your business: insurance premiums, legal and accounting fees, telephone, advertising, vehicle maintenance, equipment depreciation, business forms, office supplies, dues, memberships, and similar payments.

Overhead expenses can vary substantially from one business to another, depending on the way you operate. If you have past operating expenses to guide you, overhead is not difficult to calculate. Total all your expenses for one year, excluding labor and materials, and divide this number by your total cost of labor and materials to determine your overhead rate. For example, suppose your costs and expenses for a one-year period were as follows:

Overhead expenses	$31,200
Labor and materials Cost	$52,000
Overhead rate ($31,200 ÷ $52,000)	60%

Overhead may cost anywhere from 30% to 60% of your cost of labor and materials. You can raise or lower that figure to suit your own kind of operation. Overhead will vary greatly from one industry to another. Using an arbitrary overhead rate of 60% as just computed, and continuing with the example detailed above, we now have:

Labor and materials cost	$213
Overhead (60% of $213)	$128
Subtotal of operating costs	$341

Profit

Profit is the amount of income earned after all costs for providing the service have been met. When calculating the price of a service, profit is applied in the same manner as markup on the cost of a product. For instance, if you plan to net 20% before taxes on your gross sales, you will need to apply a profit factor of about 25% to your labor and overhead to achieve that target. Doing this in our example, we have:

Subtotal of operating costs	$341
Profit (25% of $324)	$ 85
Price you quote your customer	$426

Note that the $85 profit ends up as 20% of $426 (the "selling price") as was intended. The table presented earlier (page 195) gives you the appropriate percentage markups. Ignore references to the correct "selling price" when computing a net profit factor for your service. You can still use the table.

First, decide what percentage of the price you quote your customer is to be your net profit. Find this percentage in the left-hand column of each pair of columns. Then multiply the total of your labor, materials, and overhead by the percentage in the "Markup" (right-hand) column.

Applying the percentage in the "Markup" column will give you the desired net profit percentage in the left-hand column.

If you compare the price of $426 with the cost of labor ($201) already estimated, you will notice that one figure is almost double the other. Some contractors use this ratio as a basis for determining price. They estimate their labor costs and then double that figure to arrive at their bid price. Pricing can be tedious and time-consuming, especially if you don't have a knack for it. Some contractors seem to have a "sixth sense" when it comes to pricing and estimating; they know what they need to ask to make a job profitable to them.

If you're just starting out, you obviously won't have the skill of a seasoned pro. If your quote is too low, you will either rob yourself of some profit or be forced to lower the quality of your work to meet the price. If you estimate too high, you may lose the contract altogether, especially if you are in a competitive bidding situation. Make it your business to learn how to estimate labor time accurately and how to calculate your overhead properly, so that when you quote a price, you can be competitive and still make the profit you require.

ESTIMATING A JOB

The first step in preparing an estimate is to identify the variables that will affect the time it takes to perform your particular service or to complete work on your product. Variables are unique to each home-based business. Draw on your expertise to compose a complete list.

Calculate Your Costs

Once you estimate the number of hours required for you and your personnel (if any) to do the job according to the client's specifications, you can calculate labor costs. If you're bidding on a job that calls for a monthly fee, figure the number of hours each worker will work in a month. If the job needs to be done 5 times a week, figure 21 work-days in a month. If it is to be done 3 times a week, figure 13 workdays in a month. Then multiply the wage rate for each worker by the number of hours you schedule for the job.

Next, calculate the cost of materials and supplies. If you don't have actual cost records, estimate your supplies cost as a percentage of labor. Later, as you do business and develop records, you can prepare estimates based on actual purchases of materials.

Once you start a job, you may find that it is going to cost you more than you thought—in time commitment, materials, or labor costs. If the additional costs arise from a client's changing wishes, you can try to renegotiate with the client. Using the kitchen remodeling example, imagine that a customer originally wants the cabinets redone in a certain type of wood, then decides to ask for imported Italian marble instead. You can renegotiate the additional material costs, but what about the extra time you'll have to wait for the marble to arrive from Italy? You may not have enough time to start another job in the interim, and you could be losing money by not working. These kinds of things may be negotiable as well.

PRICING GOALS

The goal in pricing a service is to mark up the labor and materials costs sufficiently to cover overhead expenses and generate sufficient profit. First-time business owners often fail without realizing that they have priced their services too low.

If your competition is underbidding you, think carefully before lowering your price. Can you reduce your overhead? Are your cost estimates accurate? Don't forgo your budgeted profit just to get a contract. A business that does not earn an adequate profit is more vulnerable to total failure because it does not have the cushion that good profits provide for absorbing costly mistakes.

If a client wants your services but doesn't like your price, ask yourself whether it's better to turn down a project rather than set a price-cutting precedent. In fields requiring genuine expertise, price is a consideration, but seldom is it more important than qualifications.

REDUCTIONS AND PREMIUMS

On some occasions, it may be to your advantage to offer a premium or a reduced price. If a client wants immediate results and requests extended hours or increased production levels, an extra charge is reasonable.

You may want to grant price reductions to clients who can do some of the required tasks more economically than you can. Also, long-term projects ensuring long-term income, or projects that may lead to lucrative follow-up business, may warrant discounts. Then you can consider a discount an investment.

Be sure there is a good reason for any discount. If you arbitrarily lower your rate, the client may believe you were only trying to overcharge in the first place.

9

FINANCIAL MANAGEMENT

Without the means or space to hire a full-time staff of employees, you must tackle all the tasks of business ownership yourself, and that includes managing your finances. This can be a stumbling block for many new entrepreneurs—especially if they have little or no experience with financial management.

Many start-up entrepreneurs make financial faux pas. One of the most common and devastating is undercapitalization, which can mean missing payments to suppliers and vendors or having to go without a paycheck once in a while. With the right financial management techniques, you can avoid these problems.

The way you handle your business's financial assets will determine, at least in part, the degree of your entrepreneurial success. Your capital is not merely a collection of money and property; it is a powerful business tool deserving your careful attention. Making capital work for you requires careful management of your business, especially your current and future assets.

Careful financial planning is necessary throughout the life of your business. This chapter analyzes the major tools used in financial planning: the components of working capital and analysis methods, working with banks, and credit management and collections.

You must efficiently manage your money so that you can:

1. Avoid an excessive investment in fixed assets.
2. Understand banking relationships better.
3. Maintain receivables and net working capital in proper proportion to sales.
4. Plan your taxes effectively so that they become an asset instead of a necessary evil.

All financial difficulty can be traced to a violation of one or more of these principles of financial management.

WORKING CAPITAL

Most entrepreneurs fail to manage working capital properly because they don't fully understand it. It assumes various forms, and not all businesses involve the same kinds of working capital; retail stores, for example, do not need to contend with accounts receivable, just as service businesses do not keep large inventories of finished goods. Home-based entrepreneurs, meanwhile, may deal with some or all forms of working capital, albeit probably on a much smaller scale than large corporations.

To make sure you manage your working capital effectively, the functions described in the following sections are critical.

Manage Your Cash and Liquid Assets

The cash your company can most easily access includes income from sales as well as securities and short-term certificates of deposit. Maintaining an accurate and well-planned cash budgeting system is vital to the financial security of your business because it will let you know how much cash you have on hand, compared to current expenses. If for any reason the cash on hand is not enough to meet expenses that are due and payable, you will run a negative cash flow. If you own a videotaping service, for instance, and your customers don't pay you on time, you may find yourself coming up short when you need to purchase new cassettes to perform other jobs. If you can't buy the necessary materials, you won't be able to do those other jobs and your income will stall. You may be able to sustain losses like these for a short time, but running large negatives for successive months will eventually put you into bankruptcy. Determine the cycle of your cash peaks and valleys so you can meet your financial requirements by borrowing the necessary capital.

Monitor Accounts Receivable

To manufacturing or service-based entrepreneurs, we cannot stress enough the importance of managing your accounts receivable. The best way to ensure that your business will have an adequate amount of cash on hand is to require *payment upon receipt* of products or services. That may not always be possible, but there are ways to manage your accounts receivable to make sure your business gets the money owed to it.

- Ask for deposits or partial payments up front.
- Offer discounts for cash payments or payments at the time of sale.
- Check a customer's credit record before extending credit.
- Set up specific terms for credit payments; for instance, within 30 days after receipt of invoice.
- Bill immediately upon delivery of your service or product.

Don't wait for bills to be overdue before calling debtor customers. For example, a desktop publisher could call a customer about one to two weeks after delivering an invoice. This call can start as a follow-up call to make sure the customer is happy with the desktop turnout, and it can include a reminder that the bill is due. Being proactive can avoid problems later on.

Use Trade Credit Sparingly

You may be able to obtain a large amount of credit from suppliers, to offset some of your start-up costs, but don't mismanage or abuse this valuable asset. Never let accounts payable lapse beyond the prescribed terms. The effect on both your relationship with suppliers and your credit rating will be negative.

Make Timely Payments to Reduce Debts

To get your home-based venture off the ground, you may have to borrow capital. To determine which type of financing is best for you, you have to evaluate your financial situation and your capacity to manage debt. This means knowing when repayment of debts will fall and judging whether there will be funds to meet those obligations.

Take Operating Expenses and Taxes into Account

Monthly operating costs—including payroll, utilities, and insurance—fall into the category of operating expenses. Like federal, state, and local taxes, they require that enough funds are available at the due time. If you decide to hire employees and then realize you can't pay them, they will not work for you. If you don't pay your taxes, the government might shut you down until you do.

To ensure the current and future financial health of your business, you should constantly monitor these items and note any changes. By maintaining complete and accurate records of your working capital, you'll be able to react more quickly to any financial changes. If you are a home-based business owner who provides products, not services, you will have to take inventory into consideration as well.

If you plan to manufacture, assemble, or distribute products from your home, most of your capital investment (as much as 60% of current assets) will be in inventory. It's very important for you to keep track of your inventory, to protect against losing money through overstocking or shortages. For example, your business may require heavy inventory in anticipation of Christmas, Valentine's Day, and Mother's Day, and very light stock at other times of the year.

ANALYSIS METHODS

Over the years, many tools for financial management have been developed. Ratio analyses, return-on-investment guides, and break-even analyses are among the most popular. Each is discussed here in detail.

Ratio Analyses

Ratio analyses determine the stability of various financial aspects of your home-based operation, enabling you to gauge your business's financial weaknesses and strengths. Ratio analyses also let you compare your company's performance to similar businesses in your industry.

Don't assume, however, that ratio analyses will tell you everything you need to know about your business's financial performance. They have their limitations:

- *They are based only on the past performance of the company.* They don't offer any indication of present or future performance.

- *They are developed for specific periods.* If you operate a seasonal business, they may not provide an accurate measure of your financial performance.
- *Not all businesses are the same.* Ratios are based on industry averages extrapolated from a survey of financial statements. Keep in mind that businesspeople prepare their financial statements differently. The financial ratios that result may not present an accurate picture of the average business in your industry.

Measure of Liquidity

The first financial ratio we'll discuss is the measure of liquidity. This ratio analyzes the amount of available liquid assets your business has, at any given time, to meet accounts or notes payable. The measure of liquidity will tell you how much cash you have on hand, the amount of assets that can readily be turned into cash, and how quickly you can do so. A good rule of thumb to maintain your financial health is to remain as liquid as possible.

Current Ratio

Perhaps the best-known ratio analysis is the current ratio. This is the difference between your current assets and current liabilities, plus a safety margin for miscellaneous losses such as bad debts. To calculate the current ratio, divide the current assets by the current liabilities on your balance sheet. For instance, current assets of a tax preparation service could be $30,000 and current liabilities $10,000, which would give the following current ratio:

$$\$30,000 \div 10,000 = 3:1$$

Generally, a current ratio of at least 2:1 is good. You can compare your current ratio with those of competing businesses in your industry by referring to surveys conducted by various trade associations and marketing companies.

Quick Ratio

Another common ratio is the acid-test or quick ratio. Like the measure of liquidity, the acid-test ratio examines the liquidity of your business. To calculate it, total all your liquid assets: cash on hand, any government securities, receivables, and so on. Then divide these assets by your current liabilities. For example, current liquid assets of $3,000 cash, $5,000 in receivables, and another $2,000 in securities (for a total of $10,000) along with current liabilities of $5,000 would give you the following quick ratio:

$$\$10,000 \div \$5,000 = 2:1$$

For most businesses, a quick ratio of 2:1 or better is sufficient. If, however, there are factors that will slow down payment of receivables, or the due dates on your receivables exceed the time stipulation of your payables, you will need a higher ratio. For instance, if you have a mobile DJ business and you are expecting $1,500 in payments from three gigs on the 15th of the month, but you have bills you need to pay by the 1st, you're going to run into trouble.

Inventory turnover (the number of times per year an inventory investment revolves) will also help a product-oriented business determine its liquidity. The turnover provides a measure of the amount of capital invested in inventory in order to meet operation requirements.

Profitability Measures

Making money is what being in business is all about. Fortunately, there are several measures you can apply to help you determine the profitability of your home-based business once you are under way. These measures are: asset earning power, return on owner's equity, net profit on sales, investment turnover, and return on investment (ROI).

Asset Earning Power
This is a ratio calculated by taking your earnings before taxes and interest and dividing that number by your total assets. It is a measure designed to illustrate the earning power of your total assets, not just your liquid assets. For instance, total earnings (before taxes and interest) of $100,000 and total assets of $300,000 would generate an asset earning power of .33, or 33%. This shows you that your total assets are earning you 33% of their present marketable value.

Return on Owner's Equity
The ratio measures the return, or profit, you yield from the amount of equity you've invested in your home-based business. Equity in a company is usually based on capital investment, which incorporates both initial and ongoing capitalization. You can also include any intangible assets such as patents or trade secrets that have been contributed to the business in exchange for equity. If you are the only investor in your company, you control the total equity.

To compute the return on owner's equity, you first have to calculate your average equity investment in the business over a 12-month period. You can find this number on your balance sheet. Divide your net profit by the average equity to arrive at your return on owner's equity. If, for example, you run a personalized children's book business from home and have an average annual investment in the business of $10,000 and your net profit is $6,000, your return on owner's equity would be .60, or 60%.

Net Profit on Sales

This measures the difference between your net sales and what you spend to operate your business. To determine the net profit on sales, you have to divide the net profit by the net sales. The net profit of $6,000 from the above example measured against net sales of $36,000 would give you a net profit on sales of .17 or 17%.

Investment Turnover

Like inventory turnover, investment turnover is used to determine the amount of times per year that your total investment (or assets) revolves. To calculate your investment turnover, divide your total annual net sales by your total assets. If your net sales are $50,000 and your total assets are $30,000, your investment turnover would be 1.6.

Return on Investment (ROI)

This determines the performance of a business based on its profitability. There are several ways to determine ROI, but the simplest is to divide the net profit by total assets. If your annual net profit was $10,000 and total assets were $30,000, your ROI would be .33 or 33%.

You can use ROI in several different ways to measure your business's profitability. For instance, you can use ROI to measure the performance of pricing policies, inventory investment, capital equipment investment, and so forth. Some other ways to use ROI within your company are:

- Dividing net income, interest, and taxes by total liabilities to measure *rate of earnings of total capital employed.*
- Dividing net income and income taxes by proprietary equity and fixed liabilities to produce a *rate of earnings on invested capital.*
- Dividing net income by total capital plus reserves to calculate the *rate of earnings on proprietary equity and stock equity.*

Break-Even Analysis

The break-even analysis is important when you are in the planning stages of your business start-up. It is an essential piece of information which, in its most powerful application, provides quantitative support for your business plan. In other words, it shows you *and* potential investors how you plan to cover your costs and turn a profit. The break-even analysis tells you how much money you need to make—daily, weekly, or monthly—in order to pay all of your expenses.

To put together a break-even analysis, you first have to separate the variable costs from the fixed costs of your business. For the analysis, the only true variable costs are those directly related to the number of units you sell or jobs you perform. Remember that your total overhead will equal the sum of your fixed and variable expenses.

Break-Even Analysis for a Home-Based Product-Oriented Business

The following is a detailed example of a break-even analysis for a home-based mail order business. The first step is to separate monthly fixed and variable costs:

Fixed Costs

Utilities	$ 75
Office supplies	50
Professional services	50
Interest	25
Maintenance	35
Depreciation	30
Interest	25
Advertising	480
Mailing list rental	400
Insurance	110
Total	$1,280

Variable Costs

Cost of product	$1.68/unit
Cost of shipping	0.90/unit
Telemarketing commission	1.80/unit
Cost of fulfillment	1.10/unit
Total	$5.48/unit

Once you've calculated the fixed and variable costs, apply a markup factor to the product cost. The percentage you plan to charge for each item, above your cost for the item, is your gross profit margin. Refer to the markup table presented earlier (page 195). For example, if your profit margin is 54.5%, then your markup will have to be 120%. To find your selling price, take the product cost and multiply it by 120%:

$$\$5.48 \times 120\% = \$6.57$$

Your selling price would be:

$$\$5.48 + \$6.57 = \$12.05$$

Break-Even Analysis for a Home-Based Service Business

Other than having different variable costs and using *work performed* instead of *units sold* as your measurement, the process of calculating the break-even point is identical for a service-oriented business. The following example is for a home-based desktop publishing operation (the printing costs reflect the average monthly printing cost, assuming that the business spends $19,110 per year on printing):

Fixed Costs

Utilities	$ 120
Payroll	1,062
Owner's salary	1,750
Office supplies	80
Interest	—
Advertising	700
Professional services	90
Insurance	150
Maintenance	30
Transportation	100
Subscriptions/Dues	10
Depreciation	40
Miscellaneous	400
Total	$4,532

Variable Costs

Printing costs	$2.75 per book
Total	$2.75 per book

Once you know your monthly operating expenses, you are ready to apply a markup factor to the product cost—determined by applying a profit factor to the sum of your cost of labor, materials, and overhead. Your gross profit margin is the percentage you plan to charge for each item above your cost for the item. To cover expenses, book publishers often price their books at six to eight times their production costs. To find your selling price, take the product cost and multiply it by 550%:

$$\$2.75 \times 550\% = 15.13$$

Your selling price would be:

$$\$2.75 + \$15.13 = \$17.88$$

Next, take the various components in both examples and determine at what point, in terms of units sold (for the mail order business) or jobs performed (for the publishing business), these owners will pay all of their expenses and begin to make a profit. Use the break-even equation:

$$\text{Break-even} = F \div (S - V)$$

where F = fixed expenses, S = selling price, and V = variable expenses. Inserting data from the examples above, here are the results for the mail order business.

$$\text{Break-even} = \$1{,}255 \div (\$12.05 - \$5.48) = 191 \text{ units}$$

If this business doesn't raise prices or reduce expenses, it will need to sell 191 units in order to pay all expenses and start making a profit.

Here are the results for the desktop-publishing business.

$$\text{Break-even} = \$4{,}532 \div (\$17.88 - \$2.75) = 300 \text{ books}$$

According to this hypothetical break-even analysis, with no price change or reduction in expenses, this business will need to sell 300 jobs in order to pay all expenses and start making a profit.

FINANCIAL STATEMENTS

Financial statements are the tools used in business to "keep score." There are three important statements that will become familiar to you, if they are not already. They are integral for planning and attracting start-up or expansion capital, and will help you form your business plan—the blueprint that will guide your business. These statements are the balance sheet, the profit and loss or income statement, and the cash-flow statement. A brief explanation of each of these statements follows.

The Balance Sheet

A balance sheet is a table of the assets and liabilities (summary of credits and debits) as well as the capital (owner's equity) of a business at one point in time. A balance sheet is typically generated monthly, quarterly, or annually when the company's books are closed. The top (or left) portion of the balance sheet lists the company's assets, distinguished as either current or fixed (long-term).

Current assets include the following:

- Cash.
- Accounts receivable.
- Inventory.
- Supplies.

Fixed assets are also called long-term assets because they are durable and will last more than one year. Examples of this type of asset include:

- Furniture.
- Equipment.

The bottom (or right) portion of the balance sheet lists the liabilities of the business and the amount of equity or capital the owner has accumulated. These, too, are classified as current or long-term. Debts due in less than a year are tagged current, and debts due in more than a year are called long-term. Examples of current liabilities are:

- Accounts payable.
- Salaries.
- Utilities.
- Taxes.

Long-term liabilities may include:

- Bonds payable.
- Mortgage payable.
- Notes payable.

Note that capital is defined as the owner's equity in the company's assets. Capital is equal to net assets, or to the total value of the assets, minus the liabilities.

To sum up, a balance sheet follows a simple formula:

$$Assets = Liabilities + Capital$$

As an example, if you start a medical claims processing business on a $10,000 investment, the business has $10,000 in assets and you have a capital claim of $10,000. Suppose you decide to borrow an additional $20,000. Now the business has $30,000 in assets and $20,000 in liabilities. The equation would look like this:

$$Assets = Liabilities + Capital$$

$$\$30,000 = \$20,000 + \$10,000$$

From this equation, you learn what your business has and what it's worth (its assets), how the assets were financed (liabilities), and to whom they belong (capital claim).

A sample balance sheet is shown on page 212.

Income Statement

The income statement (or profit and loss statement) is a simple and straightforward report on a business's cash-generating ability. It illustrates how much a company makes or loses during the year by subtracting the cost of sales and expenses from revenue to arrive at a net result—either a profit or a loss.

Whether the primary purpose of a projected income statement is to obtain a bank loan, estimate cash requirements, or provide information for management planning, you should create such a statement before you start your home-based business. Later, as you collect operating data, you can update and refine your projections regularly.

For a service-oriented business, the steps for estimating monthly sales and profits are as follows:

1. Estimate how many of the people in your market area you can reasonably hope to attract as customers or clients.
2. Estimate the average revenue to be generated by each customer or client.
3. Calculate the total annual sales volume:

   Dollars per client $\times$ Number of clients = Total sales.

4. Estimate the seasonal sales patterns for the business, attributing varying percentages of the total volume to each month of the year.
5. Allocate the total annual sales calculated in step 3 to months:

BALANCE SHEET

STATEMENT OF FINANCIAL CONDITION AS OF _____ **, 19____**

ASSETS		TOTALS
CURRENT ASSETS		
Cash		
Accounts Receivable		
Inventory		
Total Current Assets		

FIXED ASSETS		
Capital/Plant		
Investment		
Miscellaneous Assets		
Total Fixed Assets		

TOTAL ASSETS		

LIABILITIES		TOTALS
CURRENT LIABILITIES		
Accounts Payable		
Accrued Liabilities		
Taxes		
Total Current Liabilities		

LONG-TERM LIABILITIES		
Bonds Payable		
Notes Payable		
Total Long-Term Liabilities		

TOTAL LIABILITIES		

OWNER'S EQUITY (Total Assets - Total Liabilities)		
Owner's Equity		

Total Liability + Equity		

Annual sales × Monthly percentage = Monthly sales.

6. Adjust these normal monthly sales totals to reflect the start-up period; this is strictly a value judgment.
7. Deduct from the monthly sales totals all your labor, materials, and overhead expenses. What's left is your net profit before taxes.

A sample income statement for a service-oriented business is shown on page 214. For a product-oriented home-based business, you would estimate monthly sales and profits this way:

1. Estimate the annual sales for the business, based on sales for other businesses in the same trade area and similar businesses in other areas.
2. Estimate the seasonal sales patterns for the business, attributing varying percentages of the total volume to each month of the year.
3. Allocate the total annual sales calculated in step 3 to months:

Annual sales × Monthly percentage = Monthly sales.

4. Adjust normal monthly sales totals to reflect the start-up period (same process as for a service-oriented business).
5. Deduct cost of goods sold from the monthly sales totals; the remainder is your gross profit margin. Then deduct your fixed and variable expenses. What's left is your net profit before taxes.

A sample income statement for a product-oriented business is shown on page 215.

Cash-Flow Statement

The cash-flow statement summarizes the operating, investing, and financing activities of a business as they relate to the inflow and outflow of cash. This is important in determining positive and negative cash flows, and in knowing whether your investment and financing endeavors are earning or draining cash resources.

Like the balance sheet and income statement, the cash-flow statement charts a home-based business's performance over a specific accounting period—a month, a quarter, 6 months, or a year. Most

INCOME STATEMENT

**INCOME STATEMENT
(SERVICE BUSINESS)
FOR PERIOD ENDING DECEMBER 31, 1996**

		TOTALS	
INCOME		$	155,000
Payroll	$ 34,100		
Rent	$ 545		
Utilities	$ 1,285		
Office Supplies	$ 920		
Insurance	$ 1,770		
Advertising	$ 15,272		
Professional Services	$ 855		
Travel	$ 4,655		
Maintenance & Repair	$ 1,117		
Packaging/Shipping	$ 12,328		
Miscellaneous	$ 65		
TOTAL EXPENSES		$	72,912
NET PROFIT		$	69,593
Margin %	45%		
Depreciation	$ 123		
NET PROFIT BEFORE INTEREST		$	69,467
Margin %	45%		
Interest	$ 118		
NET PROFIT BEFORE TAXES		$	69,349
Margin %	45%		

INCOME STATEMENT

**INCOME STATEMENT
(MERCHANDISER)
FOR PERIOD ENDING DECEMBER 31, 1996**

		TOTALS
INCOME		$ 155,000
Cost of Goods Sold	$ 77,281	
Margin %	50%	
GROSS PROFIT		$ 77,719
Payroll	$ 34,100	
Rent	$ 545	
Utilities	$ 1,285	
Office Supplies	$ 920	$
Insurance	$ 1,770	
Advertising	$ 15,272	$
Professional Services	$ 855	$
Travel	$ 4,655	
Maintenance & Repair	$ 1,117	
Packaging/Shipping	$ 12,328	
Miscellaneous	$ 65	
TOTAL EXPENSES		$ 72,912
NET PROFIT		$ 4,807
Margin %	3%	
Depreciation	$ 123	
NET PROFIT BEFORE INTEREST		$ 4,684
Margin %	3%	
Interest	$ 118	
NET PROFIT BEFORE TAXES		$ 4,566
Margin %	3%	

companies will prepare monthly cash-flow statements and then summarize them through an annual report for year-end meetings.

A cash-flow statement is a picture that reveals the heartbeat of your business. It shows the sources of money against the uses of that money, and indicates whether there is a cash surplus or deficit. By observing trends in the cash flow, you can monitor the influx of cash from operating activities (cash sales, accounts receivables, and interest from investments) against operating expenses to determine your liquidity. If a trend appears in which not enough income is being generated from operating revenue to meet expenses, then your liquidity will be threatened. Additional revenue will have to be obtained either through financing or from the sale of investments.

Keep in mind that the cash-flow statement doesn't reveal a profit or a loss. Just because your business has a positive cash flow doesn't mean that it generated more income from operating activities than it spent meeting its obligations. Additional revenue may have been obtained from investment and financing activities, both of which add to the business's cash position but not to its profitability.

On the other hand, a negative cash flow doesn't mean your home-based operation is not profitable. You may very well be producing a net profit for that accounting period, but may have additional obligations that do not affect the profitability of the company but do affect its cash position.

There are basically three sections of the cash-flow statement:

1. Income.
2. Expenses.
3. Cash flow.

The cash-flow statement begins with the income section. It shows all influx of revenue into the company, including some or all of the following:

- *Cash sales.* Income derived from sales paid for by cash.
- *Receivables.* Income derived from the collection of sales made by credit.
- *Investment income.* Income derived from investments, interest on loans that have been extended, and the liquidation of any assets.
- *Financing income.* Income derived from interest-bearing notes payable.

The second section represents all cash disbursements. These expenses are:

- *Material/Merchandise.* The raw material used in the manufacture of a product. (This entry applies to manufacturing operations only); also, the cash outlay for merchandise inventory during the accounting period (for merchandisers).
- *Production labor.* The labor required to manufacture a product (for manufacturing operations only).
- *Overhead.* All fixed and variable expenses required for the production of the product and the operations of the home-based business.
- *Marketing and sales.* All salaries, commissions, and other direct costs (if any) associated with marketing and sales.
- *Research and development (R&S).* All the labor expenses required to support the research and development operations of the business.
- *General and administrative (G&A).* All the labor expenses required to support the administrative functions of the business.
- *Taxes.* All taxes, except payroll, paid to the appropriate government institutions.
- *Capital.* The capital requirements to obtain any equipment elements that are needed for the generation of income.
- *Loans.* The total of all loan payments to reduce long-term debts.

A final section deals with the net and cumulative cash flow of the business. Net cash flow is the difference between income and expenses. This amount is carried over to the next reporting period through cumulative cash flow. To determine cumulative cash flow, add the net cash flow of the current period to the cumulative cash flow from the previous period.

WORKING WITH YOUR BANK

Even though your new home-based business may not be pulling in giant sums of money, you still need a business bank account. You may be happy with the bank where you have your personal accounts, but that doesn't mean you should open your business account there. It may not offer the financial services a home-based business like yours demands: checking services, transfer of funds services, linked accounts, lock boxes, and so on.

CASH FLOW	JANUARY	FEBRUARY	MARCH	APRIL	MAY	JUNE	JULY
CASH SALES	$17,113	$25,670	$34,226	$51,339	$59,896	$68,452	$72,730
RECEIVABLES	0	0	25,670	38,504	51,339	77,009	89,844
OTHER INCOME	0	0	0	0	0	0	0
TOTAL INCOME	$17,113	$25,670	$59,896	$89,843	$111,235	$145,461	$162,574
MATERIAL	0	0	0	0	0	0	0
DIRECT LABOR	7,800	11,700	15,600	23,400	27,300	31,200	35,150
OVERHEAD	0	0	0	0	0	0	0
MARKETING & SALES	8,250	9,900	11,550	11,550	12,045	12,705	13,530
R&D	3,500	4,200	4,900	4,900	5,110	5,390	5,740
G&A	1,750	2,100	2,450	2,450	2,555	2,695	2,870
TAXES	0	0	40,528	0	0	40,528	0
CAPITAL	3,430	3,430	3,430	3,430	3,430	3,430	3,430
LOANS	25,000	25,000	25,000	25,000	25,000	25,001	25,000
TOTAL EXPENSES	$49,730	$56,330	$103,458	$70,730	$75,440	$120,950	$83,720
CASH FLOW	($32,617)	($30,660)	($43,562)	$19,113	$35,795	$24,511	$78,854
CUMULATIVE CASH FLOW	($32,617)	($63,277)	($106,840)	($87,727)	($51,932)	($27,421)	$51,433

CASH FLOW	AUGUST	SEPTEMBER	OCTOBER	NOVEMBER	DECEMBER	TOTAL
CASH SALES	$81,287	$85,565	$98,400	$124,070	$136,904	$855,652
RECEIVABLES	102,678	109,096	121,931	128,348	147,600	892,019
OTHER INCOME	0	0	0	0	0	0
TOTAL INCOME	$183,965	$194,661	$220,331	$252,418	$284,504	$1,747,671
MATERIAL	0	0	0	0	0	0
DIRECT LABOR	37,050	39,000	44,850	56,550	62,400	390,000
OVERHEAD	0	0	0	0	0	0
MARKETING & SALES	15,345	17,325	17,325	17,490	17,985	165,000
R&D	6,510	7,350	7,350	7,420	7,630	70,000
G&A	3,255	3,675	3,675	3,710	3,815	35,000
TAXES	0	40,528	0	0	40,528	162,113
CAPITAL	3,430	3,430	3,430	3,430	3,430	41,164
LOANS	25,000	25,000	25,000	25,000	25,000	300,000
TOTAL EXPENSES	$90,590	$136,308	$101,630	$113,600	$160,789	$1,163,277
CASH FLOW	$93,375	$58,353	$118,701	$138,818	$123,715	$584,394
CUMULATIVE CASH FLOW	$144,808	$203,160	$321,861	$460,679	$584,394	$584,394

Here are a few tips on business banking:

1. When searching for a bank, interview bank managers in your area by phone until you find the best bank for your business. This professional approach gives you a psychological advantage with the bank manager and provides an opportunity to establish a relationship. The closer the relationship you develop with the bank manager, the better your chances of obtaining loans and special favors in marginal situations in the future.

2. Learn to talk to bankers in their language, on their terms. That approach will help your present situation and improve your position the next time you require their services.

3. Try an independent bank with no branch offices, or a small chain. In a small bank, your account will be important; and will receive personalized service. In a large bank, you may never be noticed.

4. Make your money work for you. Place it in an interest-bearing checking account.

5. If you have personal and business accounts at the same bank, arrange for "relationship banking" (linked personal and business accounts) to cut down on bank fees.

6. Deposit excess cash on hand in higher-yielding accounts, for example, money-market funds.

7. Ask for money before you need it. Your chances of obtaining a loan under marginal conditions will be improved 50% by anticipating your needs.

What to Ask Your Banker

Home-based businesses have special needs—small equipment and working capital loans. If you run a home computer business, you may need loans of $3,000 to $10,000 for equipment purchases to update your computer, but many banks don't readily dole out small loans. Small businesses—home-based ones especially—have another problem: many banks ignore small businesses and search out only big corporate accounts. To make sure you are putting your money in a bank that will help your business grow, ask these questions:

1. Is it necessary to maintain certain balances before the bank will consider a loan?

2. Will the bank advance a line of credit, and if so, what are the requirements?

3. Does the bank have limitations on the number of small loans it will grant or the types of businesses to which it will grant loans?

4. What is the bank's policy on the size or description of checks deposited to be held for collection?

5. Will checks under that size be credited immediately to your checking account balance? (This question is very important, and you must press for a definite answer.)

If you do not have a previous business account to serve as a reference, some banks will hold all checks for collection until they develop experience with you. Whether the bank exercises this precaution may depend on your personal credit rating.

EXTENDING CREDIT

Allowing your customers to pay you with a credit card can increase your business dramatically. Home-based mail order entrepreneurs know this well. Shoppers who see a mail order product advertised in a catalog or magazine are far more likely to order if they can simply phone and give their credit card number. It's far easier than making customers tear out an order sheet, fill it out, write out a check, put it in the envelope, put a stamp on it, and drop it in a mail box. Sources in the charge card industry say that extending credit can boost business by as much as 50%.

Unfortunately, obtaining merchant account status isn't easy for home-based business owners. An age-old idea that home-based businesses aren't "real" businesses often stands in the way. Don't be surprised if the bank turns you down the first time you apply for merchant account status.

Once again, this is where your relationship with your banker can play in your favor. If you have cemented a strong relationship, you may have a better chance of landing a merchant account. Also, dealing with a small, independent bank may increase your chances.

Banks aren't the only financial institutions that can give you merchant status. If you're turned down by your bank, try credit unions, savings and loans, and thrifts. You can also utilize brokers who can help you obtain merchant status through financial institutions they have relationships with. Although there aren't many such companies, their numbers are growing. Look under "Financing" in the Business-to-Business Yellow Pages.

Advantages to Extending Credit

Granting credit will give your business these advantages:

1. Extending credit promotes customer loyalty.
2. Customers usually spend money more easily when they don't have to pay cash.
3. Should you ever decide to sell your business, it will have a greater value because you can show steady accounts.
4. Extending credit may enable you to capture larger accounts.
5. Your customers will buy your products and order your services more frequently and readily.

Disadvandages to Extending Credit

There are also potential disadvantages to extending credit:

1. *Losses.* Though the customers may have fully intended to pay, they may not be able to when the time comes. Credit-card readers, however, can help you overcome this disadvantage. They let you verify that a customer has a valid card and that the charge will fall within their credit limit, before you make the sale.
2. *Increased working capital requirements.* You will need more money to keep your business going because you won't realize income from your sales as quickly as you would if you were dealing in cash sales only.
3. *Interest on the additional capital.* You may have to borrow to offset your decreased working capital.
4. *Time.* You will devote precious hours to following up on problem credit customers.
5. *Extra expense.* Credit bureau fees and memberships, collection costs, and legal fees can eat into profits.
6. *Potential resentment from your clients.* If a customer or client owes you a lot of money, he or she may be inclined to avoid you.

Collecting from Credit Customers

Create a permanent record of credit sales and maintain it separately from your sales slips and invoices. This record should show, for each customer, the date, invoice number, and amount of any new charges; a running balance of the total amount owed; the date and amount of each payment received; and a record of any invoices, collection letters, and collection phone calls made to this customer.

If an account becomes delinquent, you need to act immediately: send a copy of the most recent bill with the notation "past due" or "overdue notice" stamped on the front. If this does not bring a response in the form of payment or an arrangement for payment, follow up with a brief letter. If that doesn't work, make a personal phone call. If all of these measures fail, you may have to take more drastic action.

KEEPING YOUR MONEY IN YOUR HANDS

Here are a few financial techniques that can help improve your cash flow:

1. Pay with credit cards. This gives you upward of 30 days to pay the debt. In the meantime, the money remains in your coffers.
2. Make arrangements with suppliers to give you up to 90 days interest-free credit.
3. Use independent contractors or part-timers before hiring someone full-time.
4. Consider renting or leasing equipment rather than purchasing everything.
5. Pay bills as close to the due date as possible without being late.
6. Maintain cash on hand for emergencies. A small home-based business can fail if it is unprepared for the unexpected. Keep an extra reserve of cash for such occasions.
7. Keep all your financial records in one place. Knowing where to find your records can help you avoid missing payments, neglecting overdue bills, and similar crises.

GETTING HELP FROM AN ACCOUNTANT

If the thought of managing your finances terrifies you, don't panic. You can get help from an accountant. A good accountant can be a valuable business associate and adviser, particularly on the latest tax laws affecting your business.

Your accountant can also help you save money: you may not be aware of all the tax deductions you are entitled to take. He or she can also advise you on making equipment purchases to maximize your deductions.

Finding a good accountant takes time. During your search, use this checklist:

- Determine whether you need a Certified Public Accountant (CPA) or whether your business can make do with a licensed public accountant.
- Look for an accountant who specializes in working with home-based businesses.
- Make sure your accountant has experience in your industry.
- Find out what services your accountant will provide.

Chapter 10 provides more information on working with an accountant.

10

RECORD KEEPING AND TAXES

When starting a home-based business, you will soon discover that you need to become an organizational whiz to keep it growing. Not only do you have to offer a great product or service, be a super salesperson, and possess a good dose of persistence, but you also need to become a master at maintaining important records.

To comply with local and federal tax laws, you must maintain an accurate and thorough record-keeping system. Conducting proper record keeping will help to control cash management. Your accountant should be able to establish this type of system for you if setting up records is not your strong point. Maintaining proper records can mean the life of your business.

You can choose from several different methods for maintaining your business records. As a small, home-based entrepreneur, you may find that a manual record-keeping method, such as a single-entry system, may be best suited for your needs. In a single-entry system, the business owner monitors daily cash receipts and expenditures, which show the flow of income and expenses. The monthly receipts are recorded in a journal that also contains monthly disbursements. As your business grows, switching to a computerized system may save both time and money. A computerized record-keeping system can easily track inventory as well as daily cash transactions.

To keep track of expenses, you will need to establish a business checking account along with a petty cash fund. It is important that you maintain a business bank account that is separate from your personal bank account. This will eliminate the confusion of trying to separate expenses paid out of each account at the end of the month. The petty cash fund can be used for incidental expenses such as office supplies. When you dip into your petty cash fund, keep your receipts; they will document your purchases for tax purposes.

RECORD KEEPING

The most useful record-keeping systems are usually also the simplest to understand. Your time is valuable, and you will spend too much time maintaining your records if they are overly complex. Furthermore, complicated records may require hiring an accountant or bookkeeper to maintain them, and many start-up home-based business owners simply don't have the cash on hand to hire someone immediately. Develop a comprehensive record-keeping system, but one that is easy to understand and maintain.

RECORDS YOU SHOULD RETAIN

Keep records that support the entries on your federal tax return until the statute of limitations expires (ordinarily, three years after the return is due). You should keep copies of your federal income tax returns forever; they may even be helpful to the executor of your estate someday.

Numerous records need to be retained for tax and legal purposes. As previously mentioned, retain all receipts for the petty cash fund. Keep all paid utility bills and suppliers' bills. Retain all bank papers such as canceled checks and duplicate deposit slips. Among your shipping documents, you should keep receiving reports, purchase invoices, and customer invoices. In addition, keep copies of sales slips and any other documents you deem necessary to verify your business record entries.

You should also maintain records for these other important items: capital equipment, insurance, and payroll.

Capital Equipment

Keep equipment records for major purchases, such as a computer, fax machine, or printer, so you can determine your depreciation expenses for tax purposes. Don't keep records on small items like staplers, tape recorders, and answering machines. Don't list leased equipment in this section; it should be maintained under cash disbursements because you do not own it. Leased equipment is a liability payable each month.

Maintain records only on capital equipment you have purchased, whether outright, on a contract basis, or through a chattel mortgage. Major equipment you have purchased is considered an asset even though you may have financed it. As you pay off your loan obligation, you build equity in the equipment that can be listed on your balance sheet as an asset.

Your equipment records should include the purchase date for each piece of equipment, the vendor's name, a brief description of the item, how it was paid for, the check number if appropriate, and the full amount of the purchase.

Insurance

Keep all records pertaining to your company's insurance policies. This includes auto, life, health, fire, general liability, personal liability, and any other coverage you may obtain to decrease the risk of liability in a specific area. List the carriers of the policies and the underwriting agents who issued the policies. Also, maintain records on any claims made against your policies in order to resolve any misunderstandings that may arise.

When updating your records, enter all information about the payment of premiums: the date the check was written, the amount, and which policy it was written for. This will help with payment disputes and tax preparation.

Payroll

You need to keep all records regarding payroll taxes, even if you employ someone on a part-time basis. Payroll records can be categorized under federal unemployment tax (FUTA), social security (FICA), and income tax withholding. Keep these records for a minimum of four years after the tax has been paid or has become due, whichever occurs later.

FUTA records contain data regarding the total amount contributed for a calendar year, how much was paid into the state's fund for unemployment, how much was designated for unemployment taxes, and all other information that needs to be listed on unemployment tax returns.

FICA tax records show how much FICA tax was collected, the date of each payment, the amount of the payment designated for

FICA taxes, and a written justification for any discrepancy between the two amounts.

Income tax withholding records list the name, social security number, and address of each employee. Also required are: the date of each payment the employee received, how much of his or her wages needed to be withheld, and how much withholding tax was collected. You must attach additional statements if the taxable amount and total payment aren't the same, if an employee is a nonresident alien, or if any payments are made under sick-pay plans. If you provide any noncash compensation to your employees, be sure to provide the date and market value of that compensation. Any withholding exemption certificates or agreements allowing you to withhold additional funds should also be included. For a business where employees receive additional income such as tips, this income must be stated. If you pay your employees for nonbusiness services, the payment and date must be recorded.

Payroll for a small firm is made simple by a good pegboard or "write-it-once" system. Any office supply store can show you samples of different one-write systems. You can learn to use one in about 15 minutes. Most accountants recommend these systems because they reduce errors and save time in making payroll entries.

Bookkeeping Systems

Although you might make use of a single-entry bookkeeping system (described above), double-entry bookkeeping is the usual method of keeping business records, and it makes use of journals and ledgers. The bookkeeper (most likely you, for your first few years in business) enters transactions first in a journal, and then posts monthly totals to the appropriate ledger accounts. Five categories of ledger accounts are: (1) income; (2) expense; (3) assets; (4) liability; and (5) net worth. Income and expense accounts are closed each year; asset, liability, and net worth accounts are maintained on a permanent and continuous basis.

Balancing and Bank Reconciliations

Every page of sales, cash receipts, and disbursements should be balanced to ensure the accuracy of your records, and every month you should reconcile your checkbook against your bank statement to guarantee that your records match those of the bank. Any corrections to be made in your records should be recorded immediately. If there is a bank error, you should notify the bank within 14 working days after receipt of the reconciliation statement.

Paying with Cash vs. Check

If you are spending most of your money in cash rather than by writing checks, you should list these expenditures on an expense report form. Such forms are readily available at stationery stores and are designated by category: travel, entertainment, office supplies, and so on. Attach to the form the receipts corresponding to the expenditures. A sample form is shown on page 230.

It is essential that you try to pay as much as you can by check. This gives you a record of all debits to your company. Most bookkeepers agree that it is best to work out of one checkbook for the business. This will facilitate record keeping and make balancing your business checkbook much easier. Using different checkbooks is the cause of many financial problems when businesses begin.

CHOOSING AN ACCOUNTANT

The services of an attorney and consultant are vital during specific periods in the development of your business or in times of trouble, but your accountant will have the greatest impact on the success or failure of your business.

Once your operation begins, you will have to decide whether your volume warrants a full-time bookkeeper, an outside accounting service, or merely a year-end accounting and tax preparation service. Most likely, as a home-based business owner, you will only be able to afford an accountant on a part-time basis—possibly only once a year for tax preparation. Even the smallest unincorporated home-based businesses often employ an outside public accountant to prepare their financial statements.

When you borrow money, your bank manager will want to see your balance sheet and your operating statement. If these have been prepared by a reputable public accountant, the documents will have more credibility than if you prepared them yourself. (If you are borrowing less than $500,000, most banks will accept unaudited financial statements prepared by a licensed public accountant.)

Public accountants must meet certain proficiency levels in order to be licensed by the state in which they practice. This does not ensure that an independent business accountant will do a good job for you, but it does narrow your chances of running into an unqualified accountant.

If you are organizing a corporation, your accountant should counsel you during start-up to determine the best approach for your tax situation. If you are starting as a sole proprietor or in a partnership,

EXPENSE REPORT

NAME: _____   START DATE: _____

PURPOSE: _____   END DATE: _____

DATE	BREAKFAST	LUNCH	DINNER	TIPS	LODGINGS	PHONE	TRAVEL	PARKING/TOLLS	GAS/OIL	ENTERTAINMENT	MISCELLANEOUS	DAILY TOTAL

SUBTOTAL

LESS ADVANCE

TOTAL AMOUNT DUE

you'll want the accountant to set up a bookkeeping system you can operate internally.

Experienced independent accountants will usually be familiar with accounting problems specific to your business, and will be able to direct you wisely. For instance, if you run a bed-and-breakfast inn in a mountain resort and the majority of your guests stay during the ski season, an accountant can help you learn to manage your cash flow during the peaks and valleys of a seasonal business. Before the calendar year ends, always ask your accountant to organize your records for that tax year.

Ideally, an accountant should help organize the statistical data concerning your business, assist in charting future actions based on past performance, and advise you on your overall financial strategy with regard to purchasing, capital investment, and other matters related to your business goals. For a graphic designer working from home, an accountant can help make a decision on whether it's better to purchase a new color printer at the end of the year or to wait until the beginning of the next year. Today, however, much of an accountant's time is spent keeping clients in compliance with shifting interpretations of laws and regulations.

Accountants specialize in knowing the legal requirements that affect you. This is why you need their services if you expect to succeed. If you spend your time finding answers to perplexing questions, you will not have the time to properly manage your business. Accountants can answer these questions more efficiently. Spend your time doing what you do best, and leave the accounting to the experts.

To find a good accountant, follow these suggestions:

- Look for recommendations from other small business owners, your banker, or your lawyer. Make sure your accountant specializes in small businesses, even home-based businesses, if possible.
- Accountants' fees vary. Call several to make sure yours is within the norm for your area. Be sure to ask what is included in the fee. Is phone support included? Representation in an audit? A newsletter with tax and legal updates?
- Ask if you can pay on an annual basis.
- Set a fee in case you are audited.
- Call current clients for references. Are they happy with the service they are receiving?
- Find out whether you need a CPA or can go with a licensed public accountant. Some states require certified statements, so check your state's regulations first.

TAXES AND THE HOME-BASED BUSINESS

By running a business from your home, you not only reduce your overhead expenses but you can also gain new tax write-offs. You will be able to deduct various expenses that occur as a result of operating your business. These expenses can range from equipment and supplies for the business to redecorating the room that will house your office. The home office tax deduction is discussed in detail in Chapter 6.

Qualifying for a Home Office Tax Deduction

To be able to claim a home office tax deduction, a section of your home must be reserved for business use. Most small business owners set up in a spare bedroom, den, or garage. The IRS will not recognize a room as being used exclusively for business purposes if it contains your home entertainment center. If you do not have an entire room in which to set up your office, you can use a corner of a room, but your deductions will be restricted.

As explained in Chapter 6, the Supreme Court has ruled that the majority of your business must be conducted in your home office space, in order to qualify for a deduction. Unless business owners spend most of their work time within the home, and use it for visits from clients, customers, or patients, the IRS will not allow the deduction.

To qualify for deductions, the home office has to:

- Be your principal place of business.
- Be used as a place where clients, customers, or patients visit on a regular basis.
- Be in connection with your trade if it is in a separate place, e.g., your garage.
- Be used exclusively for business and on a regular basis.

If you meet the requirements for a home office deduction, your deductions will consist of direct and indirect expenses.

When you are establishing your home-based office, any expense you incur that is directly related to the business is labeled a direct expense. All equipment, supplies, and improvements made for your business can be deducted. Computers, pencils, mini-blinds, and any items needed to furnish and equip your office are included if they are items exclusively for business.

Indirect expenses occur when improvements made to your house benefit your office as well. Suppose you paint the inside of your entire house. You cannot deduct the entire cost as an indirect expense. Instead, you can deduct a fraction of that expense, based on how much of your total space your office occupies. You can determine the amount of your deduction in two ways. First, you can divide the square footage of your office by the total square footage your home occupies. If your office space is 200 square feet and your house is 1,500 square feet, you could deduct 13% of the total cost of any indirect expenses, such as painting.

Using the second formula, you calculate the amount of your deduction by counting the number of rooms in your home. If you use one room in an eight-room house solely as your office, you can deduct as business expenses one-eighth of your rent (or deed/mortgage payment) plus one-eighth of your utility bills and similar expenses. According to recent federal tax legislation, however, you cannot deduct any part of the base rate of the first telephone line into your residence, even if you use the telephone for business.

Standard Business Deductions

Besides the deductions your home office affords you, you can take a number of standard business deductions available to business owners in general, whether they work from home or rent office space. When claiming a deduction, make sure you have the necessary supporting documents, such as canceled checks, sales receipts, and credit card slips and statements. These deductions include a variety of business-related expenses: supplies, equipment, furniture, professional services (including attorneys and accountants), payroll, uniforms, postage and shipping, advertising, insurance, and any trade publications.

Can you deduct the cost of your computer? The Deficit Reduction Act of 1984 severely limits the conditions under which computers in the home can be used to limit tax liability. A home computer used for business over 50% of the time can qualify for appropriate business deductions or credits. As of 1985, business owners using home computers have to document business and personal use of the machine in writing.

Vehicle Expenses

Business mileage is tax-deductible. Business miles accumulate when you drive for the purpose of either *doing* business or *seeking* business; going to talk to a potential client, visiting a supplier, and doing something related to the promotional aspects of your business are all considered business mileage. The mileage you drive from your home office to any other location for business purposes is deductible. As with your other deductions, you must be able to support your claims for business miles. Keep a log by entering your business mileage after each trip. Enter your total daily business mileage on your appointment calendar at the end of each day.

At the time of this writing, the IRS allows you to deduct 28¢ for each business mile until your vehicle is fully depreciated. Once your vehicle is fully depreciated, you can deduct only 11¢ for each mile driven. Keep abreast of any changes the IRS may make in this area.

You can base your deduction on either straight mileage or actual operating costs. Calculating your straight mileage deductions is very simple. Assume you drove 10,000 miles for business this year. Multiply 28¢ per mile by 10,000 miles, and you reach a deduction of $2,800.

Calculating your actual operating expenses is somewhat more complicated. First, you need to total your yearly automobile operating expenses, which include insurance, gasoline, repairs, and depreciation. Let us assume that you spent $600 on insurance, $1,500 on gasoline, and $500 on repairs, and that your car depreciated by $2,000 last year. Your total yearly operating costs were $4,600. Suppose, furthermore, that you drove a total of 15,000 miles last year, and 10,000 of those miles were for business purposes. Your business miles make up 66% of your total mileage. To calculate your deduction, take 66% of $4,600, which equals $3,066. Our example shows that basing the deduction on actual operating expenses yields a higher deduction, but this may not actually be the case for you. If you decide to use this method, you must do so as long as you have the car.

Travel and Entertainment

If you don't want potential customers visiting your home office, you'll be meeting them in another environment: their home, their office, or a neutral area such as a restaurant or bar. As a home-based business owner, you may find that you conduct much of your business over lunch or dinner in restaurants.

If you entertain clients or potential clients to discuss a current or future project, you can deduct a portion—80%—of your entertainment costs. To qualify for this deduction, you must maintain a log of entertainment-related expenses you plan to deduct.

Use a standard appointment calendar to record whom you were entertaining, where you were, and how much you spent. You must be specific in describing the nature of the discussion; the IRS will not accept general "goodwill" as a reason. Contrary to popular belief, you do not need receipts for entertainment expenditures of less than $25, but you must maintain your log. In certain instances, you can even claim business-related entertainment that takes place in your home; ask the attending clients or prospects to sign a guest log. If you prepare a meal or serve drinks, your expenses are deductible as part of the expense of doing business.

You may have to travel to other cities or states for several days at a time on business. For instance, an importer who buys jewelry from Thailand may have to travel to Thailand several times a year to seek out and purchase new inventory. Or, you may be trying to land a client in Colorado for your public relations business, but you live in California. If the client won't do business with you unless you do a face-to-face presentation, you'll need to make a trip to Colorado.

Business travel deductions range from the cost of air, bus, or auto fares to hotels and meals, and to incidental expenditures such as dry cleaning, tips, and taxis. However, the rule is that you must stay overnight *on business* to claim travel/incidentals deductions.

YOUR RESPONSIBILITY TO COLLECT TAXES

Even though you may be a sole proprietor when you launch your business, you may eventually hire some employees. When you do, it is your responsibility to take out taxes from their paychecks. The taxes you need to be concerned with are Social Security and income tax. Once you have collected them from your employees, document the amount in your records and forward the money to the appropriate government agencies.

To collect and remit taxes as an employer, you need to use IRS Form SS-4 to receive an employer tax number. If the state in which you operate also collects income tax, you will need a state tax number. Call the local offices of the federal and state agencies, listed in the White Pages under "United States" and "State Government." The federal agency will send you your number as well as charts to calculate payroll tax deductions, quarterly and annual forms, W-4 forms, tax deposit forms, and an instruction manual explaining how to fill out the forms.

Corporations earn income. If you incorporate your business, you must file a corporate income tax return at the end of every year. Corporate tax returns may be prepared on a calendar-year or fiscal-year basis.

Operating as a sole proprietor or partner, you will not be paid a salary like an employee; therefore, no income tax will be withheld from the money you take out of your business for personal use. As a result, you must estimate what your tax liability is and pay it quarterly instead of annually. Contact an IRS office and request Form 1040 ES. This is the form you will need to report your tax liability every quarter. When applying for the form, also request the *Tax Guide for Small Business* (Publication 334).

Many home-based business owners prefer to use independent contractors to perform their service or market their product, rather than keep a staff of employees. Whether the reason is cost savings or personal preference, you should consider the advantages that independent contractors can provide you.

Hiring individuals as independent contractors requires filing an annual information return (Form 1099) to report payments totaling $600 or more made to any individual during the calendar year. If this form is not filed, you will be subject to penalties. Be sure your records list the name, address, and Social Security number of every independent contractor you hired, along with pertinent dates and the amounts paid to each person. Every payment should be supported by an invoice submitted by the contractor.

Advance tax deposits serve as insurance for states that collect taxes. A state will take a percentage of a business's projected taxable sales. For example, California's state tax bureau requires that a new business must deposit 7.25% of the taxable sales it expects to have in its first three months of operation. If your projected taxable sales for this time period are $5,000, you would be required to deposit 7.25% of that amount, or $362.50, when applying for your sales tax permit number. If the state you operate in requires an advance deposit, you might want to provide a low, but still realistic estimate for your sales. This will save you money, which you can use to start up your business. After your business is open and earning more money, you can make up the difference. Your state's tax board can help you with this process.

If you sell a product, you are responsible for collecting and recording sales tax and forwarding it to the proper local and state government bodies. Your state and/or local revenue offices will be able to inform you when your sales tax returns are due and what amount is subject to taxation.

THE SELLERS PERMIT

In many states, wholesalers or manufacturers will not sell to you at wholesale prices unless you can show them your sales tax permit or number, also called a sellers permit. You will usually have to sign a tax card for their files if you plan to sell their goods from your home-based location.

Agencies issuing permits vary with each state, but generally they are the Equalization Board, the State Sales Tax Commission, or the Franchise Tax Board. Contact the entity responsible for governing taxes in your state and apply for your resale tax or wholesale permit. You will have to provide documentation to prove you are a retailer. Usually, your business permit is acceptable.

Your resale permit allows you to avoid putting out money for sales tax on merchandise at the time you purchase it from suppliers. This does not mean you won't be remitting taxes on the merchandise; it means you'll be deferring them until you sell the merchandise to your customers. The sales taxes will be added (where applicable) to their purchases. You then remit the taxes with the appropriate forms.

When conducting business across state lines, you are not required to collect taxes for any other state except those in which you maintain offices.

SURVIVING A TAX AUDIT

Will taking a deduction for your home office increase your chances of being audited by the IRS? It could. Some things that may increase the odds that your return will be audited include making large payments to family members you claim are employees, excessive losses from a business (claiming losses of $100,000 from a business that grossed only $15,000), and excessive business expenses (claiming a new TV because it's important for you to stay abreast of the news). Your tax preparer can alert you to anything on your return that could be a red flag to auditors.

In general, if you have ample documentation for your deductions, you won't have a problem, even if you are audited. In the case of an audit, contact your accountant or tax preparer immediately. If audited, an IRS agent will most likely visit your home office to determine whether you have given accurate information regarding the size of your home office, the value of equipment purchased, and the number of employees working for you, among other things.

If your claims are found to be faulty, you will have to pay any back taxes plus interest. That's why it's important to get good tax advice from a qualified professional *before* filing your tax returns.

TAX PLANNING

Good tax planning not only minimizes your taxes, it also provides more money for your business or investments. As a home-based entrepreneur, you should view tax savings as a potential source of working capital.

There are two important rules to follow in your tax planning:

1. Don't incur an additional expense solely for the sake of getting an extra deduction.
2. Immediately deferring taxes allows you to use your money interest-free before paying it to the government.

Interest rates may justify deferring taxes; on the other hand, deferment may increase your taxes in years to come.

Estimated Tax Underpayments

If you have not paid sufficient amounts of estimated income tax, you may be able to avoid or reduce penalties for underpayment by arranging to increase the amounts withheld from the paychecks remaining in the present year. All withheld income tax is treated as if spread equally over the calendar year, even when a disproportionately large amount is withheld in the last month or months of the year. Individuals required to make estimated tax payments should pay special attention to other techniques that may be beneficial, especially if their income is irregular or seasonal.

Because of the high nondeductible penalty rates in effect, careful planning and analysis of required tax payments is warranted in any small business.

Equipment Purchases

You can deduct purchases of up to $17,000 worth of equipment in any given year. You can only take this deduction for tangible personal property used in your business (computers, tools, and similar items); it is not available for real estate or automobiles.

Inventory Valuation

Product-oriented home-based businesses don't automatically get a deduction for purchasing inventory. They must reduce the amount paid for inventory purchases by the value of the inventory at the end of the year. For example, if you paid $10,000 for merchandise in one year, and your inventory at the end of the year was $7,000, you could deduct only $3,000 for purchases.

Postponing Income

If you are a part-time entrepreneur who is still employed by someone else, and if you expect to receive a year-end bonus or other additional compensation, you may want to defer receipt until the forthcoming year, especially if you will be in a lower tax bracket in the following year. This is often the case with first-time entrepreneurs who quit their jobs without securing the steady sources of income they need until their new businesses break even. You may also want to negotiate an agreement with your employer whereby part of your earnings will be deferred and paid in either one or several future years.

11

THE PERSONNEL QUESTION

Should you hire employees or shouldn't you? Most start-up home-based businesses are small enough that they don't need to hire employees initially. Eventually, you may need an assistant on either a part-time or full-time basis. And when your home-based business reaches the point where hiring additional personnel becomes critical, then you may have to consider leaving the home nest and renting a commercial facility.

When you decide you do need help, take the necessary steps slowly. Most business owners, especially those who work from home, find the idea of hiring personnel intimidating. Some worry about being cheated or burglarized; others fear that work won't be done at all or will be done poorly; some see employees as future competitors. Afraid to leave responsibility in the hands of others, many entrepreneurs become so attached to their businesses that they never take a vacation or even a few days off. Businesses sometimes fail to move to high income and profit levels because the owner isn't able to accomplish all the tasks without hired help. With common sense and preparation, you can minimize the risk and hassle of the hiring process and put your business in a position to grow.

Home-based business owners are at a disadvantage in the hiring market. Not only are they faced with the legalities all employers must comply with (health insurance, workers' compensation, employment insurance), they are also challenged by the obstacles of zoning restrictions and limited office space.

Generally, home-based entrepreneurs are limited to hiring within their local area. A further handicap is that the best local talent may prefer employment in larger, better-known, and apparently more secure companies. By paying competitive wages and stressing the opportunity to take on responsibilities not available in a larger office, you can offset this handicap and turn it into an advantage. Aggressively selling your company can shrink some of these limitations and help secure an adequate supply of qualified job applicants.

Don't look for potential employees among your friends and relatives. Remember, if a friend or relative does not work out as an employee and you have to let him or her go, you may lose both an employee and a good relationship.

No employee is perfect. Don't expect to find someone who will fulfill your every business need. You must compromise and be satisfied with people who have most of the qualities you seek. Pay what the market requires, and give significant increases if the person works out well. Two well-paid, motivated, capable employees will serve you better than three mediocre, apathetic, underpaid ones.

If employees fail to perform as you expect and you cannot get them to change through constructive criticism, let them go. Weak employees hurt the morale of others, who must then carry a greater share of the workload.

Before hiring anyone, have the following written documents prepared:

1. A *job description,* including the objectives of the job, the work to be performed, the employee's responsibilities, the working conditions, and the relationships to other jobs.
2. A *job analysis,* a description of the qualifications required to fill the job—experience, education, special skills, and any physical requirements.
3. An *application form* that will give you the information you want (and can legally ask for) from each job applicant.

Once these duties and qualifications have been decided, begin recruiting prospective employees.

RECRUITING

Don't limit employee applications to people who happen to stop in and ask for jobs. Go out and recruit—at schools and universities (which maintain job placement bureaus for their graduates), at established government and private employment agencies, through referrals from friends, and at other business firms. Advertising in newspapers or trade publications can be effective if the position requires special training and if advertising expenses are reasonable.

Before writing a classified ad, take some time to think about the position and the qualifications you are seeking in an employee. Your ad should tell applicants what kind of education and experience you seek. Instead of focusing solely on what you are looking for, include a few words about your business and what you have to offer an employee. Remember, you need to inspire the best applicants to call your company instead of other, more established companies. If your ad includes a description of your business and explains how employees can grow with your business, you may attract better applicants.

The title of the position is no less important. Advertising a clerical position as a clerk/typist won't get as much response as advertising for an administrative assistant. Stipulate "college education required" in your ad if you want only that level of applicant to respond. Be very specific regarding the experience you require; otherwise, you will attract as many unqualified applicants as qualified ones.

SCREENING AND INTERVIEWING APPLICANTS

Hiring an employee can be very time-consuming. To streamline the process, prequalify applicants either by phone or by requesting a resume. On the phone, ask each applicant to detail his or her qualifications, and don't be timid about letting a caller know that he or she doesn't measure up to your requirements.

You can sort through resumes quickly to determine whether a person has the necessary requirements. When reviewing resumes, make three piles: a "yes" pile, a "maybe" pile, and a "no thank you" pile. Interview the people from the "yes" pile first. If they don't make the grade or don't want the job, go back to your "maybe" pile and interview the best of the lot.

Call the most qualified applicants for personal interviews. Each applicant should be required to complete a detailed application form and give references. If you are serious about the candidate after you have conducted the interview, check those references to verify his or her employment or education history.

Keep the applications squarely in front of you during interviews, and be certain to give the applicants plenty of time to present themselves thoroughly. Put the interviewees at ease; their nervousness may distract you from effectively evaluating their capabilities.

Remember that an interview is a two-way street. You want to find out as much as possible about the applicant, and the applicant wants a clear idea of the position and your company. To give the applicant an accurate idea of what the position entails, take the time to talk about your company, why you are hiring, and what you will expect from the hiree. Describe both the job and the working environment. Make sure the person is comfortable with the idea of coming to work in your home.

During the interview, concentrate on being observant. Notice the person's dress and mannerisms. If a person is reticent and answers questions with a single word such as "yes" or "no," or with stifled responses, you can assume that this applicant's personality is incompatible with a job opening for a salesperson. On the other hand, a person who is very vocal, sociable, and outgoing might not be suitable for a detail-oriented position—for example, as a bookkeeper, who chiefly works alone. By being observant, you will be able to read between the lines and can often learn more than from direct questions.

No matter how much you can glean from an interview, you may not remember your impressions if you don't write them down. You can either take notes during the interview or wait until the person leaves and then jot down your impressions.

With proper planning and effective execution, the hiring interview can become crucial for your success. Just as you shop around for the best suppliers, you should also spend time looking for the right employees. Some of the expenses of hiring new employees may be tax deductible. For more specific information, refer to IRS Publication 334, *Tax Guide for Small Businesses.*

KEEPING YOUR WORKPLACE LEGAL

The Fair Labor Standards Act (FLSA) requires minimum hourly wages for the employees of most firms. The minimum wage for employees covered by the FLSA is set by Congress; it is $4.25 per hour at this writing. The FLSA also requires employers to compensate employees at a time-and-a-half rate for hours worked in excess of 40 per week.

Not all firms engaged in interstate commerce are covered by the Fair Labor Standards Act. Among those not covered are employees of retail stores and service establishments that have annual gross sales or receipts of less than $250,000; outside salespersons; and executive, administrative, and professional personnel.

Small businesses not covered by the FLSA are most likely subject to similar minimum wage requirements in their respective states. Currently, a large majority of states, plus Puerto Rico and the District of Columbia, have minimum wage laws that come close to meeting federal standards. A smaller majority of states attempt to regulate the number of working hours by imposing overtime wage premiums.

Most state laws limit the number of working hours for children and for workers in hazardous occupations. Many states now have time-off-for-voting laws that provide paid time, particularly if employees cannot vote before or after work.

THE HIDDEN COSTS OF EMPLOYING

When you're hiring, keep in mind that, on the average, employees will cost you between 15% and 30% above their wages or salaries, depending on what benefits you offer. For example if you're paying an employee $18,000 per year in salary, your cost could be as much as $23,400. An estimate of 15% above total wages will cover payroll taxes, workers' compensation, and paid vacation. An estimate of 30% above total wages will cover all taxes and a full slate of benefits.

You must match every dollar of federal Social Security taxes that you deduct from your employees' checks. This tax is currently over 7%. In addition, you must pay state unemployment taxes (which vary from state to state; in California, they're currently at 5.4%) and an additional 0.8% (currently) for federal unemployment taxes. Social Security and unemployment tax rates can change from year to year. In some states, the employer also pays a portion of the state disability insurance premiums.

Your degree of success or failure will often be relative to the quality of employees you choose. Studying some books on how to develop professional and psychological interview techniques will help you ferret out the best workers.

CONTROL AND COMMUNICATION

Establishing clear and logical rules, along with maintaining an atmosphere of trust between yourself and your employees, will minimize disciplinary confrontations with employees. Often, the manner in which rules are established and enforced makes the difference between a smooth-running operation and a company plagued by employee-related discord.

Rules should be established with employee input whenever possible, and should always be well understood by all workers. Employees should also be familiar with the consequences of breaking these rules. Rules should be enforced impartially, and all employees should be reprimanded or rewarded for their actions equally, but you should also be flexible in the enforcement of some rules, taking into consideration all extenuating circumstances that might exist. Communication channels should be open so that employees feel free to question rules they feel are unreasonable. Stay open to change if modification or elimination of a particular rule is warranted. Consider establishing a procedure by which employees can appeal enforcement decisions they feel are unfair.

No matter how fair a system of rules might be, there will occasionally be circumstances in which employees need disciplinary action. This means developing an employee warning system that is implemented in a predictable and logical sequence and is easily adaptable to varying circumstances. For example, you might devise a system by which an employee is issued three successive warnings, each firmer than the last, in the event of an infraction. The third warning should be in writing, with a thorough account of employee performance, and should define a specific probationary period in which the problem(s) must be rectified. The employee should clearly understand that violating the probationary period will result in dismissal. Though such warnings are confidential, keep an accurate record of them in the employee's personnel file.

TERMINATING AN EMPLOYEE

Disciplining employees is a necessary evil of the business world, no matter how few of them you have or how small your facility; unfortunately, terminating them is often a mandatory course of action. Although clearly stated job responsibilities and expectations, regular performance evaluations, and a structured method of dealing with employee infractions will all contribute to having a motivated and efficient staff, situations are bound to arise where you ultimately realize that an employee is simply not inclined to do the job for which he or she was hired.

Although you may feel that an employee is not working out, consider carefully whether that person should be terminated. Is he or she exactly the type of person needed for another aspect of your business? The introverted but reliable worker who is too shy to be an effective salesperson might be indispensable as a record keeper.

Sometimes, an employee's misconduct will leave you no choice but to fire him or her. In this case, terminate the employee quickly and do not allow yourself to procrastinate or make excuses as to why the dismissal should be put off. By the time a situation reaches the point of necessary termination, the employee should be well aware of the misconduct and the meaning of the warnings about the consequences of continued violation of workplace regulations.

Although you as the employer are completely justified in terminating a problem employee, be compassionate and sensitive. Despite previous warnings about possible termination, the actual experience is always shocking and unpleasant. Be sure that the grounds for termination are clearly stated and that you limit yourself to facts that can be supported by written documentation. Also, inform the employee fully of his or her rights, such as temporary continued coverage by the group health insurance policy. Record all pertinent facts—for example, why the employee was fired, how many warnings had been issued, what compensation, if any, the employee is entitled to receive—in the employee's personnel file; this will protect you from any future legal action taken by a disgruntled employee.

HIRING OTHER HOME-BASED ENTREPRENEURS

If zoning laws prohibit you from hiring employees, you have another option. Many home-based business owners are opting for a relatively headache-free alternative: hiring people who are essentially self-employed home-based business owners themselves. The number of these self-employed home workers is on the rise: from 11.6 million workers in 1990 to 12.7 million in 1993, according to Link Resources Corp.

With these workers, you can create a home-based version of the virtual office. Using organizational systems and computer networks, home-based entrepreneurs can correspond relatively easily with workers who are based at their homes. There are special challenges with this kind of arrangement: creating spontaneous communication is difficult when you are geographically separated from your employees. You can't just walk to the next office and say, "What do you think of this?"

You can get around this problem by using computerized electronic mail, the phone, and face-to-face meetings. Communicating regularly through e-mail and the telephone alleviates some of the trouble, and regularly scheduled meetings keep everyone on track.

Creating a virtual office can be the key to helping your business grow without having your business completely take over your home or having to move out of your home into a commercial office space. If you want to keep your business home-based, this could be the answer.

Appendix A

INFORMATION RESOURCES

HOME-BASED BUSINESS ASSOCIATIONS

American Association of Home-
Based Businesses
P.O. Box 10023
Rockville, MD 20849
(202) 310-3130

Home Business Institute, Inc.
P.O. Box 301
White Plains, NY 10605
(914) 946-6600

Home Office and Business
Opportunities Association
92 Corporate Park
Suite C250
Irvine, CA 92714
(714) 261-9474

Link Resources (home-based
statistics)
79 5th Ave.
New York, NY 10003
(212) 627-1500

Mother's Home Business
Network
P.O. Box 423
East Meadow, NY 11554
(516) 997-7394

National Association for the
Cottage Industry
P.O. Box 14850
Chicago, IL 60614
(312) 472-8116

National Association of Home-
Based Businesses
10451 Mill Run Circle
Room 400
Owings Mills, MD 21117
(410) 363-3698

National Association of Private
Enterprise
P.O. Box 612147
Dallas, TX 75261
(800) 223-6273

National Small Business United
1155 15th St., N.W., Room 710
Washingon, DC 20005
(202) 293-8830

GENERAL BUSINESS ASSOCIATIONS

American Management
    Association
135 W. 50th St.
New York, NY 10020
(212) 586-8100

American Marketing Association
401 N. Michigan Ave.
Suite 2200
Chicago, IL 60606
(312) 648-0536

International Franchise
    Association
1350 New York Ave., N.W.
Suite 900
Washington, DC 20005
(202) 628-8000

Inventors Workshop
    International
Education Foundation
7332 Mason Ave.
Canoga Park, CA 91306
(818) 340-4268

National Association of Export
    Companies
P.O. Box 1330, Murray Hill
    Station
New York, NY 10156
(212) 725-3311

National Federation of
    Independent Business
    (NFIB)
600 Maryland Ave., S.W.
Suite 700
Washington, DC 20024
(202)554-9000

ADVERTISING/ MARKETING ASSOCIATIONS

Direct Marketing Association
11 W. 42nd St.
New York, NY 10036-8096
(212) 768-7277, ext. 155

The Public Relations Society of
    America
33 Irving Pl.
New York, NY 10003
(212) 995-2230

SELLING ASSOCIATION

Sales & Marketing Executives
    International
Statler Office Tower, Room 977
Cleveland, OH 44115
(800) 999-1414

FRANCHISING

International Franchise
    Association
1350 New York Ave., N.W.
Suite 900
Washington, DC 20005
(202) 628-8000

Appendix B

BOOKS

HOME-BASED BUSINESS BOOKS

Best Home Businesses for the '90s, The, Paul and Sarah Edwards (Jeremy P. Tarcher Inc., 1991)

Best Homebased Franchises, The, Gregory Matusky (Doubleday, 1992)

Complete Work-at-Home Companion, The, Herman Holtz (Prime Pub Communications, 1990)

Entrepreneur's Complete Self-Assessment Guide, The, 2nd Edition, Douglas A. Gray (Self-Counsel Press, 1990)

Home Business—Big Business: How to Launch Your Home Business and Make it a Success, Mel Cook (Collier Books, 1992)

Home Office Book: How to Set Up an Efficient Personal Workspace in the Computer Age, Mark Alvarez (Goodwood Press, 1990)

Homemade Money, 4th Edition, Barbara Brabec (Betterway Books, 1992)

How to Use a Computer in Your Home Office, Hal Schuster with Paul and Sarah Edwards (Electronic Cottage Press, 1990)

101 Franchises You Can Run from Home, Lynie Arden (John Wiley & Sons, 1990)

1101 Businesses You Can Start from Home, Daryl Allen Hall (John Wiley & Sons, 1995)

Organizing Your Home Office for Success—Expert Strategies That Can Work for You, Lisa Kanarek (Plume, 1993)

Starting & Operating a Home-Based Business, David R. Eyler (John Wiley & Sons, 1990)

Work-at-Home Sourcebook, The, 5th Edition, Lyne Arden (Live Oak Publications, 1994)

Working from Home, Paul and Sarah Edwards (Jeremy P. Tarcher, Inc., 1990)

GENERAL BUSINESS BOOKS

The Entrepreneur Magazine Small Business Advisor (John Wiley & Sons, 1995)

Entrepreneur's Road Map to Business Success, The, Lyle Maul and Dianne Mayfield (Saxtons River Publications, 1992)

Encyclopedia of Associations (Gale Research Company)—Updated annually

Fast Cash for Kids—101 Money-Making Projects for Young Entrepreneurs (Career Press, 1991)

Free Help from Uncle Sam to Start Your Own Business (Or Expand the One You Have), 3rd Edition, William Alarid and Gustav Berle (Puma Publishing, 1992)

How to Start a Business without Quitting Your Job: The Moonlighting Entrepreneur's Guide, Philip Holland (Ten Speed Press, 1992)

Making It On Your Own: Surviving the Ups and Downs of Being Self-Employed, Paul and Sarah Edwards (Jeremy P. Tarcher Inc., 1991)

Moonlighting: 148 Great Ways to Make Money on the Side, Carl Hausman (Avon Books, 1989)

Running a One-Person Business, Claude Whitmyer, Salli Rasberry, and Michael Phillips (Ten Speed Press, 1989)

Save Your Business a Bundle: 202 Ways to Cut Costs and Boost Profits Now—For Companies of Any Size, Daniel Kehrer (Simon & Schuster, 1994)

Second Coming of the Woolly Mammoth, The,—An Entrepreneur's Bible, Ted S. Frost (Ten Speed Press, 1991)

Small Time Operator—How to Start Your Own Small Business, Keep Your Books, Pay Your Taxes, and Stay Out of Trouble, 8th revised and enlarged Edition, Bernard Kamoroff, CPA (Bell Springs Publishing, 1993)

Succeeding in Small Business: The 101 Toughest Problems and How to Solve Them, Jane Applegate (NAL-Dutton, 1992)

Thomas' Register of Manufacturers (Thomas Publishing Co.)—updated annually.

ADVERTISING/MARKETING BOOKS

Big Ideas for Small Service Businesses—How to Successfully Advertise, Publicize, and Maximize Your Business or Professional Practice, Marilyn and Tom Ross (Communication Creativity, 1993)

Business Building In the '90s—A Complete Guide to Promoting and Marketing Your Service Business, Douglas J. Swanson (The Swanson Group, 2416 N.W. Norman Cir., Lawton, OK 73505; 1993)

Desktop Direct Marketing: How to Use Up-to-the-Minute Technologies to Find and Reach New Customers, Kim and Sunny Baker (McGraw-Hill, 1994)

Direct Marketing Success: What Works and Why, Freeman F. Gosden, Jr. (John Wiley & Sons, 1989)

Do-It-Yourself Advertising, David F. Ramacitti (AMACOM, 1992)

Do-It-Yourself Advertising: How to Produce Great Ads, Brochures, Catalogs, Direct Mail, and Much More, Fred Hahn (John Wiley & Sons, 1993)

Do-It-Yourself Direct Marketing: Secrets for Small Business, Mark S. Bacon (John Wiley & Sons, 1991)

Endless Referrals: Network Your Everyday Contacts into Sales Money, Bob Burg (McGraw-Hill, 1993)

Getting Business to Come to You, Paul and Sarah Edwards (Jeremy P. Tarcher Inc., 1991)

Getting Publicity—A Do-It-Yourself Guide for Small Business and Non-Profit Groups, Tana Fletcher and Julia Rockler (Self-Counsel Press, 1990)

Great Print Advertising, Tony Antin (John Wiley & Sons, 1993)

Guerilla Marketing Excellence, Jay Conrad Levinson (Houghton Mifflin, 1993)

Guerilla Marketing Attack, Jay Conrad Levinson (Houghton Mifflin, 1989)

Guide to Preparing Cost-Effective Press Releases, A, Robert H. Loeffler (The Haworth Press Inc., 1993)

How to Get Clients Jeff & Marc Slutsky (Warner Books, 1992)

How to Promote, Publicize and Advertise Your Growing Business, Kim and Sunny Baker (John Wiley & Sons, 1992)

Marketing Without Advertising, Michael Phillips and Salli Rasberry (Nolo Press, 1989)

Marketing Without Money: One Hundred Seventy Five Free, Cheap & Offbeat Ways for Small Businesses to Increase Sales, Nicholas Bade (Halle House Publishing, 1993)

Money-Making Marketing—Finding the People Who Need What You're Selling and Making Sure They Buy It, 2nd Revised Edition, Jeffrey Lant (JLA Publications, 1992)

National Directory of Mailing Lists (Oxbridge Communications, (800) 955-0231, ext. 200)

No More Cold Calls, Jeffrey Lant (JLA Publications, 1993)

Public Relations Practices: Managerial Case Studies & Problems, Allen Center and Patrick Jackson (Prentice-Hall, 1990)

Six Steps to Free Publicity and Dozens of Other Ways to Win Free Media Attention for You or Your Business, Marcia Yudkin (Plume, 1994)

Slash Your Advertising Costs Now, Jim Mantice (Dartnell Corp., 1991)

Starting & Building Your Catalog Sales Business, Herman Holtz (John Wiley & Sons, 1990)

Talk Is Cheap—Promoting Your Business Through Word-of-Mouth Advertising, Godfrey Harris (The Americas Group, 1991)

Trade Show Exhibiting: The Insider's Guide for Entrepreneurs, Diane K. Weintraub (McGraw-Hill, 1991)

Word-of-Mouth Marketing, Jerry R. Wilson (John Wiley & Sons, 1991)

Writing Effective News Releases—How to Get Free Publicity for Yourself, Your Business, or Your Organization, Catherine V. McIntyre (Piccadilly Books, 1992)

The Zen of Hype: An Insider's Guide to the Publicity Game, Raleigh Pinskey (Citadel Press, 1991)

BOOKS ON SELLING

Consultative Selling, 4th Edition, Mack Hanan (AMACOM, 1990)

Getting Past No: Negotiating Your Way from Confrontation to Cooperation, William Ury (Bantam Books, 1993)

Guerilla Selling, Bill Gallagher (Houghton Mifflin, 1992)

Opening Closed Doors: Keys to Reaching Hard-to-Reach People, C. Richard Weylman (Irwin Professional Publishing, 1994)

Selling by Phone: The Salesperson's Guide to Getting New Customers and Closing Deals, Linda Richardson (McGraw-Hill, 1992)

Selling: The Mother of All Enterprise, William H. Blades (Marketing Methods Press, 1994)

Selling Your Services—Proven Strategies for Getting Clients to Hire You (or Your Firm), Robert W. Bly (Henry Holt & Co., 1991)

Selling to Uncle Sam: How to Win Choice Government Contracts for Your Business, Clinton L. Crownover and Mark Henricks (McGraw-Hill, 1993)

Soft Selling in a Hard World: Plain Talk on the Art of Persuasion, Jerry Vass (Running Press, 1993)

Stop Telling, Start Selling: Using Customer-Focused Dialogue to Close Sales, Linda Richardson (McGraw-Hill, 1993)

BOOKS ON FINANCING

Borrowing for Your Business: Winning the Battle for the Banker's "Yes," George M. Dawson (Upstart Publishing Inc., 1991)

Guerilla Financing: Alternative Techniques to Finance Any Small Business, Bruce Blechman and Jay Conrad Levinson (Houghton Mifflin, 1992)

How to Get a Business Loan, Joseph Mancuso (Random House, 1993)

SBA Loans: A Step-by-Step Guide, 2nd. Edition, Patrick D. O'Hara (John Wiley & Sons, 1994)

BOOKS ON ACCOUNTING

Basic Accounting for the Small Business, 4th Edition, Clive G. Cornish (Self-Counsel Press, 1992)

Basics of Budgeting, Robert G. Finney (AMACOM, 1993)

Easy Financials for Your Home-Based Business: The Friendly Guide to Successful Management Systems for Busy Home Entrepreneurs, Norm Ray, CPA (Rayve Productions Inc., 1993)

Financial Management Techniques for Small Business, Art De Thomas (Oasis Press, 1992)

Keeping the Books, 2nd Revised Edition, Linda Pinson and Jerry Jinnett (Upstart Publishing, 1993)

Step-by-Step Bookkeeping: The Complete Handbook for the Small Business, Revised Edition, Robert C. Ragan (Sterling Publishing Co., 1992)

Understanding and Managing Financial Information: The Non-Financial Manager's Guide, Michael C. Coltman (Self-Counsel Press, 1993)

Up Your Cash Flow, Harvey A. Goldstein, CPA (Granville Publications, 1986)

BOOK ON EMPLOYEES

Alternative Staffing Strategies, David Nye (BNA Books, 1988)

SERVICE BOOKS

Achieving Excellence through Customer Service, John Tschohl with Steve Franzmeier (Prentice-Hall, 1991)

Keeping Customers for Life, Joan Koob Cannie with Donald Caplin (AMACOM, 1992)
Sustaining Knock Your Socks Off Service, Thomas K. Connellan and Ron Zemke (AMACOM, 1993)

BOOKS ON TAXES

Julian Block's Year-Round Tax Strategies for the $40,000 Plus Household, 1994 (Prima Publishing, 1993)
Small Business Survival Guide, The: How to Manage Your Cash, Profits and Taxes, Robert E. Fleury (Sourcebooks Trade, 1992)

BOOKS ON COPYRIGHTS AND PATENTS

Copyright Book: A Practical Guide, The, 4th Edition, William S. Strong (MIT Press, 1992)
Copyright Handbook, The, 2nd Edition, Stephen Fishman (Nolo Press, 1994)
How to Register a United States Copyright, 3rd Edition, Mark Warda (Sphinx Publishing, 1992)
Intellectual Property, Patents, Trademarks and Copyright in a Nutshell, 2nd Edition, Arthur R. Miller & Michael H. Davis (West Publishing, 1990)
Trademark: How to Name Your Business & Product, Kate McGrath and Stephen Elias (Nolo Press, 1992)

FRANCHISING BOOKS

Guide to Franchise & Business Opportunities, The, (Entrepreneur Group)
Handbook of Successful Franchising, 3rd Edition, Mark Friedlander Jr. and Gene Gurney (TAB Books, 1989)

BUSINESS PLANNING BOOKS

Business Planning Guide, The, 6th Edition, David H. Bangs, Jr. (Upstart Publishing, 1992)
Entrepreneur's Guide to Growing Up, The, Edna Sheedy (Self-Counsel Press, 1993)

BOOKS ON LEGAL ASPECTS OF BUSINESS

Complete Book of Small Business Legal Forms, The, Daniel Sitarz (Nova
    Publishing Co., 1991)
Inc. Yourself, Judith H. McQuown (Harper Business, 1993)
Make It Legal, Lee Wilson (Allworth Press, 1990)
Standard Legal Forms and Agreements for Small Business, Steve Sanderson
    (Self-Counsel Press, 1990)

INSURANCE BOOK

*Insuring Your Business—What You Need to Know to Get the Best Insurance
    Coverage for Your Business,* Sean Mooney (Insurance Information
    Institute Press, 1993)

Appendix C

MAGAZINES, NEWSLETTERS, AND OTHER MEDIA

GENERAL BUSINESS AND SMALL BUSINESS

Entrepreneur Magazine
2392 Morse Ave.
Irvine, CA 92714
(714) 261-2325

Bootstrappin' Entrepreneur
8726 S. Sepulveda Blvd., Suite B261
Los Angeles, CA 90045
(310) 568-9861

Business Radio Network:
    Working from Home

Business Start-Ups
2392 Morse Ave.
Irvine, CA 92714
(714) 261-2325

Business Week
1221 Avenue of the Americas
New York, NY 10020-1001
(212) 512-3896

Growing Your Business
Coopers & Lybrand
1251 Avenue of the Americas
New York, NY 10020
(212) 536-2960

Home & Garden Cable Network:
    Working from Home with
    Paul and Sarah Edwards

Home Office Computing
Scholastic Inc.
730 Broadway
New York, NY 10003
(212) 505-4220

Nation's Business
1615 H St., N.W.
Washington, DC 20062
(202) 463-5650

Self-Employment Survival Letter
Barbara Brabec Productions
P.O. Box 2137
Naperville, IL 60567
(708) 717-4188

ADVERTISING/ MARKETING MAGAZINES

Advertising Age
220 E. 42nd St.
New York, NY 10017
(212) 210-0171

Adweek
49 E. 21st St.
New York, NY 10010
(212) 529-5500

Direct Marketing
224 7th St.
Garden City, NY 11530
(800) 229-6700/(516) 746-6700
      in New York

Catalog Age
P.O. Box 1017
Skokie, IL 60076
(708) 647-0771

Classified Communication
P.O. Box 4242
Prescott, AZ 86302
(602) 778-6788

SELLING MAGAZINES

Selling
488 Madison Ave.
New York, NY 10022
(800) 360-5344

Sales & Marketing Managment
633 Third Ave., 32nd Fl.
New York, NY 10017-6706
(212) 986-4800

PRICING NEWSLETTER

The Pricing Advisor
3277 Roswell Rd., Room 620
Atlanta, GA 30305
(404) 509-9933

SERVICE VIDEOS

Communicating with Customers, Communication Briefings,
      (800) 888-2086
How to Give Excellent Customer Service, CareerTrack, (800) 334-1018
Power of Customer Service, Nightingale Conant, (800) 525-9000

TAX INFORMATION

IRS Help Line, (800) 829-1040
The Kiplinger Tax Letter, (800) 544-0155

Appendix D

ONLINE SERVICES

America OnLine Inc.
8619 Westwood Center Dr.
Vienna, VA 22182
(800) 827-6364

BRS Information Technologies
8000 Westpark Dr.
McLean, VA 22102
(800) 955-0906

CompuServe
5000 Arlington Centre Blvd.
Columbus, OH 43220
(800) 848-8990
(CompuServe has a Working
    from Home Forum)

Delphi
General Videotex Corp.
3 Blackstone St.
Cambridge, MA 02139
(800) 544-4005

DIALOG Information Services Inc.
3450 Hillview Ave.
Palo Alto, CA 94304
(415) 858-3785/(800) 334-2564

Dow Jones News/Retrieval
    Service
P.O. Box 300
Princeton, NJ 08543-0300
(609) 452-1511

GEnie
G.E. Information Services
401 N. Washington St.
Rockville, MD 20850
(800) 638-9636

NewsNet
945 Haverford Rd.
Bryn Mawr, PA 19010
(215) 527-8030/(800) 345-1301

NEXIS
Mead Data Central
P.O. Box 933
Dayton, OH 45401
(513) 859-5398/(800) 543-6862

Prodigy Services Company
445 Hamilton Ave.
White Plains, NY 10601
(800) 776-0845

SBA On-Line
2400-baud modems call
    (800)859-INFO
9600-baud modems call
    (800) 697-INFO
In Washington, DC:
2400-baud modems call
    (202) 205-7265
9600-baud modems call
    (202) 401-9600

The Source
5000 Arlington Centre Blvd.
Columbus, OH 43220
(614) 457-8600/(800) 336-3330

VU/TEXT Information
    Services Inc.
325 Chestnut St., Suite 1300
Philadelphia, PA 19106
(215) 574-4400/(800) 258-8080

Appendix E

GOVERNMENT AGENCIES

Small Business Administration
1441 L St., N.W.
Washington, DC 20416-0001
(202) 653-6823/(800) U-ASK-SBA
827-5722

For a list of all SBA publications, write:
SBA Publications
P.O. Box 30
Denver, CO 80201-0030

Service Corps of Retired
Executives (SCORE)
SBA, Small Business
Development Center
Headquarters
1129 20th St., N.W., Room 410
Washington, DC 20036
(800) U-ASK-SBA (827-5722)

Copyright Office
Register of Copyrights
Library of Congress
Washington, DC 20559
(202) 479-0700

Council of Better Business
Bureaus Inc.
1515 Wilson Blvd.
Arlington, VA 22209
(703) 276-0100

Export-Import Bank of the
United States
811 Vermont Ave., N.W.
Washington, DC 20571
(202) 566-2117

Federal Trade Commission
Public Reference Branch
6th St. & Pennsylvania Ave., N.W.
Washington, DC 20580
(202) 326-2222

Food and Drug Administration
5600 Fishers Lane
Rockville, MD 20857
(301) 443-6597

The Patent and Trademark Office
U.S. Department of Commerce
P.O. Box 9
Washington, DC 20231
(703) 557-4357

U.S. Department of Commerce
Office of Public Affairs
Room 5523
14th & Constitution, N.W.
Washington, DC 20230
(202) 482-6035

U.S. Department of Treasury,
    Internal Revenue Service
1111 Constitution Ave., N.W.
Room 2315
Washington, DC 20224
(202) 566-4024
New Business Tax Kit
(800) 424-3676

Appendix F

CREDIT
AGENCIES

Dun & Bradstreet
99 Church St.
New York, NY 10007
(212) 223-2937

TransUnion Credit
     Information Co.
P.O. Box 7000
N. Olmstead, OH 44070
(502) 425-7511

TRW Business Credit Services
12606 Greenville Ave.
Dallas, TX 75374
(800) 682-7654

GLOSSARY

accounts receivable: A record used to account for the total number of sales made through the extension of credit.

acid-test ratio: An analysis method used to measure the liquidity of a business by dividing total liquid assets by current liabilities.

asset earning power: A common profitability measure used to determine the profitability of a business by taking its total earnings before taxes and dividing that amount by its total assets.

Audit Bureau of Circulation (ABC): A third-party organization that verifies the circulation of print media through periodical audits.

balance sheet: A financial statement used to report a business's total assets, liabilities, and equity.

bonding: Generally used by service companies as a guarantee to their clients that they have the necessary ability and financial backing to meet their obligations.

break-even analysis: An analysis method used to determine the number of jobs or products that need to be sold to cover all expenses and begin to earn a profit for a business.

business opportunities: A venture that has potential for profit: a business or franchise that is for sale; a product, service, or piece of equipment, etc., that can be sold or leased to enable the purchaser-licensee to begin a business.

business plan: A plan used to chart a new or ongoing business's strategies, sales projections, and key personnel in order to obtain financing and provide a strategic foundation for the business's growth.

Business Publications Audit (BPA): Similar to the Audit Bureau of Circulation, the BPA is a third-party organization that verifies the circulation of print media through periodical audits.

capitalization: Capital may be in the form of money, common stock, long-term debt, or some combination of all three. With too much capital, a firm is overcapitalized; with too little capital, it is undercapitalized.

cash basis: An accounting method used for record keeping where income is logged when received and expenses are charged when they occur.

cash flow: The influx of money coming into your business through revenues, and the outlay of money through payment of expenses.

chattel mortgage contract: A credit contract used for the purchase of equipment where the purchaser receives title of the equipment upon delivery but the creditor holds a mortgage claim against it.

closing techniques: Different methods, usually verbal, used to achieve a sale.

collateral: Assets used as security for the extension of a loan.

commercial loan: A short-term loan, usually issued for a term of six months.

conditional sales contract: A credit contract used for the purchase of equipment where the purchaser doesn't receive title of the equipment until the amount specified in the contract has been paid in full.

cooperative advertising: A joint advertising strategy used by a manufacturer and another firm that distributes its products.

copyright: A form of protection used to safeguard original literary works, performing arts, sound recordings, visual arts, and renewals.

corporation: A legal form of operation that declares the business a separate legal entity guided by a group of officers known as the board of directors.

cost-of-living lease: A lease where yearly increases are tied to the government's cost of living index.

cost per thousand (CPM): Terminology used in buying media. CPM refers to the cost it takes to reach 1,000 people within a target market.

current ratio: A ratio used to determine the difference between total current assets and total current liabilities.

delegation: Handing over some managerial or service responsibilities to employees or independent contractors.

demographic characteristics: The attributes such as income, age, and occupation that best describe a target market.

depreciation: The lessening in value of fixed assets that provides the foundation for a tax deduction based on either the declining-balance or straight-line method.

disability insurance: A payroll tax required in some states that is deducted from employee paychecks to ensure income during periods when an employee is unable to work due to an injury or illness.

dollar control system: A system used in inventory management that reveals the cost and gross profit margin on individual inventory items.

Dun & Bradstreet: An agency that furnishes subscribers with market statistics and the financial standings and credit ratings of businesses.

equipment loan: A loan used for the purchase of capital equipment.

equity capital: A form of financing where equity in a business is sold to private investors.

exploratory research: A method used when gathering primary information for a market survey, where targeted consumers are asked very general questions geared toward eliciting a lengthy answer.

Fair Labor Standards Act: A federal law that enforces a group of minimum standards that employers must abide by when hiring employees.

Federal Insurance Contributions Act (FICA): A law that requires employers to match the amount of Social Security tax deducted from an employee's paycheck.

fictitious name: Often referred to as a DBA (Doing Business As). A fictitious name is frequently used by sole proprietors or partnerships to provide a name, other than those of the owners or partners, under which the business will operate.

fixed expenses: Expenses that must be paid each month and do not fluctuate with the sales volume.

franchise: A business conducted according to a standardized product presentation and sales format. The purchase of a franchise gives the new owner the right to offer, sell, or distribute goods or services covered by the franchisor's trademark.

frequency: The number of times you hope to reach your target audience through your advertising campaign.

401(k) plan: A retirement plan for employees that allows them to deduct money from their paychecks and place it in a tax-sheltered account.

income statement: A financial statement that charts the sales and operating costs of a business over a specific period of time, usually a month. Also called an operating statement.

independent contractors: Individuals who can be hired on an as-needed basis; an alternative to hiring full-time employees.

inventory loan: A loan that is extended based on the value of a business's inventory.

inventory turnover: An analysis method used to determine the amount of capital invested in inventory and the total number of times per year that investment will revolve.

investment tax credit: A tax credit that allows businesses to write off up to $17,000 of equipment purchased for business use.

investment turnover: A profitability measure used to evaluate the number of times per year that total investment or assets revolve.

liability: A term used when analyzing insurance risks; describes possible areas of exposure.

limited liability corporation: A business structure that allows the owners to distribute the income and income tax to the partners, thereby protecting themselves from personal liability for the business's debts.

market survey: A research method used to define the market parameters of a business.

markup: The amount added to the cost of goods in order to produce the desired profit.

media plan: A plan that details the usage of media in an advertising campaign, including costs, running dates, markets, reach, frequency, rationales, and strategies.

net profit on sales: A profitability measure that determines the difference between net profit and operating costs.

Occupational Safety and Health Act (OSHA): A federal law that requires employers to provide employees with a workplace that is free of hazardous conditions.

online service: Organizations that provide information to remote customers via modem.

overhead: All nonlabor expenses needed to operate a business.

partnership: A legal form of business operation between two or more individuals. The federal government recognizes several types of partnerships. The two most common are general and limited partnerships.

primary market research: An information-gathering method in which responses are obtained directly from a target market—over the telephone, in person, or through the mail.

profit: There are generally two kinds of profits: (1) gross profit, the difference between gross sales and cost of sales, and (2) net profit, the difference between gross profit and all costs associated with operating a business.

public relations: Any activity, outside of traditional paid advertising, that promotes knowledge of or a good impression of your company—contests, special events, interviews with the media, and so on.

rate card: The asked-for advertising charges for space or time in magazines or on radio or television. The published rates are often negotiable.

reach: The total number of people within a target market to be contacted through an advertising campaign.

return on investment (ROI): A ofitability measure that evaluates the performance of a business by dividing net profit by total assets.

RFM formula: A method used to choose a mailing list. R stands for recency, F for frequency, and M for money.

secondary market research: An information-gathering method that depends on published reports of government agencies, trade associations, or other businesses in the same industry.

sole proprietor: A legal form of operation where only one owner can exist.

specific research: A method used when gathering primary information for a market survey. Targeted consumers are asked very specific, in-depth questions geared toward resolving problems found through exploratory research.

Subchapter S: Under federal law, small corporations in this category can pay out all income proportionately to their shareholders, who then claim the income on their personal income tax returns.

variable expenses: Business costs that fluctuate in successive payment periods according to the sales volume.

working capital: Net current assets required for a company to carry on with its work; the surplus of a firm's current assets over its current liabilities.

INDEX

1996 Expo Schedule

LOS ANGELES
February 10-11, 1996
Los Angeles
Convention Center

NEW JERSEY
March 30-31, 1996
Meadowlands
Convention Center

CHICAGO
April 13-14, 1996
Rosemont
Convention Center

ATLANTA
May 18-19, 1996
Cobb County Galleria

SAN MATEO
June 8-9, 1996
San Mateo County
Expo Center

DALLAS
September
14-15, 1996
Dallas Market
Hall

NEW YORK
November
2-3, 1996
Nassau Veterans
Memorial Coliseum

PHILADELPHIA
November
16-17, 1996
South Jersey
Expo Center

FT. LAUDERDALE
December 7-8, 1996
Broward County
Convention Center
MJWE

**Save $5.00
when you bring this
ad to any Expo.**

For more
information, call
(800) 864-6864.

Get your FREE Small Business Development Catalog today!

Name: _____

Address: _____

City: _____

State/Zip: _____

MJWC

To receive your free catalog, return this coupon to:
ENTREPRENEUR MAGAZINE,
P.O. Box 1625, Des Plaines, IL 60017-1625.
OR CALL (800) 421-2300, Dept. MJWC
Step-by-step guidance to help you succeed.

**Get the book.
FREE!**